MUSIC IN THE
EIGHTEENTH CENTURY

Western Music in Context: A Norton History

Walter Frisch SERIES EDITOR

Music in the Medieval West, by Margot Fassler

Music in the Renaissance, by Richard Freedman

Music in the Baroque, by Wendy Heller

Music in the Eighteenth Century, by John Rice

Music in the Nineteenth Century, by Walter Frisch

Music in the Twentieth and Twenty-First Centuries, by Joseph Auner

MUSIC IN THE EIGHTEENTH CENTURY

John Rice

W. W. NORTON AND COMPANY

NEW YORK • LONDON

W. W. Norton & Company has been independent since its founding in 1923, when William Warder Norton and Mary D. Herter Norton first published lectures delivered at the People's Institute, the adult education division of New York City's Cooper Union. The firm soon expanded its program beyond the Institute, publishing books by celebrated academics from America and abroad. By midcentury, the two major pillars of Norton's publishing program— trade books and college texts—were firmly established. In the 1950s, the Norton family transferred control of the company to its employees, and today—with a staff of four hundred and a comparable number of trade, college, and professional titles published each year—W. W. Norton & Company stands as the largest and oldest publishing house owned wholly by its employees.

Editor: Maribeth Payne
Associate Editor: Justin Hoffman
Assistant Editor: Ariella Foss
Developmental Editor: Harry Haskell
Manuscript Editor: JoAnn Simony
Project Editor: Jack Borrebach
Electronic Media Editor: Steve Hoge
Marketing Manager, Music: Amy Parkin
Production Manager: Ashley Horna
Photo Editor: Stephanie Romeo
Permissions Manager: Megan Jackson
Text Design: Jillian Burr
Composition: CM Preparé
Manufacturing: Quad/Graphics—Fairfield, PA

Library of Congress Cataloging-in-Publication Data

Rice, John A.
  Music in the eighteenth century / John Rice. —1st ed.
    p.cm.— (Western music in context: a Norton history)
  Includes bibliographical references and index.
  ISBN 978-0-393-92918-8 (pbk. : alk. paper) 1. Music—18th century—History and criticism. I. Title.
  ML195.R53 2013
  780.9'033—dc23

                            2012040077

W. W. Norton & Company, Inc., 500 Fifth Avenue, New York, NY 10110-0017
wwnorton.com
W. W. Norton & Company Ltd., Castle House, 75/76 Wells Street, London W1T3QT

2 3 4 5 6 7 8 9 0

CONTENTS IN BRIEF

CONTENTS

ANTHOLOGY REPERTOIRE

1. Giovanni Battista Pergolesi, *Stabat Mater: Stabat mater dolorosa*
2. Giovanni Battista Pergolesi, *La serva padrona: A Serpina penserete*
3. Johann Adolf Hasse, *Artaserse: Per questo dolce amplesso*
4. Lodovico Giustini, Piano Sonata No. 1 in G Minor: Movement 2
5. Domenico Scarlatti, Sonata in C Major, K. 421
6. Joseph Boulogne, Chevalier de Saint-Georges, Violin Concerto in D Major, Op. 3, No. 1: Movement 2
7. Domenico Gallo, Trio Sonata No. 1 in G Major: Movement 1
8. Johann Christian Bach, Sonata in D Major, Op. 5, No. 2: Movement 1
9. Christoph Gluck, *Orfeo ed Euridice:* Act 2, Scene 1, to end of chorus *Misero giovane*
10. Johann Baptist Vanhal, *Missa Pastoralis*: Agnus Dei
11. Carl Philipp Emanuel Bach, Fantasia in C Minor, W. 63, No. 6
12. Johann Stamitz, Symphony in D Major, Op. 3, No. 2: Movement 1
13. Anna Bon, Keyboard Sonata in F Major, Op. 2, No. 3: Movement 1
14. Joseph Haydn, Symphony No. 8 in G Major (*Le soir*): Movement 1
15. Ignacio de Jerusalem, Matins for the Virgin of Guadalupe: Vidi speciosam
16. Tommaso Traetta, *Antigona: Piangi, o Tebe*
17. Giovanni Paisiello, *Il barbiere di Siviglia:* Finale of Act 4 (extract)
18. Wolfgang Amadeus Mozart, Piano Concerto No. 17 in G Major, K. 453: Movement 2
19. Joseph Haydn, String Quartet in E♭ Major, Op. 33, No. 2 ("The Joke"): Movement 4
20. Wolfgang Amadeus Mozart, String Quartet in A Major, K. 464: Movement 2

Western Music in Context: A Norton History starts from the premise that music consists of far more than the notes on a page or the sound heard on a recording. Music is a product of its time and place, of the people and institutions that bring it into being.

Many music history texts focus on musical style and on individual composers. These approaches have been a valuable part of writing about music since the beginnings of modern scholarship in the later nineteenth century. But in the past few decades, scholars have widened their scope in imaginative and illuminating ways to explore the cultural, social, intellectual, and historical contexts for music. This new perspective is reflected in the volumes of Western Music in Context. Among the themes treated across the series are:

- The ways in which music has been commissioned, created, and consumed in public and private spheres
- The role of technology in the creation and transmission of music, from the advent of notation to the digital age
- The role of women as composers, performers, and patrons
- The relationships between music and national or ethnic identity
- The training and education of musicians in both private and institutional settings

All of these topics—and more—animate the pages of Western Music in Context. Written in an engaging style by recognized experts, the series paints vivid pictures of moments, activities, locales, works, and individuals:

- A fourth-century eyewitness report on musical practices in the Holy Land, from a European nun on a pilgrimage
- A lavish wedding at the court of Savoy in the mid-fifteenth century, with Music by Guillaume Du Fay

- Broadside ballads sung on the streets of London or pasted onto walls, and enjoyed by people from all levels of society
- A choral Magnificat performed at a church in colonial Brazil in the 1770s, accompanied by an organ sent by ship and mule from Portugal
- The barely literate impresario Domenico Barbaia making a tidy fortune at Italian opera houses by simultaneously managing gambling tables and promoting Gioachino Rossini
- A "radio teaching piece" from 1930 by Kurt Weill celebrating the transatlantic flight of Charles Lindbergh

Each volume of Western Music in Context is accompanied by a concise anthology of carefully chosen works. The anthologies offer representative examples of a wide variety of musical genres, styles, and national traditions. Included are excerpts from well-known works like Aaron Copland's *Billy the Kid*, as well as lesser-known gems like Ignacio de Jerusalem's *Matins for the Virgin of Guadalupe*. Commentaries within the anthologies not only provide concise analyses of every work from both formal and stylistic points of view, but also address issues of sources and performance practice.

StudySpace, Norton's online resource for students, features links to recordings of anthology selections that can be streamed from the Naxos Music Library (individual or institutional subscription required), as well as the option to purchase and download recordings from Amazon and iTunes. In addition, students can purchase access to, and instructors can request a free DVD of, the Norton Opera Sampler, which features over two hours of video excerpts from fourteen Metropolitan Opera productions. Finally, for readers wanting to do further research or find more specialized books, articles, or web-based resources, StudySpace offers lists of further readings that supplement those at the end of each chapter in the texts.

Because the books of the Western Music in Context series are relatively compact and reasonably priced, instructors and students might use one or more volumes in a single semester, or several across an academic year. Instructors have the flexibility to supplement the books and the accompanying anthologies with other resources, including Norton Critical Scores and *Strunk's Source Readings in Music History*, as well as other readings, illustrations, scores, films, and recordings.

The contextual approach to music history offers limitless possibilities: an instructor, student, or general reader can extend the context as widely as he or she wishes. Well before the advent of the World Wide Web, the renowned anthropologist Clifford Geertz likened culture to a spider's web of interconnected meanings that humans have spun. Music has been a vital part of such webs throughout the history of the West. Western Music in Context has as its goal to highlight such connections and to invite the instructors and students to continue that exploration on their own.

Walter Frisch
Columbia University

We live in an exciting time to be studying and listening to the music of what Jacques Barzun has called "The Encyclopedic Century." More of it than ever can be enjoyed in concert, on CD, or on the Internet in performances that seek to re-create the period's sonic values and performance styles. Since the mid-1990s, musicological research has revolutionized how we think about and hear the music of the era.

This book takes advantage of these developments, exploring music and musical life in Europe between 1715 and 1815, with brief glimpses of music in the European colonies of the New World. Like the authors of the other volumes in the Western Music in Context series, I have focused on the ways in which music emerged from, reflected, and influenced the culture of which it was a part. While following the broadly chronological approach of the series as a whole, this book is also organized geographically. Chapters examining the musical life of particular cities, or groups of cities or courts, allow readers to experience something of the Grand Tour so characteristic of the eighteenth century.

In place of the traditional chronological and stylistic categories of "Classical" and "pre-Classical," I emphasize the continuities that link the music of such pioneers of the galant style as Pergolesi and Hasse with the works of Haydn, Mozart, and Beethoven. I give the great Austro-German triumvirate a little less prominence than most other surveys of eighteenth-century music. No one would dispute the beauty, importance, and value of their music; no one would wish to teach or take a course on eighteenth-century music in which their accomplishments were minimized. Because their intricately crafted scores offer special rewards to those who analyze them closely, I have included a substantial number of movements by them in the accompanying *Anthology for Music in the Eighteenth Century*. Yet a modest shifting of emphasis away from Haydn, Mozart, and Beethoven will,

I hope, prove useful as we seek fresh insights into and a deeper understanding of eighteenth-century music and its place in European culture and society.

Music in the Eighteenth Century takes account of the most recent scholarly research and perspectives; to assure readability, endnotes and references are kept to a minimum. A short list of further readings at the end of each chapter points the student to some of this more specialized literature; an expanded bibliography is available on StudySpace, Norton's online resource for students. I hope this book will convey some of the excitement I have felt in trying to come to terms with the new ideas now circulating among writers on eighteenth-century music. If my readers turn quickly to their books, and to the music they bring to life, I will consider mine a success.

Throughout the book, frequent quotations from primary sources, many drawn from *Strunk's Source Readings in Music History*, keep the narrative lively. For readers who wish to explore these sources in more detail, page references for both the single-volume and seven-volume editions of *Strunk* appear in parentheses after quotations drawn from this text. Bibliographic information for other source readings appears in endnotes.

The text is also sparing in its use of musical examples and analytical remarks. For those who wish to delve deeper into individual works, twenty-nine full musical scores, each with detailed commentary, are included in the accompanying *Anthology for Music in the Eighteenth Century*. Links to recordings of anthology repertoire are also available on StudySpace.

ACKNOWLEDGMENTS

Many scholars have contributed to this book, and I am delighted to have an opportunity to thank some of them here. In doing so, I am reminded of how lucky I am to have so many knowledgeable and generous colleagues who share with me an interest in and a love of the eighteenth century and its music.

Among the many librarians and archivists from whose expertise and generosity I have benefited, James Cassaro stands out for all that he did for me during my three semesters as a visiting professor at the University of Pittsburgh. I am also indebted to Kristen Castellana and Nola Reed Knouse for sending me copies of unpublished scores in their collections.

Anna Nisnevich helped me with the Russian text of Giuseppe Sarti's *Now the Powers of Heaven*. Daniel Freeman sent me a copy of his edition of one of Joseph Mysliveček's most brilliant arias. David Black gave me the benefit of his knowledge of eighteenth-century Viennese church music. To Kurt Markstrom I owe thanks for advice on the operas of Leonardo Vinci. Rogerio Budasz guided me to sources of information on Brazilian colonial music and shared with me his publications and recordings.

Bruce Alan Brown read and commented on early drafts of several chapters, and has been a frequent source of advice and encouragement throughout this book's long gestation. Lucio Tufano introduced me to the website Internet Culturale, indispensable for students of eighteenth-century Italian music. Margaret Butler gave me valuable advice on Italian opera. Robert Gjerdingen helped me apply his promising new analytical framework to a wide variety of eighteenth-century music.

Elisabeth Le Guin, Melanie Lowe, Pierpaolo Polzonetti, Stephen Rumph, and Jessica Waldoff read drafts of the book. I thank them for their warm encouragement and thoughtful, constructive criticism. They inspired me to rewrite several chapters, and I hope they will agree with me that in doing so I have improved them. Richard Freedman and Elizabeth Le Guin used an early version of this text in their classes at Haverford College and the University of California, Los Angeles; their students provided very detailed feedback and helpful suggestions.

The geographical organization of this book owes much to Neal Zaslaw's *The Classical Era*, a book (now out of print) to which I had the honor of contributing a chapter on Vienna in the 1780s. In Chapter 14 of the present book I have incorporated some of the material from my earlier treatment of the same subject.

I am grateful to Walter Frisch for his friendly and inspirational leadership of this project from its inception more than decade ago, and to all my coauthors for their ideas and support. Like the orchestra at Mannheim, the team at Norton is an army of generals. I thank them, and especially Maribeth Payne (their Stamitz) for all the work they have done to bring this project to fruition.

My most heartfelt thanks go to the scholar to whom this book is most indebted, Daniel Heartz. When he kindly read and commented on an early draft, he must have found much of it strangely familiar. The focus on political and musical institutions that characterize his books *Haydn, Mozart, and the Viennese School, 1740–1780*; *Music in European Capitals: The Galant Style, 1720–1780*; and *Mozart, Haydn, and Early Beethoven, 1780–1802* is reflected in this book. But those who know Heartz's books will recognize his influence in many parts of this one. They would not be far off the mark to call this book a radical abridgment, in one small volume, of his big three. As such, I offer it to him as a token of my admiration and friendship.

John Rice

MUSIC IN THE EIGHTEENTH CENTURY

CHAPTER ONE

The Encyclopedic Century

"We live in this world in order to learn industriously and, by exchanging our ideas, to enlighten one another and thus endeavor to promote the sciences and the fine arts." Writing in 1776, at the age of 20, Wolfgang Amadeus Mozart expressed ideals typical of his century: a fundamentally optimistic era that believed in the value of education and the possibility of improving human life through the spread of knowledge. It called itself the "Age of Enlightenment," and the term has been used ever since. The historian Jacques Barzun has proposed an equally appropriate name, the "Encyclopedic Century":

> Encyclopedia—"the circle of teachings"—may be taken as the emblem of the eighteenth century. Like the Renaissance, the age was confident that the new knowledge, the fullness of knowledge, was in its grasp and was a means of emancipation. Confidence came from the visible progress of scientific thought. Science was the application of reason to all questions, no matter what tradition might have handed down. Everything will ultimately be known and "encircled." The goal of exploring nature and mind and broadcasting results was to make Man everywhere of one mind, rational and humane. Language, nation, mores, and religion would cease to create differences, deadly as everybody knew. With a single religion and its universal morals and with French as the international medium of the educated, it would be a world peopled with—or at least managed by—*philosophes*.

1

The encyclopedia to which Barzun referred was not the *Encyclopedia Britannica* (although it too was a product of the eighteenth century) but rather the *Encyclopédie, ou dictionnaire raisonné des sciences, des arts et des métiers* (Systematic Dictionary of the Sciences, Arts, and Crafts) that Denis Diderot conceived, edited, and largely wrote during the third quarter of the eighteenth century. Diderot (1713–1784) was the greatest of the *philosophes*, the French intellectuals whose writings embodied the Enlightenment's values of clarity, elegance, accessibility, and optimism.

Music also expressed those values. The didactic impulse that drove Diderot to complete the *Encyclopédie* also drove Johann Sebastian Bach (1685–1750) to assemble the great series of *Clavier-Übungen* (keyboard exercises) that we might call Bach's "circle of teachings" and that constitute one of Europe's finest musical achievements. The publication in 1735 of the first edition of Carl Linnaeus's *Systema naturae* (Organization of Nature, which led eventually to the system of binomial nomenclature that assigns every animal and plant to a genus and species) followed by ten years the publication of Johann Joseph Fux's *Gradus ad Parnassum* (Steps up Mount Parnassus, 1725), which divides counterpoint into five rhythmic species. (Fux thus systematized an approach to the teaching of counterpoint that went back to the Renaissance, as discussed by Richard Freedman in Chapter 2 of his book in this series.)

"Vaghezza, chiarezza, e buona modulazione" (charm, clarity, and good melody), a recipe for good music by the Italian composer Baldassare Galuppi, represented ideals—characteristic of the Enlightenment—to which many musicians aspired. Mozart wrote of his Piano Concertos K. 413–15 in terms of which Diderot and Galuppi would have approved, and that elegantly capture the encyclopedic century's ideals: "These concertos are a happy medium between what is too easy and too difficult; they are very brilliant, pleasing to the ear, and natural, without being vapid. There are passages here and there from which connoisseurs alone can derive satisfaction; but these passages are written in such a way that the less learned cannot fail to be pleased, though without knowing why."

Musicians born in the eighteenth century expressed the optimism of their age in favoring major keys over minor, not only in the choice of keys for whole works but in the tendency to end in the major mode works that begin in the minor, such as Mozart's Piano Concerto in D Minor, K. 466, and Ludwig van Beethoven's Fifth Symphony in C Minor. Most eighteenth-century operas have happy endings, in which one critic found "certain proof of the progress humankind has made in peacefulness, sophistication, and clemency." In his opera *Romeo und Julie* (Romeo and Juliet, 1776), Georg Benda went so far as to allow the lovers to live happily ever after.

It is characteristic of the eighteenth century that even music mourning the death of Christ contains moments of pure joy. In 1736 Giovanni Battista Pergolesi (1710–1736) made a setting of the *Stabat Mater* (The Mother Was Standing), a medieval poem about the crucifixion. The text of the duet *Inflammatus et accensus* (Lest I burn in the flames of hell) is a fervent prayer to the Virgin Mary for intercession on Judgment Day. Perhaps to inspire confidence in Mary's goodness, Pergolesi departed from the work's prevailing somberness and wrote music whose fast tempo, major mode, jaunty syncopations, and ubiquitous trills convey unmistakable cheerfulness. So does the echo-like repetition pervading the movement (Ex. 1.1).

Example 1.1: *Giovanni Battista Pergolesi*, Stabat Mater, Inflammatus et accensus, *mm. 14–26*

Lest I burn in the flames of hell, let me be defended by you, Virgin, on the day of judgment.

Pergolesi's *Stabat Mater* (about which we'll have more to say in Chapter 2) was performed often, in many parts of Europe, during the rest of the century. It found an early admirer in J. S. Bach, who arranged parts of it as a cantata. The philosopher and novelist Jean-Jacques Rousseau (1712–1778), who wrote on music for Diderot's *Encyclopédie*, praised Pergolesi's opening duet (see Anthology 1) as the most perfect ever written. But the *Stabat Mater* also earned censure for straying too far, even by eighteenth-century standards, from the solemnity of sacred music. The musical scholar Giovanni Battista Martini (to whom Mozart addressed the remark quoted at the beginning of this chapter) may have had *Inflammatus* in mind when he criticized Pergolesi for writing music more suitable for comic opera than for the church.

In stating their opinions of Pergolesi's *Stabat Mater*, Rousseau and Martini participated in a culture of writing about music that flourished in our period. This first great age of musical historiography saw the publication of Charles Burney's four-volume *General History of Music* (1776–89), encyclopedic in its depth and breadth. Fux, in *Gradus ad Parnassum*, presented a manual for the study of counterpoint remarkable for its systematic, pedagogically oriented structure. No books on the playing of the flute, keyboard, or violin have superseded those published in the 1750s by the flutist Johann Joachim Quantz, the keyboard virtuoso Carl Philipp Emanuel Bach, and the violinist Leopold Mozart (excerpts from all three in SR 125: 129, 130; 5/4: 8, 9). One of Quantz's contemporaries referred to the wide-ranging content of his book, which goes far beyond flute technique, by praising it as "a musical encyclopedia."

THE GRAND TOUR

Most of the writers and musicians just mentioned traveled extensively, exemplifying another aspect of eighteenth-century culture. Europe's relatively peaceful and prosperous state after 1715 led to an increase in international travel. The nobility and upper middle classes of Britain, Germany, and France went south to Italy. They toured palaces, visited picture galleries, and sampled the local cuisine. Their travels, collectively, have come to be called the Grand Tour.

Many professional musicians traveled around Europe as well, to enhance their skills, to make money, or to do both at once. Although their travels often differed considerably from those of the noble and wealthy travelers whose experiences typified the Grand Tour, this term will be applied here to all the great travels across Europe made in the eighteenth century, whether for business or pleasure.

The Grand Tour affected music in many ways. It broadened the tastes of both musicians and patrons, bringing foreigners into the theaters of Italy and exposing Italian singers and composers to visitors who might later make recommendations or decisions about hiring those musicians in London, Paris, Berlin, or Vienna. Among the most popular souvenirs that tourists brought home were musical scores.

No musician benefited more from travel than Mozart (1756–1791). His father Leopold's primary motive in organizing the tour that the Mozart family undertook in 1763–66 was to make money from the performances of his two prodigious children, Nannerl and Wolfgang (who was only seven when they left Salzburg). But the trip, to Germany, France, England, the Netherlands, and Switzerland, also benefited the children by exposing them to the languages, customs, and musical styles of Europe's cities and courts. Not by accident did Mozart and his father, on their first trip to Italy in 1769, cross the Alps in December—risking an early winter snowstorm—so as to arrive in Italy near the beginning of the carnival opera season (see Chapter 4). Traveling quickly from one city to another, 13-year-old Wolfgang received a crash course in Italian musical dramaturgy.

In the memoirs of a musician who did not make a Grand Tour, C. P. E. Bach (1714–1788), one senses both defensiveness and regret:

> This lack of foreign travel would have been more disadvantageous to me in my profession if I had not had the special good fortune since my youth to hear, close by, the finest of all kinds of music and to make a great many acquaintances among masters of the first rank, sometimes winning their friendship. . . . I do not deny that it would have been of exceptional pleasure as well as advantage to me if I could have had the opportunity to visit foreign lands.

THE "FISH-TAIL"

The Age of Enlightenment had its dark side. Carl Theodor, ruler of the Palatinate (one of the many small principalities into which the German-speaking part of Europe was divided), whose musical patronage we will examine in Chapter 10, summed up his age's contradictions in a letter to the great French writer Voltaire. After saying that in some respects the eighteenth century deserved to be called a golden age, he continued: "It seems to me that our century resembles those mermaids of whom one half is a lovely nymph and the other a loathsome fish-tail."

Europe built its prosperity largely on the labor of impoverished and illiterate peasants who made up a majority of the population, and on international trade that depended on the buying and selling of human beings and the exploitation of their labor in Europe's colonies (see Chapter 11). The coffee that stimulated intellectuals and artists, and the sugar that made the coffee palatable, were both products of slave labor. Close to slavery was the serfdom that prevailed in parts of central and eastern Europe and that gave noblemen ownership of the peasants who worked their land. The lord of the manor not only had the right to his serfs' labor, but also could legally keep them and their descendants from leaving his property, determine their occupations, and arrange their marriages.

Enlightenment ideals formed the foundations of the Declaration of Independence and the American Constitution, largely written by slave owners. Opera embodied the same paradox. In the first-act finale of Mozart's *Die Zauberflöte* (The Magic Flute, 1791), we enter an enlightened realm dedicated to wisdom and reason. It is also a slave-owning society in which the wise ruler Sarastro uses brutal, even sadistic means to keep the overseer of his slaves in line. He orders that Monostatos be given 77 lashes to the soles of his feet, a punishment that would leave its recipient unable to walk for weeks. Sarastro's subjects approve, singing in chorus: "Long live Sarastro! In his divine wisdom, he rewards and punishes with equal justice."

Slavery and serfdom benefited European music more directly than in producing the wealth that paid for it and the coffee that sustained its production and consumption. The large mixed-race population that resulted from sexual relations between male slave owners and female slaves included several musicians who adopted European musical styles, the most famous being the violinist and composer Joseph Boulogne, Chevalier de Saint-Georges (1745–1799), born on the French Caribbean island of Guadeloupe. The wealthy Russian nobleman Nicholas Sheremetev trained some of his 200,000 serfs to sing, dance, and play in the orchestra of his private theaters (see Chapter 12).

Another institution representing the dark side of our period—and an essential part of its music—was the castration of boys to produce adult male sopranos and altos (see Chapter 3). Viewing musical castration from the perspective of our twenty-first century Western moral system, we might consider it close to slavery in its cruelty. Yet it inspired some of the era's most remarkable musical achievements. The fish-tail was indeed loathsome; but sometimes it glistened with strange, iridescent beauty.

DEMOGRAPHICS AND RELIGION

Western Europe in the eighteenth century was one of the three most populous parts of the world; the other two were India and China. In all three regions peasants made up the vast majority. Peasants constituted about 85 percent of Europe's population. In some colonies, where slaves took the place of peasants in the generation of agricultural wealth, Africans and their descendents constituted an even larger majority; slaves made up 90 percent of the population of mid-eighteenth-century British Jamaica.

At the beginning of the century fewer than 9 percent of Europeans lived in cities with more than 10,000 inhabitants. But the number of large cities in Europe, and the size of the urban population as a whole, increased rapidly. Table 1.1 illustrates these trends; the accompanying map (Fig. 1.1) shows the location of all the cities listed in the table. Bigger cities encouraged greater specialization and greater efficiency in the production and distribution of musical goods and services. The table also illustrates a change in the relative size of cities in different parts of Europe: a shift in the balance of population between south and north. The size of Italy's urban centers, relative to northern Europe, declined. In 1700 Italy had four of the ten largest cities; in 1800 it had only one. ("Italy" here means the geographical area roughly corresponding to the modern republic of Italy, which in the eighteenth century consisted of several separate political entities.) Looked at from a religious point of view, most of the fastest growing cities were predominantly Protestant (London and Berlin) or Russian Orthodox (St. Petersburg and Moscow), while most of the cities that fell in rank were predominantly Catholic. We will see that music thrived in many of the expanding cities. Vienna, Berlin, London, and St. Petersburg all attracted immigrants, including many musicians and instrument builders.

As Wendy Heller notes in *Music in the Baroque*, much of the warfare that afflicted seventeenth-century Europe involved conflict between Catholics and Protestants. They took their religious differences seriously, using music as well as guns in a quest for cultural and military domination. Outstanding musicians emerged from both camps: the best-remembered composers born in the seventeenth century include both Protestants (Dietrich Buxtehude, Henry Purcell, Georg Philipp Telemann, J. S. Bach, George Frideric Handel) and Catholics (Jean-Baptiste Lully, François Couperin, Arcangelo Corelli, Alessandro Scarlatti, Antonio Vivaldi, Jean-Philippe Rameau).

Religious differences continued to exist in the eighteenth century, of course, but they were taken less seriously and treated with more tolerance. Protestants gained the upper hand in military power and commerce; Britain's wealth and Prussia's military strength increased. But in the cultural arena Protestants ceded territory to Catholics. The Grand Tour, largely involving English Protestants traveling to Catholic Italy, was one manifestation of a cultural system in which (broadly speaking) Catholics produced art and Protestants consumed it.

The most prominent composers born in the eighteenth century, from Galuppi and Pergolesi to Ludwig van Beethoven and Franz Schubert, were overwhelmingly Catholic. This was partly a matter of education. Two Catholic lands, Bohemia and Italy, excelled in the training of musicians and became exporters of musical talent—performers as well as composers—to the rest of Europe, including Protestant and Russian Orthodox cities. Catholic composers dominated the composition of opera, which Catholic courts and cities had cultivated from its invention. That two of the greatest opera composers of the century, Johann Adolf Hasse and Johann Christian Bach, were born into Lutheran families but converted to Catholicism reinforced the association between opera and Catholicism. Also associated with Catholic culture were the castrated singers

Table 1.1: *Europe's 16 largest cities in 1700, 1750, and 1800. Each city's predominant religious affiliation is given as Catholic (C), Protestant (P), or Russian Orthodox (O).*

RANK	1700		1750		1800	
	CITY	POPULATION (IN THOUSANDS)	CITY	POPULATION (IN THOUSANDS)	CITY	POPULATION (IN THOUSANDS)
1	London (P)	575	London	675	London	948
2	Paris (C)	500	Paris	570	Paris	550
3	Naples (C)	300	Naples	339	Naples	430
4	Amsterdam (P)	200	Amsterdam	210	Moscow	300
5	Lisbon (C)	180	Lisbon	185	Vienna	247
6	Madrid (C)	140	Vienna	175	St. Petersburg	220
7	Venice (C)	138	Madrid	160	Amsterdam	217
8	Rome (C)	135	Rome	158	Dublin	200
9	Moscow (O)	130	Venice	150	Lisbon	195
10	Milan (C)	125	Moscow	130	Berlin	172
11	Vienna (C)	114	Dublin (C)	129	Madrid	168
12	Palermo (C)	100	Milan	124	Rome	153
13	Lyon (C)	97	Palermo	124	Palermo	139
14	Marseille (C)	90	Lyon	114	Venice	138
15	Brussels (C)	80	Berlin (P)	113	Milan	135
16	Florence (C)	72	St. Petersburg (O)	95	Hamburg (P)	130

Source: Paul Bairoch et al., La population des villes européenes, 800–1850 (Geneva: Droz, 1988). Religious data added by the author.

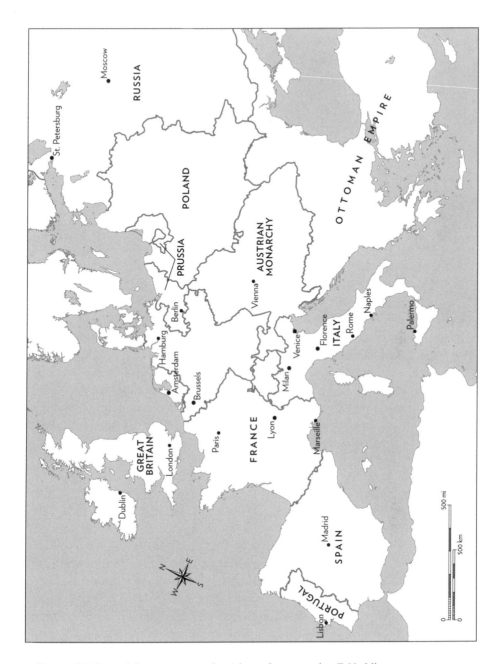

Figure 1.1: *Europe's largest cities in the eighteenth century (see Table 1.1)*

who performed in opera houses and Catholic churches. A characteristic feature of our century is the spread of Catholic musical culture, especially Italian opera, to Protestant London and Berlin and to Russian Orthodox St. Petersburg.

A MUSICOLOGICAL GRAND TOUR

This book discusses aspects of music and musical life in Europe during the century between 1715 and 1815, with a brief glimpse across the Atlantic to music in the European colonies. It devotes considerable attention to musical style, but also explores some of the ways in which music grew out of, reflected, and influenced the culture of which it was a part. Although following the broadly chronological approach of the series as a whole, it is also organized geographically, with chapters that examine the musical life of particular cities, or groups of cities or courts, thus allowing readers to experience something of the Grand Tour so characteristic of our period.

Walter Frisch, in the book that follows this one in the series, demonstrates the usefulness of the terms "Classicism" and "Classical" in defining certain aspects of European culture of the second half of the eighteenth century, and especially in highlighting differences between the cultures of the late eighteenth century ("Classical") and the early nineteenth century ("Romantic"). But in relation to musical style, the term "Classical" has been subject to much criticism in recent years. The music historian James Webster has argued for its abandonment, largely because it leaves music of the period before 1780 in a terminological and analytical limbo. The expression "Viennese Classical Style" has the additional weakness of suggesting that Vienna, alone among Europe's great cities, produced music of lasting value. If we accept Joseph Haydn's late symphonies (written in the 1790s for London, not Vienna!) as definitive examples of the Classical style, how are we to explain and appreciate his earlier symphonies except as "pre-Classical"—interesting but only half-successful attempts to write in a style that came to fruition only later?

No single term can fully acknowledge the stylistic diversity of any period's music; but two words that musicians of the eighteenth century applied frequently to music of their own time—"galant" and "learned"—are used often in this book. So is "Enlightenment," a term sanctioned by the eighteenth century's frequent use of it. Barzun's "Encyclopedic Century" is a richly suggestive phrase with important musical implications. These terms bring with them their own problems, but they have the advantage of allowing us to go beyond the stylistic diversity of eighteenth-century music and to think in general terms about the civilization that produced it.

However obvious it may seem, it may be useful to state that this book deals largely with written music—and therefore with only a small fraction of the music made during the Encyclopedic Century. The music of the vast majority of Europeans—the peasants and the urban working class—was mostly unwritten, and has therefore largely disappeared. So too has the music of the Africans who labored for Europeans in the New World's fields and mines. What remains for us to enjoy and study is the music of the elites: the courts, the aristocracy and other wealthy landowners, the clergy, and the relatively small, urban upper-middle class of professionals and merchants.

When Mozart referred to his "less learned" listeners, he had in mind an audience consisting largely of the Viennese nobility. The complexity of the music that survives from the eighteenth century—even music that Mozart called "pleasing to the ear"—is part of its character. It required years of training and practice to compose and perform. Musicians had to learn an esoteric system of notation with origins in the Middle Ages; they used sophisticated and expensive instruments, difficult to build and play. The urban elites (personified comically by William Hogarth as a violinist who, enraged by the racket outside his window, turns momentarily away from his music stand; Fig. 1.2) treasured their music not only because it gave them pleasure but also because it communicated and confirmed their wealth, education, and good taste.

Figure 1.2: *William Hogarth,* Enrag'd Musician, *1741. The elegant coat, the wig, and the musical notation all identify the violinist at the window (possibly Pietro Castrucci, concertmaster at the King's Theatre) as a representative of the elite musical culture with which this book is almost exclusively concerned.*

Because the music with which this book is concerned was closely associated with the most powerful and richest parts of society, it should come as no surprise that political events contributed to changes in musical life. It makes sense to take politics into account when deciding the chronological limits of the material to be covered.

A cluster of developments that occurred around 1715—the Treaty of Utrecht (which ended the War of the Spanish Succession, the century's first "world war," in 1713), the founding of the Hanoverian dynasty in Britain (1714), and the death of King Louis XIV of France (1715)—helps to define that year as a turning point in European history. The death of the Sun King was followed in France by a period known as the Regency, which saw radical change in the cultural as well as the political climate. Among the musical innovations that followed, perhaps the most important was the development in Italy of what came to be known as the galant style.

While composers of galant music (mostly born after 1700) cultivated a new musical language from the 1720s onward, older composers—J. S. Bach, Handel, and several others—continued to cultivate the genres and styles characteristic of the seventeenth century and the earliest years of the eighteenth. Much of their music came to be described by eighteenth-century musicians as "learned."

This coexistence of old and new, learned and galant, helps to explain and to justify the chronological overlap between this book and Wendy Heller's volume on music in the Baroque. There are good practical reasons, however, to avoid as much as possible overlapping the musical repertory covered in our series, and especially in the anthologies that accompany it. Heller and I have thus generally distinguished between composers born before and after 1700. Heller focuses her attention on the older generation; I focus my attention on the younger generation.

The eighteenth century ended in revolution and war. The Enlightenment produced not only the light of understanding and knowledge but the fire of destruction. It gave rise not only to the *liberté, égalité,* and *fraternité* (liberty, equality, and brotherhood) of the French Revolution, but to the Terror under Robespierre and the militaristic empire building of Napoleon. The Revolution broke out in 1789, and in the following 25 years Europe's great powers were often at war.

Artistic change accompanied the political and military upheavals; the Romantic movement began to transform European culture. But music lagged behind some of the other arts—literature in particular—in responding to the changing world. Frisch, in Chapter 2 of *Music in the Nineteenth Century*, locates the origins of German Romanticism (a term as problematic, he makes clear, as "Classicism") among writers of the 1790s; but he also shows that the Romantic spirit did not begin to dominate music until the 1820s.

The French Revolution marked the beginning of this period of rapid change; the Congress of Vienna (1814–15), which Frisch discusses in his Chapter 3, marked its conclusion. In the aftermath of Napoleon's defeat, diplomats from all over Europe met to decide the Continent's political fate, as they had done a century earlier at Utrecht. Both the Revolution and the Congress offer useful points of orientation; a history of the eighteenth century or of the Age of Enlightenment could legitimately end in 1789 or 1815. But the Congress of Vienna offers a particularly attractive punctuation mark for music historians, for several reasons. One is music's late embrace of Romanticism. Another is the fact that Haydn (1732–1809), one of the greatest composers of the eighteenth century, wrote some of his most important and influential music after the French Revolution. And a third is the remarkable novelty of the works that Beethoven (1770–1827) produced after 1815, which differ in many respects from his earlier music; Beethoven's late works belong, more obviously than his earlier ones, to the aesthetic world of the nineteenth century.

In avoiding such terms as "Viennese Classicism," we almost automatically encourage ourselves to question the prominence most previous surveys of eighteenth-century music have granted to the Austro-German triumvirate of Haydn, Mozart, and Beethoven. No one would dispute the beauty, importance, and value of their music. No one would wish to teach or take a course on eighteenth-century music in which their accomplishments were minimized. Because their intricately crafted scores offer special rewards to those who analyze them closely, I have included a substantial number of movements by them in the accompanying anthology. Yet a modest shifting of emphasis away from the three great composers will, I hope, prove useful as we seek fresh insights into and a deeper understanding of eighteenth-century music and its place in European culture and society.

Some previous books on eighteenth-century music have emphasized instrumental music—in which German composers excelled, which most closely represents the ideals of purely abstract, "absolute" music, and in which nineteenth- and twentieth-century analytical techniques can be most conveniently and fruitfully applied—at the expense of vocal music. I devote less attention to such genres as the string quartet and piano sonata and correspondingly more to church music, opera, and other kinds of vocal music. In discussing instrumental music I call attention to the use of "topics" (various combinations of rhythm, key, meter, melody, harmony, and tempo that carried associations from opera, church music, and elsewhere) to communicate extramusical meaning. One function of my discussion of vocal music, indeed, will be to provide a context for the study of such programmatic works as Haydn's symphony *Le soir* (The Evening) and Beethoven's Sixth (*Pastoral*) Symphony.

One result of my shift in emphasis from instrumental to vocal music is to call attention to the participation of performers, especially singers, in the compositional process. Dennis Libby wrote of improvisation in Italian opera: "The composer determined the general character and structure of the composition and filled in its main outlines, leaving the surface detail to be supplied spontaneously by the performer in the heightened state induced by performance." Most previous surveys of eighteenth-century music have concentrated on the lives and works of composers; this book examines music-making in a wider sense, recognizing the importance of performers in the creative process.

Allowing performers to share the spotlight with composers encourages us to examine the work of more women than would be possible in a study in which composers are viewed as the sole or primary creators. As performers, especially singers and keyboard players, women played a crucial role in music (more important than their role as composers), and this book considers several of them in some detail.

Our musical Grand Tour will revisit many of the cities to which Charles Burney traveled in 1770–72, a little past the midpoint of our century. Even in an age of international travel, Burney's two trips are remarkable for the vast distances he covered, the number of places he visited, and the importance of the musicians he heard and met. In Berlin, Naples, Paris, Vienna, and many other cities, he studied with equal curiosity the manuscripts and old books on which he based his *General History of Music* and the living musical culture in which he found himself. The lively accounts of these journeys that he published on his return to London constitute the successful marriage of two kinds of writing typical of the eighteenth century: travel books and musical criticism. Readers who notice how frequently I quote Burney's eyewitness reports and judgments will agree, I hope, that it would be unwise to write a book about music in eighteenth-century Europe without acknowledging that Burney was there first and learning as much as we can from him.

This is an exciting time to be studying and listening to music of the Encyclopedic Century. More of it than ever can be enjoyed on recordings that seek to re-create the period's sonic values and performance styles. During the last several decades, several books have revolutionized the way we hear and think about this music; I have recommended many of them in lists at the end of each chapter. I hope this book will express some of the excitement I have felt in trying to come to terms with the new ideas now circulating among these and other students of eighteenth-century music. If readers turn quickly to their books, I will consider mine a success.

FOR FURTHER READING

Black, Jeremy, *The British Abroad: The Grand Tour in the Eighteenth Century* (New York: St. Martin's Press, 1992)

Blanning, Tim, *The Pursuit of Glory: Europe, 1648–1815* (New York: Viking Penguin, 2007)

The Cambridge History of Eighteenth-Century Music, ed. Simon P. Keefe (Cambridge: Cambridge University Press, 2009)

The Classical Era: From the 1740s to the End of the 18th Century, ed. Neal Zaslaw (Englewood Cliffs, NJ: Prentice Hall, 1989)

The Eighteenth Century: Europe in the Age of Enlightenment, ed. Alfred Cobban (New York: McGraw Hill, 1969)

Heartz, Daniel, *Music in European Capitals: The Galant Style, 1720–1780* (New York: W. W. Norton, 2003)

Taruskin, Richard, *The Oxford History of Western Music,* vol. 2, *The Seventeenth and Eighteenth Centuries* (New York: Oxford University Press, 2005)

Webster, James, "The Eighteenth Century as a Music-Historical Period?" *Eighteenth-Century Music* 1 (2004): 47–60

Ⓢ **Additional resources available at wwnorton.com/studyspace**

CHAPTER TWO

Learned and Galant

In 1713 the Treaty of Utrecht ended the War of the Spanish Succession, in which England, Holland, Austria, and France had been involved since 1701. Taking a longer view: the treaty, together with the death of Louis XIV two years later, marked the end of a series of wars of which the French king had been a major instigator during much of his 72-year reign, and which, in combination with the Thirty Years' War (1618–48) and the English Civil War (1642–51), had made the seventeenth century and the beginning of the eighteenth a period of great bloodshed and destruction in much of Europe. The decades that followed Utrecht, although not free of war, were considerably more peaceful than those that preceded it.

No ruler shaped the cultural life of seventeenth-century Europe more completely than Louis XIV (1638–1715; see Wendy Heller's *Music in the Baroque*), and his influence continued to be felt in the eighteenth century. Yet in many respects the Regency—the eight-year period (1715–23) following the Sun King's death, when the Duke of Orléans ruled as regent for Louis's underage great-grandson—saw a reaction against the tastes of Louis and his court. The Regency initiated a period that simultaneously embraced two cultures: one that aspired to preserve seventeenth-century values and one that sought to replace them. The dichotomy was partly a matter of generations. People born in the seventeenth century tended to support the old culture; people who came of age during the Regency or after tended to support the new one. Older men wore long hair or wigs in the style of Louis XIV, younger ones wore shorter hair (Fig. 2.1).

16

Figure 2.1: *August the Strong (1670–1733), elector of Saxony and king of Poland, and King Frederick William I of Prussia (1688–1740); double portrait by Louis de Silvestre, ca. 1730 (detail). With his long wig August declares allegiance to the tastes of the court of Louis XIV. Frederick William's much shorter hair identifies him not only as an officer in the Prussian army (where the fashion for shorter hair was adopted very early) but also as a man considerably younger than the elector of Saxony.*

The old and new cultures coexisted and interacted. While preserving some aspects of the grand formality and complicated etiquette of the court of Louis XIV, Parisian society under the Regency favored the informality and intimacy of the salon. The enormous palace at Versailles continued to impress visitors, but the aristocracy preferred Paris and built residences that delighted those who entered with the intricate play of curved surfaces and delicate ornamentation inspired by foliage, garlands of flowers, cresting waves, and seashells (for an example of this kind of decoration in a musical context, see Fig. 7.3). They opened up their interiors to sunlight that fell on lightly colored surfaces: white, pastels, and gold leaf. While some artists cultivated the grand traditions of

Figure 2.2: *Antoine Watteau,* La gamme d'Amour *(The Scale of Love), ca. 1717*

historical and religious painting promoted under Louis XIV, others, led by Antoine Watteau, charmed their viewers with small images of theatrical scenes and of amorous couples in pleasant outdoor surroundings (Fig. 2.2). The plays of the great seventeenth-century dramatists Pierre Corneille and Jean Racine continued to be performed and imitated in Paris, but now they had to compete with Italian commedia dell'arte (improvised comedy involving stock characters and plotlines), in the form of a company summoned by the regent himself in 1716.

The Grand Tour and the climate of cosmopolitanism that it promoted allowed the innovations and contradictions associated with the Regency to spread quickly. Imitating Versailles, rulers in Germany, Italy, and elsewhere built big palaces, such as Eszterháza in Hungary (see Fig. 10.3). Yet the palace of Sanssouci (French for "without a care") that King Frederick the Great of Prussia built at Potsdam reflected a different taste: in its modest size, its architectural style and decoration, and its very name, it conveyed values associated with the Regency. Dozens of churches were built or remodeled in the countryside of Catholic Bavaria and Austria. Instead of the bare stone with which seventeenth-century architects clothed many of their buildings in shades of gray, these new churches glowed with brightly painted stucco; their interiors enveloped congregations and pilgrims in lovely visions of light and color (Fig. 2.3).

Figure 2.3: *The Church of St. Peter and St. Paul, Steinhausen, designed by Domenicus Zimmermann with ceiling fresco by Johann Baptist Zimmermann, 1733*

OLD AND NEW MUSICAL STYLES

Music felt the effects of the coexistence of new and old so characteristic of the Regency and the years that followed. Many of the musicians who came of age during the reign of Louis XIV continued to express the aesthetic ideals of his era well into the eighteenth century, while musicians born after 1700 tended to express a very different taste, exploring genres, forms, and techniques that together constitute the basis for many of the greatest musical achievements of the later eighteenth century.

Johann Sebastian Bach (to whom Wendy Heller devotes a full chapter in *Music in the Baroque*) and George Frideric Handel, both born in 1685, were among several composers who evoked the musical values of the age of Louis XIV for many years after his death. Their musical language came to be called the "learned style"; other eighteenth-century terms that sometimes carried the same meaning were "fugal," "strict," and "ecclesiastical." Composers in the learned style shared with the musical culture of their childhood a fondness for counterpoint (though few of them used it as much as Bach). They would have agreed with Friedrich Wilhelm Marpurg's view, in his *Abhandlung von der Fuge* (Treatise on Fugue) of 1753–54, of counterpoint as a universal language that transcended national boundaries and changing fashions: "An advantage of counterpoint is that it is not based on the changeable style of the day and its wretched traits, which creates a dubious taste; at the present time there is neither a German, nor a French, nor an Italian counterpoint, while at the same time all nations agree that counterpoint is truth in music."

Learned composers applied the century-old technique of basso continuo (a bass part whose harmonic implications are realized in performance by one or more chordal instruments) to a line that shared melodic interest with the upper parts, which resulted in a fast harmonic rhythm. A melodic style that involved the spinning out of lines, primarily by means of sequence and the repetition of short motives, accompanied a tonal fluidity by which passages move seamlessly from one key to another. Among the instrumental genres most closely associated with the learned style were the French overture, the trio sonata, the keyboard suite, and the concerto grosso.

In France the most obvious musical embodiment of the reign of Louis XIV was the operatic oeuvre of Jean-Baptiste Lully (1632–1687), whose works continued to be performed and admired in Paris during much of the eighteenth century. The operas that Jean-Philippe Rameau (1683–1764) wrote in the 1730s and 1740s are built on the solid foundation of the Lullian tradition, though some devotees of Lully failed to recognize this at the time.

But just as the Regency encouraged new tastes to develop in French architecture and painting, so too did French music turn in new directions. Composers of instrumental music, in emphasizing brevity, simple harmony, and transparent, homophonic textures, produced a sonic counterpart to the bright, airy interiors created by Regency architects and decorators. François Couperin (1668–1733), in his second book of *Pièces de clavecin* (Keyboard Pieces, published in 1716), included a piece that in its title as well as its musical substance perfectly evokes the spirit of the Regency: *Les graces naturelles* (The Natural Graces; Ex. 2.1). Utterly simple in texture and phrase structure, the first strain uses only tonic and dominant harmony. The melodic descent in the second strain, from the sixth scale degree down to the third over a bass descending from the fourth scale degree to the tonic, was to be repeated countless times by composers all over Europe during the eighteenth century. This music's goal is to charm and delight the player and listener; and it does that perfectly.

Meanwhile, beginning during the 1720s, a new generation of operatic composers came to the fore in Naples (see Chapter 3). Their innovations, while not directly inspired by French music, expressed some of the values of the Regency: lightness, clarity, playfulness, and elegance. The music by which such Naples-trained composers as Johann Adolf Hasse and Giovanni Battista

Example 2.1: *François Couperin,* Les graces naturelles, *mm. 1–12, from the second book of* Pièces de clavecin *(Paris, 1716)*

Pergolesi projected these values rapidly won acclaim in much of Europe, and composers throughout the continent adopted their style, which came to be called *galant*—a French word adopted by the Germans and, in the form *galante*, by the Italians and Spanish as well. (Writers in English, in contrast, seem to have been reluctant to use it, or its English cognate "gallant," in a specifically musical sense. It has come into common use only recently.)

Hasse, Pergolesi, and their contemporaries largely rejected counterpoint and divorced the melodic function of the upper part from the accompanimental function of the bass. The lean textures that resulted often involved just melody and bass, or two upper parts in parallel thirds and sixths above the bass. Harmonic rhythm slowed down, often to a rate of one or two chords per measure. The bass line, shorn of its melodic interest, often imparted a sense of momentum and excitement by moving in repeated quarter notes or eighth notes. Melodies were often laid out in phrases of two (or multiples of two) measures, with frequent use of antecedent-consequent phrase structure. Galant composers especially loved **ABB** or **ABB'** melodies consisting of three phrases, usually of equal length, of which the second and third are similar or identical. They favored particular rhythmic devices, such as Lombard rhythms (reverse dotted rhythms), triplets, and syncopations.

Galant composers liked to emphasize subdominant harmony, often in the form of a subdominant chord above a tonic pedal. Half cadences often served to articulate important breaks in the musical discourse. Augmented-sixth chords, rarely used by composers born in the seventeenth century, became popular with young composers in the 1720s. Among the instrumental genres frequently cultivated by galant composers were the three-movement concerto and two relatively new genres: the keyboard sonata and the symphony.

The first movement of a sonata in F major for keyboard (see Anthology 13) composed by a precocious teenage girl, Anna Bon (ca. 1740–?), and published in the mid-1750s exemplifies the galant in genre and style (see Chapter 10 for more on Bon). In her dedicatory message Bon referred to her sonatas as *divertimenti*, a word used often in the context of eighteenth-century music, emphasizing their role as entertainment. A two-part texture directs our attention to a graceful, triplet-laden melodic line. The six-measure melody ends with a descending three-note scale segment on the downbeat—one of several similar decorative elements that galant composers loved. We have already seen similar three-note slides in *Inflammatus et accensus*, the duet from Pergolesi's *Stabat Mater* illustrated in Example 1.1.

BINARY AND DA CAPO FORM: MUSICAL COMMON GROUND

Learned and galant composers also shared some musical forms. Composers young and old, born in the seventeenth century or the eighteenth, all relied on two of the age's most ubiquitous formal schemes: binary form and da capo form.

It was largely through French dance movements that binary form spread throughout Europe during the late seventeenth and early eighteenth centuries. It spread not only geographically but also across musical genres, becoming as common in opera and church music as in dance music. Movements in binary form have two parts. The first part usually modulates to a new key (typically the dominant or relative major) and cadences there. The second part usually begins in a foreign key (often the key in which the first part ends) and modulates back to the tonic. Composers of instrumental movements in binary form usually called for both parts to be repeated.

Within these basic parameters, eighteenth-century composers produced an astonishing variety of movements, vocal as well as instrumental. In what is often called "parallel binary form," the two parts are closely parallel in length and melodic content; such movements can be represented ‖:A:‖ ‖:A′:‖. In what is known as "rounded binary form," the second part (longer than the first part) ends with a restatement of some or all of the material from the first part (but arranged so that it now ends in the tonic); such movements can be represented ‖:A:‖ ‖:B A′:‖. The first movement of Bon's Keyboard Sonata in F Major offers a good example of rounded binary form. Sonata form (to be discussed in Chapter 7), one the most productive of eighteenth-century musical forms, is itself an elaboration of binary form, whose diversity helps to explain the analogous diversity that we will encounter in sonata-form movements.

Vocal movements in binary form rarely require that both parts be repeated; that lack of repetition sometimes obscures their binary framework. Pergolesi's duet *Stabat mater dolorosa* (see Anthology 1) exemplifies parallel binary form. After an instrumental introduction, the first part begins with an ascending chain of suspensions in the tonic, F minor, modulates to the dominant, C minor, and ends with cadential material in the orchestra. The second part, three measures longer, presents the same text and most of the same melodic material, beginning in C minor and modulating back to the tonic.

Composers used binary form not only for whole movements, but also (especially in the later part of our period) for melodies. To cite just two examples, the final movement of Joseph Haydn's String Quartet in E♭ Major, from the set of six quartets published in 1781 as Opus 33 (see Anthology 19), is a rondo, in which a theme is presented several times in the tonic, interspersed with contrasting material called "episodes"; this theme is in rounded binary form. The slow movement of Haydn's Symphony No. 97 in C Major (see Anthology 24) is a set of variations on a theme, the theme itself being in binary form.

Composers of the early eighteenth century such as Alessandro Scarlatti wrote da capo and dal segno arias, in which a binary movement, performed twice, serves as the first and third elements of a larger **ABA** structure. The dal segno aria differs from the da capo aria only in that after the **B** section the performer returns not to the beginning (*capo*) of the **A** section but to a point later in the **A** section marked with a sign (*segno*); thus the second **A** section is shorter than the first. These arias gave singers an opportunity, in the second **A** section, to embellish a vocal line already familiar to listeners. Galant composers, however innovative in texture, harmony, and melodic style, made few changes in the large-scale form of the aria they inherited from Scarlatti and his contemporaries.

COEXISTENCE AND INTERACTION OF STYLES

The flutist Johann Joachim Quantz (1697–1773) traveled through Europe as a young man. After a trip to Prague in 1724 for the coronation of Charles VI as king of Bohemia, he began a Grand Tour that took him to Italy, France, and England. Quantz's reminiscences help to clarify the stylistic dichotomy he encountered. In Prague, the opera *Costanza e fortezza* (Constancy and Strength) by Johann Joseph Fux (1660–1741) was part of the coronation festivities:

> The opera was performed outdoors by 100 singers and 200 instrumental-ists. It was written more in the ecclesiastical style than theatrically, but made a magnificent effect. . . . Although consisting of movements that might appear stiff and dry on paper, [it] mostly made, with so numerous a band, an excellent effect, indeed a much better one than would have a more galant melody ornamented with many small figures and quick notes.

Quantz's opinion that the galant style was particularly suited to small-scale music-making, while the learned or ecclesiastical style made a better impression in music played outdoors by a large orchestra, calls to mind the parallel paths in eighteenth-century architecture that led, more or less simultaneously, to the jewel-like churches of Bavaria and the awe-inspiring palaces at Eszterháza and elsewhere. The association between massed performing forces and the learned style would eventually find expression in the Handel festivals of late eighteenth-century London, where hundreds of instrumentalists and singers performed his oratorios in Westminster Abbey.

As Quantz continued his discussion of Fux's opera, he mentioned Lully in such a way as to imply that Fux's style in some respects resembled that of the great seventeenth-century opera composer:

> It goes without saying that a more galant song for the instruments, admittedly better in a smaller locale and with fewer players, would be impossible to perform with appropriate ensembles here, especially being executed by so many musicians who were unused to playing with each other. . . . The truth of this observation convinced me on many other occasions, including at Dresden, where the otherwise rather dry overtures of Lully, when played by a full orchestra, make a better effect than do many more pleasant and galant overtures by other famous composers, works that, in a chamber, unquestionably receive preference.

Quantz's mention of Lully in connection with *Costanza e fortezza* begins to make sense when we consider what the performance of Fux's opera looked like (Fig. 2.4): it was clearly intended to remind its audience of the great spectacles at the court of Louis XIV.

In Italy, Quantz met both Alessandro Scarlatti (1660–1725), now near the end of his career, and his son Domenico (1685–1757). Alessandro, whom he called "one of the greatest contrapuntists of his time," played the keyboard "in a learned manner." Domenico, in contrast, was "a galant keyboard player in the manner of the time." There is no clearer testimony to the generational component in eighteenth-century music's stylistic dichotomy, even if the younger Scarlatti, an exact contemporary of Handel and J. S. Bach, was unusually old when he found his galant voice (see Chapter 5).

Although Quantz treasured some aspects of galant music, he also criticized it. An attack on contemporary Italian composers in his book on flute playing is largely directed toward what he perceived as the excessive simplicity of galant part-writing:

> Their basses are neither majestic nor melodious, and have no particular connection with the principal part. Neither the fruits of labor nor anything

Figure 2.4: *Johann Joseph Fux's* Costanza e fortezza, *performed on an outdoor stage in Prague in celebration of the coronation of Emperor Charles VI as king of Bohemia, August 1723, in an attempt to evoke the splendor of the court of Louis XIV. Engraving by Birckart after designs by Giuseppe Galli.*

venturesome is apparent in their middle parts; you find simply dry harmony. And even in their solos they cannot endure a bass that occasionally has some melodic motion. They much prefer it if the bass moves along quite tediously, is but rarely heard, or always drums upon the same note.

Other musicians were equally critical of the learned style. One of the earliest to articulate the galant aesthetic in writing was Johann David Heinichen (1683–1729), author of a book on figured bass realization. Heinichen was a child of the seventeenth century; in his youth, he wrote, he had been "an ardent adherent" of counterpoint. But having spent the years 1711–17 in Italy, he experienced something of a midlife crisis in regard to the learned style. To "embittered contrapuntists" who defended themselves by saying that "one can unite art with good taste," Heinichen responded:

These gentlemen never observe their own watchword, for if one listens to their very best music it sounds as if someone were beating the dust out

of an old woman's fur coat, or (as others say) as if a child who is learning to read were spelling out something, understandable as syllables and
words, but not the full sense or connection [of these words in a sentence].
In short, when the performance is finished one does not know what the
fellow meant to say.

Heinichen's views, probably exceptional among musicians born in the 1680s,
found easy converts among the young. In 1737 the thirty-year-old composer
Johann Adolf Scheibe published his notorious put-down of his former teacher,
J. S. Bach, who at 52 was old enough to be his father: "This great man would be
the admiration of whole nations if he had more amenity, if he did not take away
the natural element in his pieces by giving them a turgid and confused style, and
if he did not darken their beauty by an excess of art [that is, artifice]."

When not preoccupied with such polemics, most eighteenth-century musicians would have agreed that there was a time and place for both galant and
learned music. Indeed, a stylistic dualism continued to be a feature of music
throughout our period. The composer Johann Philipp Kirnberger (1721–1783), a
student of J. S. Bach, published in the 1770s a book on composition in the learned
style, which he characterized as particularly appropriate for the church, whereas
the galant style was suitable for the theater and concert room.

Even as late as the 1790s, the violinist and composer Heinrich Christoph
Koch (1749–1816) still saw the dichotomy between the galant and the learned
(which he called "strict" or "fugal" style) as crucial to an understanding of the
music of his time. On the composing of a string quartet, he wrote: "If it really is
to consist of four obbligato [essential] voices of which none has priority over the
others, then it must be treated according to fugal method. But because the modern quartets are composed in the *galant* style, there are four main voices which
alternately predominate and sometimes this one, sometimes that one forms the
customary bass" (SR 126: 813–14; 5/5: 79–80).

Koch acknowledged the importance of the learned style in Mozart's string
quartets, which he praised as "unique in their special mixture of strict and free
styles." But the uniqueness of these quartets consists less in the coexistence
of galant and learned than in the skill and inventiveness with which Mozart
achieved that interaction. Such stylistic mixture characterizes much of the century's best music, as illustrated by two masterpieces, one from the first half of
our period and one from the second half. Almost 70 years after Pergolesi wrote
his *Stabat Mater*, Beethoven revolutionized orchestral music with his huge Third
Symphony, the *Sinfonia eroica* (Heroic Symphony, 1804). Its slow movement, like
Pergolesi's work, is a meditation on death; Beethoven entitled it *Marcia funebre*
(Funeral March).

Pergolesi's *Stabat mater dolorosa* (see Anthology 1) is dominated by a steady
walking bass and suspensions in the upper parts: learned music, and clearly

derived from the trio-sonata textures cultivated by Arcangelo Corelli in the late seventeenth century (as discussed by Wendy Heller). But the movement is punctuated three times by homophonic drives to the cadence with antecedent–consequent phrases, treble parts in parallel thirds, and a bass line (on the scale degrees $\hat{3}$–$\hat{4}$–$\hat{5}$–$\hat{6}$, $\hat{3}$–$\hat{4}$–$\hat{5}$–$\hat{1}$), a favorite cadential formula of the early galant composers.

The slow movement of Beethoven's *Eroica* Symphony (see Anthology 28) begins with music whose grandeur and monumentality are characteristic of the revolutionary age in which it was written, yet its balanced phrase structure, slow harmonic rhythm, homophonic texture, and Lombard rhythms are all galant; so is the use of augmented-sixth harmony (at m. 22) as part of a half cadence. The sustaining of dominant harmony (V of C minor) over the following measures takes to its extreme the slow harmonic rhythm typical of the galant style. Yet at the core of this movement is a splendid fugato (a fugue-like passage) in the most learned style.

The march and the fugato are worlds apart, yet they are both products of a musical culture that valued a synthesis of learned and galant—not only in the obvious sense that they are both parts of the same movement, but also in the fugato's incorporation of galant elements. The ascending fourth in its principal subject is an inversion of the descending fourth heard earlier in a completely homophonic context. Anyone who has looked (in vain) for dynamic marks in J. S. Bach's fugues will notice that Beethoven's interest in dynamic contrast and gradation—which he shared with other composers born in the eighteenth century—is just as apparent in his fugato as in his march.

TEACHING AND LEARNING

Eighteenth-century musical education, at its best, often involved instruction in both the learned and the galant. Quantz, during his visit to Italy in the 1720s, studied with old Francesco Gasparini (1668–1727), whose contrapuntal skills he admired. But in his early attempts at composition he was drawn to instrumental genres that favored a galant approach:

> After I had become rather tired of the contrived "eye music" I turned again to "ear music," and again composed solos [that is, pieces for a single treble instrument and basso continuo], trios [for two treble instruments and basso continuo], and a concerto. Although my studies had given me a decided advantage in the kind of composition that served me well in the writing of trios and quartets, yet I had to discard much of that learning when composing solos and concertos, so as not to fall into the stiffness and dryness so often associated with artificial counterpoint. I resolved to

keep in view the aim of always combining art with nature, to keep a steady balance between melody and harmony, and to look upon good invention and well-chosen ideas as the most essential thing in music.

Quantz's dichotomy of "eye music" (learned) and "ear music" (galant) is typical of his century, whose polemics were often marred by superficial name calling. But this dichotomy is not quite as simplistic as it might seem. It invokes the tendency of galant scores to serve as frameworks for performances that included elaborate improvisation. Such works are "ear music" in the sense that they cannot be fully appreciated except in the context of a particular performance. Quantz's ambition to find a balance between galant and learned exemplifies the eighteenth-century's approach to musical education.

Studying the learned style often involved working through Fux's *Gradus ad Parnassum*. The Viennese composer Johann Schenk (1753–1836) studied during the 1770s with Georg Christoph Wagenseil (1715–1777). A composer of galant instrumental music, Wagenseil in his teaching balanced two stylistic worlds, according to Schenk:

> Wagenseil's method of teaching composition was based on the theories of Johann Fux, who had been his teacher. . . . In the course of my studies I devoted some of my time to practicing the keyboard. Sebastian Bach's preludes and fugues as well as the keyboard suites by Handel served for my practice material. . . . My wise teacher guided me to the art of composing in a freer style. His intentions seemed to have been to wean me from the dry movement and to direct me toward a beautifully blossoming melody. Here my paragon was Adolf Hasse for the serious compositions and Baldassare Galuppi for the comic ones.

Schenk, in turn, taught Beethoven shortly after his arrival in Vienna in 1792. Schenk heard the brilliant young pianist from Bonn improvise: "The beauty of the manifold motifs, interwoven so clearly with utter loveliness, compelled my attention and I let myself be carried away by this delightful impression." But Schenk soon discovered a weakness in Beethoven's musical skills, when he chanced to see some of his counterpoint exercises on a table and found them riddled with errors. Seeking to instill in Beethoven the same breadth of musical values and skills that he had inherited from Wagenseil, Schenk gave him a copy of *Gradus ad Parnassum* and guided him through it. Their work together was to pay off in such passages as the fugato in the second movement of the *Eroica* Symphony.

Although composers born in the eighteenth century generally favored the galant style in writing operas and instrumental music, in the church they often had recourse to the learned style, whose connotations of antiquity added weight and solemnity to their music. Composers born in the seventeenth century, who tended to be more comfortable in the learned style, were drawn to instrumental genres (such as the trio sonata and French overture) that demanded contrapuntal textures. As composers of vocal music, they tended to devote much of their energy to church music (J. S. Bach) or oratorio (Handel). But Italian opera demanded modernity. When older composers such as Handel and Antonio Vivaldi tried to compete with their younger, more galant contemporaries on the operatic stage, the younger composers often prevailed.

Because churches employed many of Europe's professional musicians, it made sense for aspiring composers to be trained in counterpoint. But there was another good reason to study the learned style as well as the galant: for those like Pergolesi and Beethoven who became expert at both, the possibilities of combining them were limitless.

FOR FURTHER READING

Heartz, Daniel, *Music in European Capitals: The Galant Style, 1720–1780* (New York: W. W. Norton, 2003), 3–65

Quantz, Johann Joachim, *On Playing the Flute*, trans. Edward R. Reilly (New York: Schirmer, 1966)

Ratner, Leonard G., *Classic Music: Expression, Form, and Style* (New York: Schirmer, 1980)

Rosen, Charles, *Sonata Forms* (New York: W. W. Norton, 1988), 16–70

Schönberger, Arno, and Halldor Soehner, *The Rococo Age: Art and Civilization of the Eighteenth Century* (New York: McGraw Hill, 1960)

Sheldon, David A., "The Galant Style Revisited and Re-evaluated," *Acta musicologica* 47 (1975): 240–70

Sisman, Elaine, *Mozart: The "Jupiter" Symphony* (Cambridge: Cambridge University Press, 1993), 68–79

Yearsley, David, *Bach and the Meanings of Counterpoint* (Cambridge: Cambridge University Press, 2002)

Ⓖ Additional resources available at wwnorton.com/studyspace

CHAPTER THREE

Naples

The tenor Michael Kelly (1762–1826) personified eighteenth-century musical cosmopolitanism. Born in Dublin, he studied in Naples, sang in the premiere of Mozart's *Le nozze di Figaro* (The Marriage of Figaro, 1786) in Vienna, and enjoyed a successful career as a singer and impresario in London. At the age of 17 he sailed from Ireland to Italy on a Swedish merchant ship. His arrival, as he described it in his memoirs, followed a nocturnal storm that left him terrified and seasick:

> I was awakened by the cabin-boy on the following morning, the 30th of May 1779, who to my great joy, told me that we were in the Bay of Naples.
>
> The astonishment and delight I experienced when I got on deck, can never be effaced from my recollection. The morning was beautiful; I was restored to health, and safe in the wished-for port.
>
> The Bay, full of shipping, the Island of Caprea [Capri] where Augustus and Tiberius once held their revels; to the West the Isles of Procida, and Ischia, the picturesque and varied scenery of Pozzuoli, Posilipo . . . the King's Palace at Portici, the Campagna Felice, the Castle and Fort of St. Elmo, the delightful coast of Tarentum, the Castel a Mare, and the City of Naples, with its numerous palaces and convents, have beauties far, far beyond my feeble powers of description.

Figure 3.1: *View of Naples and Mount Vesuvius*

Kelly's destination was Europe's third-largest city (after London and Paris) and Italy's largest by far: the capital of a kingdom comprising most of southern Italy. Situated in a splendid natural amphitheater with views of the Mediterranean and Mount Vesuvius (Fig. 3.1), it attracted visitors from all over Europe. Its wonders of nature (the volcano was more active than now) and of art (Greek and Roman antiquities, churches, palaces, castles, and theaters) made it one of the principal destinations of the Grand Tour. Emblematic of sensual, even dangerous beauty, Naples was the setting of Mozart's study in seduction, *Così fan tutte* (All Women Act Like That, 1790; to be discussed in Chapter 14).

Naples gained almost mythical status as a musical city. Jean-Jacques Rousseau singled it out in 1768 as the place where young musicians could go to learn if they had real talent for composition:

> So you want to know if some spark of this devouring flame inspires you? Run, fly to Naples to hear the masterpieces of Leo, Durante, Jommelli, and Pergolesi. If your eyes fill with tears, if you feel your heart palpitate, if you are seized with trembling, if oppressive feelings suffocate you in the midst of your rapture, then take up Metastasio and go to work. His genius will warm yours. You will create by his example. That is what makes genius.

Rousseau himself never went to Naples, and the music of most of the composers he named was no longer performed there much in the 1760s. The great librettist Pietro Metastasio (to be discussed in Chapter 4) did indeed begin his career in Naples, but soon left. Rousseau alluded to a golden age of Neapolitan music that existed largely in his imagination. Yet his advice reflects the exalted reputation enjoyed by composers trained in Naples.

MUSICAL EDUCATION

Naples established itself by the end of the seventeenth century as Italy's leading center of musical education. Here, aspiring musicians could not only learn their craft at one of several conservatories, but could count on early and frequent opportunities—in the city's many churches, theaters, and private music rooms—to display their abilities. Charles Burney, who visited Naples in 1770, had a more realistic view than Rousseau of the musical education the city provided. He recorded his impressions of one of the conservatories:

> I . . . visited all the rooms where the boys practise, sleep, and eat. On the first flight of stairs was a trumpeter, screaming upon his instrument till he was ready to burst; on the second was a French horn, bellowing in the same manner. In the common practising room there was a *Dutch concert*, consisting of seven or eight harpsichords, more than as many violins, and several voices, all performing different things, and in different keys: other boys were writing in the same room; but it being holiday time, many were absent who usually study and practise in this room. (SR 144: 994; 5/23: 260)

The situation did not favor the production of outstanding instrumental soloists, but could turn out many musicians able to play in the orchestras of Italy's theaters and churches:

> The jumbling them all together in this manner may be convenient for the house, and may teach the boys to attend to their own parts with firmness, whatever else may be going forward at the same time; it may likewise give them force, by obliging them to play loud in order to hear themselves; but in the midst of such jargon [noise], and continued dissonance, it is wholly impossible to give any kind of polish or finishing to their performance; hence the slovenly coarseness so remarkable in their public exhibitions; and the total want of taste, neatness, and expression in all these young musicians, till they have acquired them elsewhere.
>
> The beds, which are in the same room, serve for seats to the harpsichords and other instruments. Out of thirty or forty boys who were

practising, I could discover but two that were playing the same piece; some of those who were practising on the violin seemed to have a great deal of hand [dexterity]. The violoncellos practise in another room; and the flutes, oboes, and other wind instruments in a third, except the trumpets and horns, which are obliged to fag [practice], either on the stairs, or on the top of the house.

There are in this college sixteen young *castrati* [see below], and these lie upstairs, by themselves, in warmer apartments than the other boys, for fear of colds, which might not only render their delicate voices unfit for exercise at present, but hazard the entire loss of them forever. (SR 144: 994–95; 5/23: 260–61)

Years of intensive practice compensated to some extent for the terrible conditions under which it took place. At least so Burney hoped, describing a daily schedule that required the students to rise two hours before dawn and to practice, except for an hour and a half for meals, until eight in the evening. (Conditions had changed little since the Franciscan missionary Michelangelo Guattini visited a Neapolitan orphanage in the 1670s, as Wendy Heller describes in *Music in the Baroque*.) The variety of abilities that such a rigorous education fostered allowed musicians, on leaving the conservatory, to develop their careers in any of several directions, according to their talents and circumstances, and to handle the various artistic and administrative demands placed on music directors.

PARTIMENTI AND GALANT SCHEMATA

One of the most important tools of musical training in Naples was the *partimento*, a bass line whose harmonic and melodic implications students realized at the keyboard. *Partimenti* helped budding composers build up a repertory of essential musical gestures. They also played a role in the training of singers, whose music was often notated in the form of vocal scores consisting only of the vocal part and the bass. Practice in the realization of *partimenti* made it easier for singers to accompany themselves at the keyboard, as well as facilitating vocal improvisation—an essential skill for eighteenth-century singers.

In these *partimenti* the theorist Robert Gjerdingen has recently (2007) identified what he calls "schemata" (singular, "schema"): voice-leading patterns involving combinations of melody and bass, consisting of particular phrases, cadences, and sequences that every eighteenth-century musician—singer, accompanist, or composer—was expected to use over and over in various combinations. Gjerdingen has shown that the schemata found in *partimenti* are ubiquitous in galant music. By isolating and naming the schemata, and showing how composers used them, Gjerdingen has given us a promising new set of tools for the analysis of eighteenth-century music.

Table 3.1: *Prototype of the Galant Romanesca*

Tables 3.1, 3.2, and 3.3 adapted from Robert O. Gjerdingen, Music in the Galant Style *(New York: Oxford University Press, 2007), Appendix A*

METRICAL CONTEXT	Strong	Weak	Strong	Weak
SCALE DEGREES IN MELODY	$\hat{1}$	$\hat{5}$	$\hat{1}$	$\hat{1}$
SCALE DEGREES IN BASS	$\hat{1}$	$\hat{7}$	$\hat{6}$	$\hat{3}$

Among the melodic–harmonic schemata taught in Naples through the realization of *partimenti* is the romanesca, which has a long history going back to the Renaissance. In its most common galant form it involves a bass descending by step from scale degree $\hat{1}$ down to $\hat{7}$, $\hat{6}$, and then (often but not always) leaping down to $\hat{3}$ (Table 3.1). The overture to the opera *La finta cameriera* (The Pretend Chambermaid) by Gaetano Latilla (1711–1788), who studied in Naples, exemplifies the romanesca (Ex. 3.1).

Example 3.1: *Gaetano Latilla,* La finta cameriera, *overture, movement 1, mm. 53–56*

Another schema combines a bass descending by step from the fourth to the first scale degree and a melodic line descending by step from the sixth scale degree to the third (Table 3.2). As eighteenth-century musicians do not seem to have referred to this schema in writing, Gjerdingen named it the Prinner, after Johann Jakob Prinner (1624–1694), who included an example of it in a treatise published in 1677. Composers found the Prinner particularly useful as a response to or continuation of a musical idea stated earlier; they rarely began a melody with it. We have already referred to two pieces that use it: François Couperin's *Les graces naturelles*, published in 1716 (see Ex. 2.1, mm. 5–8), and Anna Bon's Keyboard Sonata in F Major, published in 1757 (see Anthology 13,

Table 3.2: *Prototype of the Prinner*

METRICAL CONTEXT	Strong	Weak	Strong	Weak
SCALE DEGREES IN MELODY	$\hat{6}$	$\hat{5}$	$\hat{4}$	$\hat{3}$
SCALE DEGREES IN BASS	$\hat{4}$	$\hat{3}$	$\hat{2}$	$\hat{1}$

Table 3.3: *Prototype of the Fonte*

MODE	Minor		Major (whole step lower)	
SCALE DEGREES IN MELODY	$\hat{4}$	$\hat{3}$	$\hat{4}$	$\hat{3}$
SCALE DEGREES IN BASS	$\hat{\#7}$	$\hat{1}$	$\hat{7}$	$\hat{1}$

mm. 3–4, 5–6, and elsewhere). These passages differ in surface detail, genre, and geographic origin, but they belong to a common musical language familiar to eighteenth-century composers, performers, and listeners alike.

A third schema, the Fonte (meaning "spring" or "fountain," named by the eighteenth-century theorist Joseph Riepel), is a descending sequence consisting of two segments: the first in the minor mode, the second (a whole step lower) in the major (Table 3.3). In the first movement of a trio sonata in G major attributed to one Domenico Gallo (see Anthology 7), a modulatory passage uses a Fonte to return to the tonic (Ex. 3.2).

Example 3.2: *Domenico Gallo, Sonata No. 1, movement 1, mm. 29–30*

Strings, basso continuo

In the following pages and in the commentaries that accompany the anthology, I will occasionally point to these and other galant schemata, using Gjerdingen's terminology. Readers need to keep in mind, however, that this terminology and the theory on which it rests are quite new and their usefulness still subject to debate. For example, some might object to the naming of things that apparently had no names in the eighteenth century. The $\hat{6}$–$\hat{5}$–$\hat{4}$–$\hat{3}$ descent over a $\hat{4}$–$\hat{3}$–$\hat{2}$–$\hat{1}$ bass obviously existed, but the fact that no one named it suggests that eighteenth-century musicians did not think of it as an entity that needed to be recognized, discussed, and taught. By giving it a name (the Prinner), Gjerdingen emphasizes its existence in a way that eighteenth-century musicians might have found strange.

THE *MUSICO* AND VOCAL IMPROVISATION

In mentioning "sixteen young *castrati*" studying at the conservatory he visited in Naples, Burney alluded to one of the strangest yet most characteristic features of eighteenth-century music: the crucial role played in the opera, church music, and concerts of many parts of Europe by castrated singers. They preferred to be called *musici* (singular, *musico*), the generic Italian term for professional musicians; the word *castrato* often carried derogatory or humorous connotations because it also meant "mutton." The *musici* sang not only in Italy, where most of them were born, castrated, and trained, but in London, Lisbon, Madrid, Munich, Vienna, Berlin, and several other cities. (As we will see in Chapter 4, they played a particularly important role in the theaters of Rome.) Combining a boy's vocal apparatus with a man's chest cavity and lung power, they delighted audiences with their sweet, powerful alto and soprano voices and their extraordinary improvisatory abilities. Some were also great actors, portraying with memorable intensity the young lovers who were their operatic specialty.

In the early twenty-first century it may seem barbarous that parents of a preadolescent boy with a beautiful treble voice and other signs of musical talent would consign him (or allow him to consign himself) to the scalpel. Those parents, however, might have seen little difference between the celibacy imposed by priestly vows and the limits to sexual activity resulting from castration (limits that apparently varied a great deal depending on the exact nature of the surgical procedure and a particular patient's anatomy and constitution). Christ himself apparently sanctioned castration as a way to come closer to God (Matthew 19:12). Puberty, moreover, generally occurred later—often around the age of 15 or 16—than today, giving boys more time than we might expect for vocal training and their parents and teachers more time to assess their skills before deciding about castration.

Many (probably most) *musici* ended up singing in Catholic churches, sharing the words of the liturgy with priests. This probably suppressed the scruples that some parents may have felt in allowing the castration of their sons. The religious role that *musici* played may also have encouraged eighteenth-century listeners, even in theaters, to think of them as sacred vessels, their unearthly voices communicating to ordinary mortals intimations of heaven. When the *musico* Luigi Marchesi sang in Florence in 1779, the effect of his aria *Mia speranza* (My hope) overwhelmed listeners, who, according to a contemporary report, "cried out loud at the height of their rapture, 'Questa è musica dell' altro mondo!'" (This is music of the other world!)

The large amount of literal repetition in the scores of eighteenth-century arias (including, but not limited to, da capo arias) only begins to make sense when we think of these scores as vehicles for vocal improvisation. Composers wrote for *musici* and other professional singers with the expectation that they would contribute their own musicianship and creativity to the performance in the form of embellishments. A review of Marchesi's performances in London in 1788 emphasized how much the singer's improvised embellishments contributed to his effect on stage. The opera in which he appeared, wrote the critic, "is not very striking nor moving. However some part of it has much merit, and what made it appear most brilliant last Saturday was the appearance in it of Signor Marchesi. Though it must always be understood that the modulations, flights, and variations which he utters are his own, and not the master's [composer's]."

That kind of improvisation required many years of training. It was at such institutions as the conservatory in Naples that Burney visited that *musici* developed their astonishing virtuosity. That they kept to themselves, well away from the deplorable conditions under which the instrumentalists practiced, makes sense because they were the school's most valuable product. At their lessons as well, the singers were shielded from the racket that prevailed elsewhere: "the ears of both master and scholar are respected when lessons in singing are given, for that work is done in a quiet room." All the taste, expression, and delicacy denied the instrumentalists were instilled in the *musici*, and that is what made them the royalty of eighteenth-century music.

THEATERS

At the center of Neapolitan life—and the ultimate goal for those studying in its conservatories—were its royal theaters: the Teatro San Bartolomeo and, replacing it in 1737, the even grander Teatro San Carlo. Both specialized in the production of opera seria, the most expensive and prestigious form of Italian opera. Burney attended a rehearsal and the premiere of Niccolò Jommelli's *Demofoonte* at the San Carlo in 1770. He carefully looked around at the huge auditorium:

> The theatre of San Carlo is a noble and elegant structure: the form is oval, or rather the section of an egg, the end next the stage being cut. There are seven ranges of boxes, sufficient in size to contain ten or twelve persons in each, who sit in chairs, in the same manner as in a private house. In every range there are thirty boxes, except the three lowest ranges, which, by the King's box being taken out of them, are reduced to twenty-nine. In the pit there are fourteen or fifteen rows of seats, which are very roomy and commodious, with leather cushions and stuffed backs, each separated from the other by a broad rest for the elbow: in the middle of the pit there are thirty of these seats in a row. (SR 144: 995–96; 5/23: 261–62)

Operatic premieres at the Teatro San Carlo were timed to coincide with dynastic celebrations: the birthdays and name days of the king, the queen, and their closest relatives. November 4, the day of the premiere of *Demofoonte*, was St. Charles's Day, the name day of both Queen Carolina of Naples and her father-in-law, King Charles of Spain. Burney found the theater completely transformed for the festive occasion:

It is not easy to imagine or describe the grandeur and magnificence of this spectacle. . . . [T]he court was in grand gala, and the house was not only doubly illuminated, but amazingly crowded with well-dressed company. In the front of each box there is a mirror, three or four feet long by two or three wide, before which are two large wax tapers; these, by reflection, being multiplied, and added to the lights of the stage and to those within the boxes, make the splendor too much for the aching sight. . . . The stage is of an immense size, and the scenes, dresses, and decorations were extremely magnificent; and I think this theatre superior, in these particulars, as well as in the music, to that of the great French opera in Paris. (SR 144: 996; 5/23: 262)

The vastness of the auditorium and the noise of the audience (more vocal than the solemnly silent audience in most opera houses these days) made it difficult for Burney to hear the music that had given him so much pleasure at the rehearsal. But he understood that an operatic premiere at the San Carlo was a political celebration as much as (maybe more than) a musical event. The evening's visual marvels, surpassing "all that poetry and romance have painted," compensated, at least in part, for its musical disappointments.

THE AUSTRIANS IN NAPLES, VINCI, AND THE EMERGENCE OF THE GALANT STYLE

Naples had witnessed a momentous political change in 1707. After almost two centuries of rule by Spain, it came under the power of the Austrian Habsburgs, who ruled their Italian kingdom through a series of governors. Musical changes quickly followed the change of regime.

It was almost certainly through the initiative of the Austrian and Bohemian noblemen who ruled Naples that the horn, which composers in Vienna, Dresden, and other German cities had begun to use in opera orchestras during the first few years of the eighteenth century, became part of orchestras in Naples as well. In 1713 Alessandro Scarlatti's cantata *Il genio austriaco* (The Spirit of Austria) was performed in celebration of the birthday of the Habsburg empress, Elizabeth Christina. An eyewitness praised the orchestra: "There were countless harmonious instruments: timpani, trumpets, hunting horns, as well as flutes and all sorts of strings and organ." One of the first Neapolitan operas to use horns in the orchestra was Scarlatti's *Tigrane* of 1715; the libretto for that opera was dedicated to Count Daun, the Austrian governor. Soon a pair of horns became a standard part of opera orchestras throughout Italy; and so it remained.

Two years after the arrival of the Austrians a new theater, the Teatro de' Fiorentini, opened. With it, a new operatic genre was born: full-length comic opera with most of the roles sung in Neapolitan dialect. The comic operas performed at the Teatro de' Fiorentini quickly became associated with young musicians, eager to make a name for themselves and open to new ideas. Students in the conservatories and recent graduates such as Leonardo Vinci (ca. 1690–1730) quickly came to regard comic operas as ideal vehicles for their debuts as opera composers.

The music of most of these Neapolitan comedies is unfortunately lost. But one of the surviving scores, Vinci's *Li zite 'n galera* (The Lovers on the Galley, 1722), shows that the new genre encouraged the development by its youthful composers of a musical style quite different from that of serious operas performed in the larger, more glamorous Teatro San Bartolomeo. Homophonic texture predominates in Vinci's opera, with many passages in two parts (melody and bass) and frequent unison passages. Melodies generally fall into short phrases, most often of two measures; and one phrase often answers another in antecedent-consequent patterns, as in the aria *Si' masto mio* (Master, please don't beat me; Ex. 3.3). Vinci made frequent use of the melodic-harmonic schemata that he had learned from his work with *partimenti*; the passage quoted here contains a good example of a Fonte (at the words "te ccà vedite": C minor, B♭ major). These are all features of what eventually came to be called the galant style, whose emergence in Naples during the 1720s probably owed its initial impetus to stylistic experimentation in Neapolitan comic opera.

Example 3.3: *Leonardo Vinci,* Li zite 'n galera, *aria:* Si' masto mio, *mm. 5–14.*

Master, please don't beat me. Take a look: I'm sick.

Many of the characters in eighteenth-century comic operas are from the lower and middle classes (as distinguished from the almost exclusively royal and noble characters in opera seria). This has led some historians to conclude that comic operas appealed to audiences less aristocratic than those that supported opera seria. If this were true, then we might be justified in calling the galant style a product of the entry of the middle classes into the previously aristocratic world of opera. But the reality is more complicated. The audience that applauded *Li zite 'n galera* included the Habsburg governor (to whose wife the libretto was dedicated) and most of the Neapolitan nobility. And its success led to Vinci's immediately being awarded the commission to compose an opera seria for the royal Teatro San Bartolomeo.

For the rest of his short life Vinci devoted himself mostly to opera seria, into which he brought many of the stylistic novelties of comic opera and encouraged his younger contemporaries to do the same. It was primarily in regard to serious opera that Burney, many years later, wrote: "Vinci seems to have been the first opera composer who . . . without degrading his art, rendered it the friend, though not the slave to poetry, by simplifying and polishing melody, and calling the attention of the audience chiefly to the voice-part, by disentangling it from fugue, complication, and laboured contrivance."

Silla dittatore (Silla the Dictator), Vinci's second serious opera, performed in 1723 in celebration of Emperor Charles's birthday, contains an illustration of this "disentangling" in the aria *Non ha quell'augelletto* (The little bird; Ex. 3.4), where the bass line accompanying the opening vocal solo moves entirely in eighth notes and the violins (not shown in the example), in unison, mostly double the vocal line. Vinci made a clear distinction—typical of the galant style—between melodic and modulatory passages. In the first two measures of the vocal part, a Prinner serves as a response to a romanesca. This antecedent–consequent phrase pair is then treated as the first half of a larger, four-measure antecedent–consequent melody (mm. 3–6). Three-note slides dominate the modulatory passage that follows (mm. 7–9); it ends with a half cadence (V of V), preparing for a three-measure passage in the dominant (mm. 10–12).

Because opera seria, unlike comedies in Neapolitan dialect, appealed to audiences throughout Italy and in many cities and courts throughout Europe, it was a perfect vehicle for the dissemination of the new style. Vinci himself wrote serious operas not only for Naples but for Rome and Venice. His younger contemporary Johann Adolf Hasse (1699–1783) studied in Naples during the 1720s and brought galant opera seria first to Venice (where his *Artaserse*, to be discussed in Chapter 4, was performed in 1730) and then to Dresden (where he became music director of the court opera later the same year).

Naples came back into the Spanish orbit in 1734, when Charles, son of the king of Spain, became king of Naples. But 17 years of Austrian rule had changed Neapolitan music for good. The Teatro San Carlo, named after the Spanish ruler

Example 3.4: *Leonardo Vinci,* Silla dittatore, *aria:* Non ha quell' augelletto, *mm. 3–12*

The little bird caught in a snare has no crueler enemy than the one who imprisoned it

who built it in 1737, resounded with music in the galant style that had emerged while Naples was under Austrian control.

PERGOLESI AND THE COMIC *INTERMEZZO*

Giovanni Battista Pergolesi, one of the first stars of the galant style, was born in 1710 and died, probably of tuberculosis, at the age of 26. From 1725 he studied at one of the conservatories of Naples. Among his teachers, at least for a few months, may have been Vinci. Pergolesi must have shown extraordinary promise. In 1732, when he was just 22, the Teatro San Bartolomeo produced his first opera, *Salustia*. He wrote several more operas during the next four years and completed his famous *Stabat Mater* (see Chapter 2) during or shortly before his final illness.

Serious operas in Naples in the 1720s and 1730s were often performed in conjunction with much shorter, simpler comic operas called *intermezzi*. During the two intermissions between the three acts of an opera seria, a small comic troupe (usually just two or three singers) performed an *intermezzo* in two parts. They differed from Neapolitan comic operas such as *Li zite 'n galera* in their brevity, their very small casts, and their use of standard Italian rather than Neapolitan dialect. For performance between the acts of his serious opera *Il prigionier superbo* (The Proud Prisoner), performed at Teatro San Bartolomeo in 1733, Pergolesi wrote the intermezzo *La serva padrona* (The Servant Turned Mistress).

Two singing characters gave Pergolesi and his librettist, Gennaro Antonio Federico, all they needed to make a delightful miniature opera that uses many aspects of the galant style to good dramatic and comic effect. Serpina, a clever and seductive servant girl (her name means "little snake"), tries to persuade her master Uberto to marry her. The blustering Uberto is caught, like many old men in comic opera, between his sexual urges and his wish to remain independent and to keep his money to himself.

Serpina sets about her seduction by pretending she is to be married to a soldier, thus arousing Uberto's jealousy. In her aria *A Serpina penserete* (You will think of Serpina; see Anthology 2), she bids Uberto farewell. She pretends to be sad and tells her master—quoting his future words—that he too will be sad when she is gone. But in an aside she gleefully confides to the audience that her trick is having its intended effect: little by little Uberto is beginning to weaken.

Pergolesi's early death and the beauty of his music combined to generate legends about his life (said to have been full of love affairs) and his death (another composer, jealous of his genius, was said to have poisoned him). The Pergolesi myth transformed the *Stabat Mater* into a swan song completed on the day of his death. These legends helped Pergolesi gain a posthumous reputation that set him above even the best of his compositional contemporaries. Already in 1739 a French music lover visiting Italy, having named many of the leading Italian composers, wrote: "Of all these musicians my favorite composer is Pergolesi. Ah! What charming talent, simple and natural. It is impossible to write with more ease, grace, and taste." By the second half of the century admiration for Pergolesi had grown into something of a cult, inspiring the French composer André Grétry to declare: "Pergolesi was born, and the truth was revealed." Copyists and publishers, hoping to increase the value of their wares, attached Pergolesi's name to music he did not write, including the sonata in G major now attributed to Domenico Gallo (see Anthology 7).

That Michael Kelly, the young Irish musician with whom we began this chapter, came all the way from Dublin to Naples to study singing testifies to the enormous prestige that Naples enjoyed as a center of musical education, composition, and performance. One aspect of musical training in Naples that deserved its high reputation was its use of *partimenti* to inculcate in future composers and performers a repertory of voice-leading schemata that constituted the basic vocabulary of the galant style.

When Kelly toured the countryside around Naples in 1779, Giovanni Battista Pergolesi had been dead for more than 40 years. Yet Kelly's guide pointed to a house that was supposedly Pergolesi's "favorite retreat," as if it were a shrine. Pergolesi's music contributed to the establishment and spread of the galant style; his life and the myths that it inspired provided biographers with a narrative that nineteenth-century writers applied to another great composer, born in Salzburg two decades after Pergolesi's death: Wolfgang Amadeus Mozart.

FOR FURTHER READING

Feldman, Martha, *Opera and Sovereignty: Transforming Myths in Eighteenth-Century Italy* (Chicago: University of Chicago Press, 2007), 188–225

Gjerdingen, Robert O., *Music in the Galant Style* (New York: Oxford University Press, 2007)

The Golden Age of Naples: Art and Civilization under the Bourbons, 1734–1805, exhibition catalog (Detroit: Detroit Institute of Arts, 1981)

Heartz, Daniel, *Music in European Capitals: The Galant Style, 1720–1780* (New York: W. W. Norton, 2003), 67–169

Libby, Dennis, "Italy: Two Opera Centres." in *The Classical Era: From the 1740s to the End of the 18th Century*, ed. Neal Zaslaw (Englewood Cliffs, NJ: Prentice Hall, 1989), 15–39

Markstrom, Kurt, *The Operas of Leonardo Vinci, Napoletano* (Hillsdale, NY: Pendragon, 2007)

Naples in the Eighteenth Century: The Birth and Death of a Nation State, ed. Girolamo Imbruglia (Cambridge: Cambridge University Press, 2000)

Robinson, Michael, *Naples and Neapolitan Opera* (Oxford: Clarendon, 1972)

Ⓢ Additional resources available at wwnorton.com/studyspace

CHAPTER FOUR

Carnival Opera in Rome and Venice

At the beginning of the eighteenth century Italy had the largest concentration of big cities in Europe (see Table 1.1 in Chapter 1). Genoa, Turin, Milan, Venice, Bologna, and Florence all lay within a few days' travel of each other, Rome and Naples a few days farther south. In this respect Italy, before its unification in the nineteenth century, differed from some other parts of Europe, such as Spain, France, and England, which were dominated by single capitals. The quantity and proximity of Italian cities encouraged the development of a distinctive system of operatic production that prevailed throughout the eighteenth century and into the nineteenth (as Walter Frisch relates in Chapter 4 of *Music in the Nineteenth Century*).

The operatic year consisted of a series of seasons, in which theatrical exigencies interacted with the Catholic liturgical calendar. Carnival, the most important season, extended (in most of Italy) from the day after Christmas to Shrove Tuesday (Mardi Gras, the day before the beginning of Lent). After Lent (the penitential period of 40 days preceding Easter, when theaters were closed) came the spring season; some theaters also presented a summer season; and a fall season completed the operatic year. This calendar was subject to local variation but uniform enough, given the short distances between cities, to allow singers to go from town to town, spending a season in each. They enjoyed steady employment while audiences enjoyed a wide variety of singers.

Each theater normally presented two operas during carnival, the first performed nightly until about halfway through the season, when the second opera replaced it. In anticipation of these productions, each theater's impresario, or general manager, engaged a group of singers for both operas. The theaters of only a few major cities, including Venice, Rome, and Naples, specialized in the production of newly composed operas. Most other cities made do with revivals or *pasticci* (operatic "pies" filled with existing arias by various composers).

Rome and Venice played distinctive roles in this system of operatic production. Two of Europe's most celebrated centers of art, architecture, and music, they were both political as well as cultural capitals. The pope not only led the Catholic Church but ruled Rome and the Papal States, which included a substantial part of Italy. The doge and the Venetian oligarchy that elected him ruled not only the city of Venice but a large part of northern Italy.

Rome and Venice greatly differed—an ecclesiastical center built on the ruins of an ancient city and a commercial capital and naval base rising from the middle of an Adriatic lagoon—and their opera reflected these differences. Rome concentrated all operatic activity into carnival (the pope prohibited opera during the rest of the year), whereas Venice timed the spring season to coincide with the festival of the Ascension, when the doge renewed the city's symbolic marriage to the sea by dropping a ring into the lagoon. In Rome the pope forbade women from appearing on stage during most of our period; men portrayed female characters in both opera and ballet. Venice had several institutions that specialized in the education of female musicians, including singers, and its theaters welcomed the finest female singers. (In *Music in the Baroque,* Wendy Heller discusses the rise of commercial opera in seventeenth-century Venice.) Yet for all their operatic differences, Rome and Venice were similar in their promotion of galant music in the 1720s and 1730s.

METASTASIO AND OPERA SERIA

The spread of the galant style through Italy coincided with the rise of Pietro Metastasio (1698–1782), a dramatist and poet whose name became synonymous with Italian opera seria. Between 1723 and 1771 Metastasio wrote 27 three-act librettos, basing most of them loosely on historical events in Greek or Roman antiquity, and peopling them mostly with royal and noble characters. (As Heller notes, Metastasio had close ties to the classicizing Accademia degli Arcadi in Rome.) Composers, singers, and audiences alike recognized the excellence of Metastasio's librettos, and over the course of the century composers made hundreds of settings of them. In their fine craftmanship, liveliness, optimism, accessibility, and cosmopolitan appeal to opera lovers all over Europe, Metastasio's librettos embody many of the Enlightenment's ideals.

Fascinated by the intricacies of human emotion, Metastasio followed with exquisite detail the feelings of men and women caught up in moral and emotional dilemmas. He focused interest on struggles within his characters as well as between them. Following the example of Pierre Corneille and Jean Racine, the seventeenth-century French playwrights, he set up situations in which characters have to decide between love and duty, between private interest and public good. The resolution of the dilemma often turns on an act of will by which a noble hero or heroine triumphs over the temptation to give way to some merely personal feeling.

The polarity between external and internal conflict is reflected in the structure of Metastasio's librettos, divided into dialogue on the one hand and soliloquies on the other. The dialogue, in blank verse of 7 or 11 syllables per line, is the realm of action. Here the dramatic situation is defined, the characters presented and developed; here the characters interact, much as in a spoken play. The soliloquies, mostly in the form of solo arias, are the realms of emotion. Here the characters express their individual thoughts and feelings.

Metastasio wrote his blank verse with the understanding that singers would declaim it in a free, speechlike rhythm, using a musical language of melodic formulas over an equally conventional harmonic foundation supplied by one or more chordal instruments and sometimes also a low melodic instrument, such as a cello. Italians called this conventional musical language *recitativo semplice* (simple recitative), a term preferable to *recitativo secco* (dry recitative), which came into fashion in the nineteenth century and has pejorative implications. Metastasio typically wrote aria texts in two stanzas, the first meant to serve as the **A** section in da capo form, the second as the **B** section. He placed most arias so that characters would sing them just before leaving the stage (hence the term "exit aria"). Ensembles are rare in Metastasio's dramas, choruses even rarer.

This description of Metastasian opera might leave the impression of excessive solemnity, conventionality, and predictability; and indeed many nineteenth- and twentieth-century critics, applying the operatic standards of their own time, dismissed the opera seria genre as hopelessly undramatic. They might have thought differently about it had they considered its primary function: to celebrate carnival and other festive occasions such as rulers' birthdays, weddings, and coronations.

CARNIVAL

The carnival season, which took up most of the time between the penitential seasons of Advent and Lent, granted Catholics a respite from the rules and obligations of everyday life. The wearing of masks and costumes encouraged interaction between strangers, between the sexes, and between classes—whether in ballrooms, theaters, or the street—that were unthinkable at other times of the year. Food, wine, dance, and gambling presented temptations hard to resist for those who knew that the approaching Lent would give them plenty of time to atone for their excesses.

Opera seria was one of the essential pleasures of carnival. A painting of a performance in Turin's Teatro Regio, probably in the 1740s, perfectly conveys the festive, carnivalesque atmosphere of Italian theaters (Fig. 4.1). On stage a climactic scene appears to be unfolding. The prima donna weeps, two young

Figure 4.1: *The performance of an opera seria in Turin's Teatro Regio during the second third of the eighteenth century; previously attributed to Pietro Domenico Olivero, but more likely the work of Giovanni Michele Graneri*

children at her side; front and center, a man suggests with an imperious gesture that he is portraying a king; before him, pleading for mercy or forgiveness,
kneels a young man (probably a *musico*) who may be portraying the woman's
lover. Their elaborate costumes correspond to no historical period, but suggest a fantastic world of the imagination, or a carnival ball. The scenery likewise
makes no attempt to represent anything from the real world, except perhaps the auditorium itself. The stage holds up a mirror to the audience: a make-believe carnival reflecting the real one being celebrated by the Turinese. The candles illuminating
the theater continue to flicker during the performance, allowing the audience
to divide its attention between the stage and auditorium. Some turn their backs
to the stage and look around at their neighbors; some engage in conversation,
others study their librettos. Waiters circulate with food and drink. What we
call opera seria, the painting makes clear, was not completely (or even mostly)
serious; it was a joyful expression of the carnival spirit.

An equally carnivalesque verbal picture, from about 50 years later, emerges from
the diaries of Susannah Burney (daughter of the music historian Charles and sister
of the novelist Fanny), who often attended rehearsals and performances of opera
seria in London in the 1770s and 1780s and recorded in vivid detail the topsy-turvy
world that she witnessed on stage, behind the scenery, in the orchestra, and in the
audience (for excerpts, see SR 145; 5/24).

During the 1720s and 1730s Metastasio provided galant composers with librettos that encouraged them to display their fresh approach to operatic composition.
When, many years later, Jean-Jaques Rousseau urged ambitious young musicians
to go to Naples and to find inspiration in Metastasio's librettos, he evoked the aesthetic climate of Naples during the second quarter of the eighteenth century and
the crucial role Metastasio played in the consolidation and dissemination of the
galant style. Those innovations traveled quickly. By the time Metastasio's career
had taken off, most of his musical collaborators and most of the premieres of his
operas were not in Naples but in Rome or Venice.

OPERA SERIA IN VENICE: HASSE'S *ARTASERSE*

Born near Hamburg, Johann Adolf Hasse (1699–1783) was an almost exact contemporary of Metastasio, with whom he collaborated often. In 1719, as a 20-year-
old tenor, he joined an opera troupe at the court of Braunschweig; but he did
not stay for long. A stipend allowed him to spend three years in Italy on an edu-
cational Grand Tour. In Naples he studied composition with old Alessandro
Scarlatti, but he paid more attention to the music of younger composers such as
Leonardo Vinci.

One of Hasse's first great operatic successes was the setting of Metastasio's
Artaserse (Artaxerxes) that he made (in direct competition with Vinci, who had
just presented his setting of the same libretto in Rome) for the Venetian carnival

of 1730. The libretto, set to music many times during our period, is ostensibly based on events in ancient Persian history. But a powerful sense of unreality—of carnivalesque make-believe—pervades the drama, in part because the plot is set in motion by an improbable action: Prince Artabano, having assassinated the king of Persia, exchanges his bloody sword with that of his son Arbace, thereby implicating Arbace in the crime.

In preparation for the Venetian production of *Artaserse*, a local poet revised the libretto, replacing some of Metastasio's aria texts. Among the new texts are two that, with Hasse's music, became famous arias. In *Per questo dolce amplesso* (Through this sweet embrace), Arbace, who thinks he is about to be executed, bids farewell to his father, asking him to take care of his beloved Mandane after his death. In *Pallido il sole* (The sun is pale), Artabano, tortured by remorse, expresses horror at the idea of his son dying in his place. Both arias show Hasse expertly using galant elements within the da capo form he had inherited from Alessandro Scarlatti and his contemporaries.

The great *musico* Farinelli (the stage name of Carlo Broschi, 1705–1782) created the role of Arbace in Venice; it was for him that Hasse wrote *Per questo dolce amplesso* (a dal segno aria; see Anthology 3). Hasse gave Farinelli plenty of opportunity to show off his low notes, which must have been particularly sonorous. He took advantage of the second syllable in the aria's last word, "amato," to exploit the facility with which Farinelli sang coloratura. The singer, in taking the aria with him on his triumphant progress through Europe, made it famous.

In *Pallido il sole* (Fig. 4.2), Hasse gave his music urgency by banning all vocal coloratura—in contrast with *Per questo dolce amplesso*. A continuous fabric of sixteenth notes in the muted violins and violas unfolds over a bass line whose repeated notes convey inexorable momentum. The slow harmonic rhythm allows listeners to feel the full force of what was in 1730 a striking effect that Hasse used repeatedly in this aria (first in m. 5): the augmented-sixth chord. Rarely used by composers born before 1700, augmented-sixth harmony was welcomed by younger composers as a means of expressing intense emotion; later it became a standard way of approaching the dominant chord as part of a half cadence.

THEATRICAL TRANSVESTISM AND THE ROMAN CARNIVAL: LATILLA'S *LA FINTA CAMERIERA*

The law prohibiting women from appearing on the stage in Rome gave castrated men a particularly important role in that city's theaters. *Musici* portrayed not only the young male heroes that they portrayed elsewhere, but also female characters in both serious and comic opera. A caricature by Pier Leone Ghezzi shows Farinelli in women's clothes in Rome in 1724, near the beginning of his career (Fig. 4.3).

Figure 4.2: *The first page of a reduced score of Johann Adolf Hasse's* Pallido il sole, *printed in London by John Walsh* (The Favourite Songs in the Opera Call'd Artaxerxes by Sig.ʳ Hasse). "The sun is pale, the sky is dark, pain threatens, death approaches, everything fills me with remorse and horror."

Figure 4.3: *Farinelli in a woman's role in Rome, 1724. Caricature by Pier Leone Ghezzi.*

Like William Shakespeare, Italian librettists found inspiration in cross-dressing and its resulting gender ambiguities. Metastasio, who grew up in Rome and whose operatic tastes were formed in its theaters, wrote for the Roman carnival of 1729 a libretto in which the main female character, Queen Semiramide, disguises herself as a man during most of the drama. In Vinci's setting, a *musico* created the title role: a castrated man portrayed a woman pretending to be a man. A few years later Metastasio took as the hero of *Achille in Sciro* (Achilles on Scyros) a man who dresses as a woman so as to escape the dangers of the Trojan War. Although *Achille in Sciro* was first performed in Vienna (in 1736, in celebration of a royal wedding), its Italian premiere took place two years later in Rome, where *musici* portrayed both Achilles and Deidamia, Achilles's beloved. A Greek hero disguised as a woman and sung by a male soprano expressed his passion for a maiden sung by another male soprano.

Roman audiences must have especially enjoyed such gender games; the pope would have banned them if he had wanted to. The renowned philosopher Charles-Louis de Montesquieu, in Rome during carnival 1729, found that theatrical transvestism aroused sexual passion both homosexual and heterosexual:

> It has a very bad effect on morals, for I know of nothing that so inflames the Romans with *l'amour philosophique* [homosexual desire]. . . . During my stay in Rome, in the Capranica theater there were two little eunuchs, Mariotti and Chiostra, dressed as women, who were the most beautiful creatures I ever saw in my life, and who would have inspired the taste of Gomorrah in people whose inclinations were the least depraved in this respect. A young Englishman, believing one of them was a woman, fell madly in love with him and entertained this passion for more than a month.

The dramatic delights of Neapolitan comic opera (as exemplified by Vinci's *Li zite 'n galera*—see Chapter 3) and the new musical style that it helped to establish in Naples found fertile ground in Rome, where the use of men in female roles added spice to plots that already involved a good deal of sexual ambiguity. Gaetano Latilla (1711–1788) was one of the handful of composers who transformed Neapolitan comic opera into first a pan-Italian, and then a pan-European genre (Fig. 4.4). Latilla's comic opera *Gismondo*, based on a libretto by Gennaro Antonio Federico (the poet of Pergolesi's *La serva padrona*), was performed in Naples in 1737. It gave rise to one of the century's great operatic success stories when it was re-vised for Rome the following year. Under the title *La finta cameriera* (The Pretend Chambermaid, 1738), Latilla's opera took Italy by storm, and within a few years delighted audiences beyond the Alps as well. The international success of *La finta cameriera* helped to make Italian comic opera, often referred to as opera buffa, popular in many of Europe's cities, though it supplanted opera seria only in a few cities (most notably Vienna).

Giocondo, a young man (soprano), loves Erosmina (soprano), whose wid-owed father Pancrazio (bass) has promised her in marriage to Don Calascione, a rich old fool (bass). Giocondo, to be close to his beloved, disguises himself as a girl ("Alessandra") and gets hired as a servant in Pancrazio's household. He tells Erosmina that a handsome stranger loves her. Pancrazio soon falls in love with the new chambermaid. This increases his eagerness to marry off his daughter, so that he will feel free to marry "Alessandra." Calascione arrives to claim his bride, but is dis-tracted by the sexual allure of the various female servants, both real and counterfeit.

Figure 4.4: *Gaetano Latilla in a caricature by Pier Leone Ghezzi, 1739. On the floor are the three bound volumes of a manuscript full score. The unbound papers are probably vocal parts consisting of just the vocal line and bass, used by singers to learn their music.*

With all the soprano parts created in Rome by men, this plot resulted in cross-dressing arrangements as complicated as those in *Achille in Sciro*. They reach their climax at the end of Act 2, when "Alessandra" tells Pancrazio she loves him. The old man's response is about as explicitly erotic as an eighteenth-century operatic text could be: "Oh God! These sweet words of yours, my sunshine, bring me death. I feel joy mixed with pain flow in my veins. I still can't quite believe that you shall be my bride."

Now desperate to get his daughter out of the house, Pancrazio tells her she must wed in the aria *O questo o quello* (This or that). With a primarily disjunct melody that goes through the text quickly, and an absence of coloratura, Pancrazio's vocal line exemplifies the music with which *buffi* (male comic singers) delighted eighteenth-century audiences. The grotesquely abrupt augmented-sixth chord at measure 13 makes even the expected modulation to the dominant a part of the comedy (Ex. 4.1). The aria is in da capo form, but, reflecting Pancrazio's impatience, it is short and ignores some of the conventions associated with the da capo aria. The **A** section is in the expected binary form, but it lacks the ritornello that normally marks the end of the first part. And instead of going through the text twice, Pancrazio presents the text once and then, in the second part of the binary structure, mixes up the words in meaningless but amusing patter. With this fine example of the comic aria for bass, Latilla contributed to a tradition that stretched

Example 4.1: *Gaetano Latilla,* La finta cameriera, *aria:* O questo o quello, *mm. 7–13.*

This or that, that or this: you must resolve to stay here no longer. Think and think again, and then decide what you want. . . .

unbroken to the music that Mozart wrote for Figaro and Leporello in the 1780s (see Chapters 14 and 15).

Pancrazio's *O questo o quello* stands at one end of a full spectrum of aria types in *La finta cameriera*. At the other end are the elegant, serious arias of the lovers Giocondo and Erosmina. Giocondo's *Agitato il mio cor si confonde* (My agitated heart is confused), for example, is a setting of a shipwreck simile—a standard way of expressing emotional turmoil in an era in which travelers at sea (like Kelly on his way to Naples) still faced considerable discomfort and danger. Latilla spun out a long melody over a busy accompaniment; huge leaps in the vocal line and intricate coloratura on the word *mar* (sea) simultaneously convey Giocondo's nobility (despite his being disguised as a chambermaid) and the violence of the storm he describes.

VENETIAN OSPEDALI

In the account of his visits to one of the conservatories of Naples, quoted in Chapter 3, Charles Burney referred to the students as boys and castrati. There was no place for girls at these institutions. Many daughters of the nobility and upper middle classes learned at home, with private teachers, enough music to participate in private performances. Daughters of professional opera singers often traveled with their parents, absorbing musical and theatrical skills as they grew; many became professional singers themselves. And in Venice a group of institutions provided yet a third kind of musical education for girls. During the seventeenth century several foundling hospitals (that is, orphanages) for girls, known as *ospedali*, came to specialize in musical education and performance. An Englishman traveling in Italy in the 1720s reported that before the construction of orphanages, large numbers of unwanted babies had been regularly thrown into the city's canals. The ospedali offered not only a refuge for abandoned children but musical education for girls and young women, not all of whom were foundlings or orphans. Their public concerts, under the leadership of such prominent composers as Antonio Vivaldi and Johann Adolf Hasse, contributed substantially to Venetian music.

We know little about the training these women received, but the many enthusiastic accounts of their concerts suggest that it was excellent. The music filled Rousseau, who visited Venice in the early 1740s, with delight: "I cannot conceive of anything so pleasurable or so moving as that music: the artistic riches, the exquisite taste of the singing, the beauty of the voices, the delicacy of execution, everything about those delightful concerts combines to produce an impression which is certainly not a fashionable one, but against which I doubt whether any man's heart is proof."

Most of the women eventually left the orphanages for marriage or the convent; a few became professional singers. Faustina Bordoni achieved international success and fame during a career that began in 1716 and took her to Munich, Vienna, Dresden, and London. Adriana Ferrarese eloped from one of the ospedali with a lover and quickly found her way to the operatic stage. Within a few years she had established herself as Vienna's prima donna, creating in 1790 the role of Fiordiligi in Mozart's *Così fan tutte*; we will consider some of her music in Chapter 14.

"I BOAST OF MY STRENGTH": THE LIFE AND MUSIC OF CATERINA GABRIELLI

Although the playwright Friedrich Schiller had one of his characters call the 1700s "the century of the castrato," it was also an era of great female singers, several of them trained in Venice. Many women parlayed their vocal and histrionic talents into lucrative careers, in the course of which they contributed much to musical life. Students of women and music have paid too little attention to these extraordinary musicians, who attained success in the face of obstacles that did not affect their male counterparts, castrated or not.

The edict against women on the Roman stage meant that money and prestige that could have gone to women in this operatic capital went instead to *musici*. Even women who had established flourishing careers often left the theater after marriage, aware that many operagoers did not bother to differentiate between female opera singers and prostitutes. ("A chaste actress and opera singer," wrote Burney, "is a still more uncommon phenomenon in Italy, than in Great Britain.") Marriage to another singer sometimes allowed a woman to combine married life with a career. Even so, audiences generally preferred young women to older ones; a female singer whose youthful beauty was fading might find it difficult to sustain her career for long.

The life of the soprano Caterina Gabrielli (1730–1796) and the music written for and sung by her may serve to demonstrate the challenges, rewards, and achievements of a career as a professional female singer. She regularly appeared on stage with a singer named Francesca Gabrielli, whom she identified as her sister. But her other important relations were with men—teachers, composers, patrons, and lovers—and with an audience as fickle and cruel as it was adulatory. In the course of her long career she developed a reputation as a difficult prima donna, which she probably projected, at least in part, to hide the disappointments and losses that marred her life.

Born in Rome, Gabrielli may have studied at one of the Venetian ospedali; she is said to have been a pupil of Nicola Porpora (who had earlier taught Farinelli). After some performances in Venice she went to Vienna, where she was engaged at a large salary. She created several roles for Christoph Gluck (see Chapter 8), the first of several major composers with whom she established fruitful working relations. She received instruction in declamation and acting from Metastasio, who called her the "new star in the musical heavens." She enjoyed the protection of a wealthy patron, the powerful minister of state, Count Kaunitz, probably in exchange for sexual favors; a court official referred to her as "the favorite of the minister's harem."

Back in Italy, in 1759 Gabrielli began an association with the composer Tommaso Traetta (1727–1779) that lasted for several productive years. In *Ippolito ed Aricia* (Hippolytus and Aricia; Parma, 1759), she sang *In questo estremo addio* (In this final farewell), the first in a series of big, passionate arias in E♭ that Traetta would write for her (Ex. 4.2). No aria more perfectly embodies the galant spirit than this one, with its six-measure **ABB'** melody, Lombard rhythms, and three-note slide. This melody gave Gabrielli a fine opportunity to display her cantabile (her ability to spin out long, lyrical lines); later in the aria she could show off her equally admirable coloratura (florid passagework) and *messa di voce* (sustaining a note over several measures, building from *piano* to *forte*, in this case high above the churning full orchestra).

Gabrielli's performance in *Ippolito ed Aricia* dominated its critical reception. "The singers are the greatest now practicing," wrote one critic, "Mademoiselle Gabrielli being perhaps the greatest musician Italy has ever had. She joins an admirable taste to the most astonishing voice: tender, expressive, and nimble. The first man, Elisi, was a worthy partner to her."

The distance that separated Naples from the cities of northern Italy kept it from being a regular part of the system by which singers moved between seasons

Example 4.2: *Tommaso Traetta,* Ippolito ed Aricia, *aria:* In questo estremo addio, *mm. 15–20*

In saying a final farewell, I feel as if I am about to faint

from one city to another. The Teatro San Carlo normally engaged singers for a year or more. Gabrielli sang in Naples from 1763 to 1767, creating, among other roles, that of Argene in *Bellerofonte* (Bellerophon), the opera with which the Bohemian composer Joseph Mysliveček (1737–1781) made his Neapolitan debut.

In the four arias he wrote for Gabrielli as Argene, Mysliveček created a vivid portrait of a singer equally skillful at spinning out cantabile lines and setting off incendiary coloratura. In *Palesar vorrei col pianto* (I would like to reveal through tears), she did both. Faced with insurmountable misfortunes, Argene declares in simple recitative:

Vanto fortezza, è vero,	*I boast of my strength, it is true,*
Negli atti, e nel sembiante,	*in my actions and my face,*
Ma, oh Dio, tanto è maggiore	*but—oh God!—so much the greater is*
L'interna pena che m'opprime	*the pain within that weighs on*
il core.	*my heart.*

The bravura aria that follows, about ten minutes long, expresses both Argene's outwardly projected strength and the pain she feels. Mysliveček must have had an exceptional hornist in Naples. The aria begins with an orchestral introduction that presents the horn as *concertante* instrument (that is, treated as if it were the solo instrument in a concerto). Later the soprano launches the first of several coloratura passages, some in parallel thirds and sixths with the horn. This coloratura expresses Argene's strength by requiring a singer of great power and agility; but it also suggests that her suffering has brought her near madness.

Gabrielli renewed her ties with Traetta in St. Petersburg in the early 1770s. For the Russian court she created the title part in Traetta's *Antigona*, a tragedy rich in dance and choral music as well as opportunities for the prima donna to display her abilities as actress and singer. *Non piangete i casi miei* (Do not bewail my fate), discussed in Chapter 12, is yet another in the series of arias in E♭ that Traetta and Mysliveček wrote for her. From Russia she went to England, where she made her debut in the tragic role of Dido in November 1775. As rebellion stirred in North America, Gabrielli charmed London.

Thirteen years after their triumph in *Bellerofonte*, Mysliveček and Gabrielli joined forces again. When she appeared in his *Armida* in Milan in 1780, at the age of 49, her voice and looks were past their prime. She had to compete with the young *musico* Luigi Marchesi, who was entering the period of his greatest fame. To make matters worse, Gabrielli alienated the audience, which applauded her aria at the end of Act 1 and demanded an encore. She initially refused to return to the stage, and by the time she finally appeared, she had lost the audience's good-will and had to retreat under a hail of jeers, "the cruelest of which," wrote an eyewitness, "was the echoing cry 'old woman!'" That terrible evening effectively brought her career to an end. After a few appearances in Venice, she retired. Of the rest of her life we know nothing, except that she died in 1796 in her native Rome, the city that had throughout her career denied her access to its stages.

———————————

Readers may have noticed that a chapter ostensibly about opera in Venice and Rome ends with the career of a singer who, although born in Rome and possibly a student in Venice, performed all over Italy and in many of Europe's largest cities. Caterina Gabrielli's career exemplifies a phenomenon that helped to shape European music during the eighteenth century: the activity of Italian musicians—composers, instrumentalists, and singers—throughout Europe. The rest of this book is largely devoted to musical life in cities outside of Italy, but this does not mean that Italian musicians will be lacking. On the contrary, a result of the Italian musical diaspora is that every chapter that follows—whether it deals with Paris, London, Vienna, or St. Petersburg—refers to musicians born and trained in Italy. It was thanks largely to these traveling musicians that the galant style became a musical language understood, cultivated, and loved throughout Europe.

FOR FURTHER READING

Art in Rome in the Eighteenth Century, ed. Edgar Peters Bowron and Joseph J. Rishel (London: Merrell, 2000)

Butler, Margaret, "Italian Opera in the Eighteenth Century," in *The Cambridge History of Eighteenth-Century Music*, ed. Simon Keefe (Cambridge: Cambridge University Press, 2009), 203–71

Feldman, Martha, *Opera and Sovereignty: Transforming Myths in Eighteenth-Century Italy* (Chicago: University of Chicago Press, 2007), 141–87, 226–83

Heartz, Daniel, *Music in European Capitals: The Galant Style, 1720–1780* (New York: W. W. Norton, 2003), 171–293

Italy's Eighteenth Century: Gender and Culture in the Age of the Grand Tour, ed. Paula Findlen et al. (Palo Alto, CA: Stanford University Press, 2009)

Johnson, James H., *Venice Incognito: Masks in the Serene Republic* (Berkeley: University of California Press, 2011)

Libby, Dennis, "Italy: Two Opera Centers," in *The Classical Era: From the 1740s to the End of the 18th Century*, ed. Neal Zaslaw (Englewood Cliffs, NJ: Prentice Hall, 1989), 15–60

Strohm, Reinhard, *Dramma per musica: Italian Opera Seria of the Eighteenth Century* (New Haven: Yale University Press, 1997)

Ⓢ Additional resources available at wwnorton.com/studyspace

CHAPTER FIVE

Instrumental Music in Italy and Spain

In composing instrumental music, musicians born in the late seventeenth century such as Johann Sebastian Bach, George Frideric Handel, and Antonio Vivaldi focused much of their attention on concertos (both solo concertos and concerti grossi) and trio sonatas, discussed by Wendy Heller in *Music in the Baroque*. Younger musicians continued to cultivate the solo concerto—especially virtuosos for whom it offered the ideal vehicle for display during concerts. But they also favored two newer genres: the symphony and the keyboard sonata.

Both the symphony and the keyboard sonata emerged in Italy in the early eighteenth century and soon became characteristic elements of the musical scene all over Europe. They developed in conjunction with an ensemble (the orchestra with strings and pairs of oboes and horns) and an instrument (the piano, also an Italian invention), for which many symphonies and sonatas were written. Both the symphony and the keyboard sonata made early and conspicuous use of an elaboration of binary form that eventually became known as sonata form, as discussed in Chapter 7.

The careers of two masters of instrumental music, Domenico Scarlatti (1685–1757) and Luigi Boccherini (1743–1805), offer us examples of the musical diaspora by which Italian musicians, genres, and styles radiated throughout the Continent. They also exemplify two competing economic models of musical production, one based on private patronage, the other on the open market, with the latter gradually coming to predominate in the course of the eighteenth century.

THE OPERATIC SINFONIA, THE SYMPHONY, AND THE ORCHESTRA

The dichotomy between the learned and galant styles manifested itself in the orchestral music that composers wrote for performance at the beginning of operas and other big vocal works. Some adherents to the learned style (such as Handel) preferred the two-part French overture, so called because it had been cultivated with great success by Jean-Baptiste Lully and his successors at Versailles. As late as 1791, Mozart paid tribute to the conventions of the French overture in the overture to *Die Zauberflöte* (The Magic Flute), with the dotted rhythms of its opening Adagio and the fugal textures of the Allegro. The slow introduction of Beethoven's *Pathétique* Sonata, to be discussed in Chapter 17, also carries, in its pervasive dotted rhythms, traces of the French overture. But the polyphonic texture expected in the second, fast part of the French overture made it largely unacceptable to galant composers. They preferred a kind of overture that had been popularized by Alessandro Scarlatti (1660–1725): the three-part *sinfonia* (accent on the penultimate syllable), consisting of two fast movements framing a slow one. They standardized the form and character of the sinfonia's movements. It usually began with a vigorous, festive movement in the major mode; continued with a gentle, quiet slow movement, often in the minor; and ended with a minuet or minuet-like movement in binary form with repeats.

The sinfonia to Gaetano Latilla's *La finta cameriera* (The Pretend Chambermaid; Rome, 1738; see Chapter 4) is a good example of the early galant operatic overture. A brilliant opening Presto scored for strings, a pair of horns, and a single oboe is followed by a subdued Larghetto labeled "Sotto voce" for strings alone. Latilla brought back the horns and oboe for the final movement, in binary form with repeats, whose form, regular phrase structure, and $\frac{3}{8}$ meter conspire to give it the character of a minuet. The coda with which this movement ends serves also to signal the end of the overture as a whole.

The sinfonia developed at more or less the same time as the institution of the public concert began to establish itself, first in London and Paris, and later in much of the rest of Europe. It was not long before works intended for performance at the beginning of operas were being played at the beginning or end of concerts; and soon composers were writing symphonies especially for concert use. The three-movement layout of the operatic sinfonia and the character of all three of its movements served as an important model for composers of the concert symphony. Some (such as Johann Stamitz in Mannheim, to be discussed in Chapter 10) experimented with the addition of a fourth movement (in the sequence fast-slow-minuet-fast), but others stuck with three movements. The four-movement format eventually won out, thanks largely to its adoption by Haydn (see Chapters 10 and 16).

In settling on the ensemble of strings, oboes, and horns as the standard orchestra for the sinfonia, Italian composers of the 1720s and 1730s established what was to be probably the most common orchestra of the rest of the eighteenth century. (Latilla's orchestra differs from the soon-to-be-standard ensemble only in requiring one oboe instead of two.) Because the oboists and horn players were often expected to be able to play flute and trumpet, respectively, composers rarely required both oboes and flutes, or both horns and trumpets, in a single movement until later in the century.

Figure 4.1 shows an orchestra of 32 musicians, most of whom are arranged, in typical eighteenth-century fashion, facing each other along a desk parallel to the edge of the stage. This is the kind of orchestra for which Latilla wrote the overture to *La finta cameriera*. It had no conductor in the modern sense of the word. The man sitting at the keyboard on the left directs the performance. Although it is not possible to identify all the instruments (especially those being held by the players facing the stage), the orchestra seems to consist (in addition to the two keyboard instruments) of 18 violins and violas, 4 cellos, 2 double basses, 2 oboes, 2 bassoons (which would have doubled the bass line in playing Latilla's overture), and 2 horns. Note that the oboists sit apart from one another, among the violinists. Because they often doubled the first and second violin parts (a practice that became less common in the second half of the century), they may have found it convenient to sit next to the strings.

A cellist and double bassist surround both keyboard players; all three musicians in each group appear to be reading from the same part on the keyboard instrument's music stand. These two clearly defined groups were ideally suited to the realization (both linear and chordal) of a basso continuo; we might be tempted to call them continuo groups. But the keyboard players did not necessarily serve this function throughout the evening. The one on the left was probably the opera's composer, required by a widespread and long-lasting tradition to direct the first three performances from the keyboard. He did so with some combination of gestures and sounds, which must have included chordal realization of the bass to accompany the recitative.

Elsewhere in the opera, the director might have recourse to other kinds of aural or visual cues. A caricature by Pier Leone Ghezzi, dated 1753, depicts the opera composer Nicola Logroscino at the keyboard, with a cellist close behind him reading from the same music stand (Fig. 5.1). Another continuo group? In this case, probably yes; but not always. At the moment depicted by Ghezzi, Logroscino must have felt that slapping the side of his instrument with the fingers of his right hand was a more effective means of keeping his orchestra together than strumming chords.

Figure 5.1: *Nicola Logroscino directing an opera from the keyboard. Caricature by Pier Leone Ghezzi, 1753*

Ghezzi's drawing serves as a reminder that the presence of a keyboard instrument in an eighteenth-century orchestra does not necessarily mean that its player was constantly improvising chords with his right hand.

THE PIANO

The previous section refers to keyboard instruments without specifying harpsichord or piano, as both instruments were in use through most of the eighteenth century. From pictures of keyboard instruments (such as Figs. 4.4, 5.1, 9.2, and 14.1), it is often unclear whether a particular instrument is a piano or a harpsichord, and terminology was often ambiguous: the French *clavecin*, the Italian *cembalo*, and the German *Clavier* could all mean harpsichord or piano. (*Clavier*, in addition, could mean clavichord, an instrument to be discussed in Chapter 9.)

The instrument maker Bartolomeo Cristofori (1655–1732) invented the *gravicembalo con piano e forte* (stringed keyboard instrument with soft and loud, from which we get the word *pianoforte*) in Florence around 1700. He replaced the mechanism by which harpsichord players caused a plectrum to pluck a string with a new mechanism by which players caused a leather-covered wooden hammer to strike the string. By varying the speed at which they depressed the key, players of the piano affected the speed of the hammer and thus the loudness of the sound. Cristofori's new instrument had roughly the same shape as a modern grand piano, but was much smaller and lighter, with a case built entirely of wood and a simpler mechanism for transmitting movement from the key to the hammer. It also had a much shorter keyboard of four octaves, just over half the range of modern grands. (The term *fortepiano*, which was interchangeable with *pianoforte* in our period, is often used today to refer to instruments made in, or modeled on those of, the eighteenth century.)

The new piano did not excite much immediate interest among performers or composers. Harpsichords—gorgeous and brilliant in sound, technologically perfected after centuries of development, and familiar to builders, repairers, and players—continued to be built and played all over Europe during most of our period. The piano eventually won out, but only after a long coexistence with the harpsichord, which we can understand as one aspect of the coexistence of the learned and galant styles: the harpsichord was particularly suitable for the performance of contrapuntal music, whereas the piano excelled at the expression of dynamic nuance and at the differentiation of melody from accompaniment.

Charles Burney, looking back on the whole span of the eighteenth century, explained both why the harpsichord maintained its popularity for so long and why it finally succumbed to the piano: "We were unwilling to give up the harpsichord, and thought the tone of the pianoforte spiritless and insipid, till experience and better instruments vanquished our prejudices and the expression and the *chiar'oscuro* [light and shade] in performing music expressly composed for that instrument, made us amends for the want of brilliancy in the tone so much, that we soon found the scratching of the quill in the harpsichord intolerable, compared with the tone produced by the hammer."

By the time Daniel Gottlob Türk published his *Clavierschule* (School of Clavier Playing, 1789), the keyboard instrument he had primarily in mind was the piano, and he devoted a great deal of attention to subtle shadings of dynamics: "Even with the most painstaking marking [by the composer], it is not possible to specify every degree of loudness and softness of tone. . . . The player must himself feel and learn to judge what degree of loudness and softness of tone is required by the character of the music to be expressed in any given case" (SR 132: 878; 5/11: 144).

Türk's interest in dynamic gradations was typical of the galant style, which made the crescendo and the diminuendo essential elements of the musical language. The great *musico* Farinelli, who appeared in London in the mid-1730s, owed part of his success to an extraordinary ability to manipulate dynamics. Of his performance of the aria *Son qual nave* (I'm like a ship), Burney wrote: "The first note he sung was taken with such delicacy, swelled by minute degrees to such an amazing volume, and afterwards diminished in the same manner, that it was applauded for full five minutes." Farinelli's *messa di voce* expressed galant values as dramatically as the orchestral crescendo perfected later at Mannheim (see Chapter 10).

The piano's flexibility of dynamics likewise conveyed some of the galant style's most characteristic features. Johann Joachim Quantz, whose interest in subtle shadings of dynamics was one of his most modern traits, recommended (already in the 1750s) the piano as the ideal keyboard instrument for accompanying; his employer, King Frederick the Great of Prussia, owned several pianos. Farinelli's favorite instrument was a piano made in Florence in 1730; he was so attached to it (and so impressed by its coloristic effects) that he named it after one of the most famous painters of the Renaissance. In 1770 Burney visited Farinelli in Bologna, where he lived in prosperous retirement: the old man "played a considerable time upon his Raphael, with great judgment and delicacy." Burney referred to the "delicacy" of both Farinelli's singing in London and his playing in Bologna. The piano allowed Farinelli to re-create with his fingers some of the dynamic contrasts and gradations with which he had triumphed as a singer.

GIUSTINI'S SONATAS

Another Italian musician who used the piano much earlier, when Farinelli was at the peak of his career, to express the galant fascination with the subtleties of dynamic gradations was Lodovico Giustini (1685–1743). Born in Pistoia (a small town near Florence), he lived quietly in his hometown, carrying out his duties as organist for a local religious institution. It is ironic, then, that Giustini's *Dodici sonate da cimbalo di piano e forte detto volgarmente di martelletti* (Twelve Sonatas for Harpsichord with Soft and Loud, Commonly Called "with Little Hammers"), published in Florence in 1732, has emerged as a document of such importance in the history of the piano and its literature. The first works published explicitly for the piano, Giustini's sonatas are also among the first keyboard works published under this generic term. Although they reflect the operatic style of his day, they disguise their modernity by being in four or five movements (instead of the three movements that became common around the middle of the eighteenth century) and by their use of dance terms associated with the seventeenth-century French suite and the sonata da camera, genres that after 1715 attracted the attention mostly of composers in the learned style.

Giustini's Sonata No. 1 in G Minor consists of five movements: Balletto, Corrente, Sarabanda, Giga, and Minuet. It supplements the old-fashioned titles with more modern instructions about tempo or character of performance; thus the Balletto is to be played "spiritoso, ma non presto" (with spirit, but not quickly) the Corrente "allegro" (fast), the Sarabanda "grave" (solemnly), the Giga "presto" (quickly), and the Minuet "affettuoso" (with feeling). All five movements are in binary form with repeats. The Balletto ends on a half cadence—odd for a binary-form movement—that encourages us to hear it as an introduction to the Corrente. Although the three- and four-part textures typical of the learned style predominate in the Balletto, the Corrente (see Anthology 4) unfolds mostly in two parts. The opening melody, six measures long, has the same **ABB'** phrase

Example 5.1: *Lodovico Giustini, Sonata No. 1 in G Minor, movement 3 (Sarabanda), mm. 1–8*

structure as the tune at the beginning of Tommaso Traetta's aria *In questo estremo addio* (see Ex. 4.2). Opera composers sometimes gave phrase **B'** the character of an echo by having it played quietly. Giustini used his instrument's "little hammers" to capture this effect at the keyboard—the first of many dynamic contrasts in the Corrente.

Another surprisingly modern sound in Giustini's Sonata No. 1 is that of augmented-sixth chords. We heard prominent deployment of emotionally intense augmented-sixth harmony in Johann Adolf Hasse's *Pallido il sole* (see Fig. 4.2), first performed two years before the publication of the sonatas. Giustini was one of the first keyboard composers to make augmented-sixth chords a distinctive part of his harmonic language (Ex. 5.1, mm. 2 and 6).

The piano and its earliest literature seem to have found a particularly warm welcome in Portugal. João de Seixas, a globetrotting Brazilian bishop and music lover with close contacts at the highest levels of both the Portuguese court and the grand-ducal court of Florence, probably heard Giustini's sonatas in Italy during his residence there between 1727 and 1734. He sponsored their publication, dedicating them to Prince Antonio, younger brother of King John V of Portugal. Thus he preserved evidence of a culture of Tuscan piano composition more or less contemporary with Cristofori's activities as a builder of pianos; and he strengthened a chain of evidence linking Cristofori with early use of the piano on the Iberian peninsula. King John's music-loving daughter Maria Barbara owned, at the time of her death in 1758, twelve keyboard instruments, of which five were pianos made in Florence. A piano built in Lisbon in the 1760s was clearly inspired by early eighteenth-century Florentine designs (Fig. 5.2). A performance of Giustini's sonatas on this instrument makes audible the musical connections between Florence and Lisbon, of which the publication of these sonatas was one product.

Figure 5.2: *A grand piano by Manuel Antunes of Lisbon, 1767*

DOMENICO SCARLATTI

Princess Maria Barbara of Portugal studied keyboard with the music director at her father's court, Domenico Scarlatti. They must have established strong ties, because when Maria Barbara married Crown Prince Ferdinand of Spain in 1729, she brought Scarlatti with her. He spent the rest of his life at the Spanish court, teaching both Maria Barbara and her husband, and writing for her, the more talented of the two royal musicians, the great corpus of keyboard music for which he is famous.

FROM ITALY TO PORTUGAL

Scarlatti was an amazingly precocious musician, but he also took a surprisingly long time to find the genre and style with which he made his mark on music history. Born in Naples in 1685, the same year as J. S. Bach, Handel, and Giustini, he received an appointment as organist and composer in the royal chapel of Naples at the age of 15. While still a teenager he composed and directed the performance of his first opera. Early travels to Rome, Florence, and Venice brought him into contact with leading patrons and musicians and with a German composer who was exactly his age, Handel.

Unlike Handel (and unlike his own father, Alessandro), Domenico Scarlatti seems to have found the theater an uncongenial venue for his compositional ambitions. During his long life he wrote only a handful of operas, most of them for private performance. Alessandro Scarlatti, Handel, and other opera composers made a good living writing works for public theaters. But if Domenico was to be a professional composer, he would need private patrons or steady employment. He found both in Rome. From 1709 to 1714 he served Maria Casimira, the exiled queen of Poland, as music director; and from 1714 to 1719 he was music director at the Cappella Giulia in the Vatican.

Approaching the age of 35, Scarlatti had composed much competent vocal music, sacred and secular, and had won a position that brought him prestige and a dependable income. But he had not managed to escape his father's shadow. Perhaps this is one of the reasons why in 1719 he quit his position at the Vatican and took a new job far from Italy, as music director to King John V of Portugal. He spent the next decade in Lisbon, composing vocal music for the Portuguese court, directing its performance, and giving keyboard lessons to Princess Maria Barbara.

"THAT WILD BUT MASTERLY COMPOSER":
SCARLATTI IN SPAIN

Accompanying his royal pupil from Portugal to Spain in 1729, Scarlatti had good reason to expect that when the princess became queen he would be given a position at the Spanish court equivalent to the one he had earlier held in Lisbon. But his career took a different path.

Although Madrid was the largest city in Spain, and its capital, the court spent relatively little time there during Scarlatti's tenure. Instead it migrated from one palace to another, most of them in the countryside around Madrid, following a regular schedule that reflected the changing seasons. Although Scarlatti and his family maintained a residence in Madrid, he probably spent most of his time outside the city.

The itinerant court to which Scarlatti belonged cultivated Italian music, and especially Italian opera, with increasing energy and enthusiasm. In 1737 Queen Isabella Farnese invited Farinelli to Spain, to sing privately at court and to supervise the production of Italian opera. She hoped that his singing might improve the mental state of her husband, the deeply depressed and emotionally unstable King Philip V. Farinelli's musical therapy seems to have reinforced rather than cured the king's eccentricity. It consisted of singing the same four arias every night, including *Pallido il sole* and *Per questo dolce amplesso*, the two numbers from Hasse's *Artaserse* (Venice, 1730) that we examined in Chapter 4. More successful were Farinelli's efforts to improve opera at the Spanish court. His arrival in Spain initiated a golden age of Italian opera, with settings of many of Pietro Metastasio's librettos sung by some of Europe's leading singers. The production of opera seria reached an even higher level of artistic brilliance after Philip's death in 1746 and the accession to the throne of Ferdinand and Maria Barbara.

Scarlatti's patron loved opera as much as keyboard music; she supported Farinelli as strongly as Scarlatti. Farinelli's supervision of opera, and the presence of other Italians who directed and composed music for the stage and church, allowed Scarlatti's activities, in contrast, to take place strictly in the private sphere. He remained Maria Barbara's personal musician, directing his musical energy to an intensive exploration of keyboard technique and the development of a distinctive musical language.

Scarlatti's surviving keyboard works consist of an astounding 555 sonatas in one movement, most of which are in binary form. Although he had displayed exceptional abilities as a keyboard player in Italy, there is no reason to think that he wrote any of the surviving sonatas before he came to the Iberian Peninsula: none is preserved in Italian sources that date from before his departure. The musical relations that developed between composer and patron, and the freedom from his former obligations to compose and conduct vocal music, seem to have stimulated Scarlatti's creativity in ways that not even he could have foreseen. Working with Maria Barbara, he became acutely receptive not only to aspects of Spanish musical culture (especially its cultivation of the guitar) but also to the galant style that pervaded the operas performed at the Spanish court at midcentury. Scarlatti himself understood his music as belonging on the modern side of the divide between learned and galant. "Do not expect any profound learning," he wrote in the preface to his *Essercizi per gravicembalo* (Exercises for Keyboard), the set of 30 sonatas published in London in 1739, "but rather an ingenious jesting with art." Scarlatti was indeed, as Quantz put it, "a galant keyboard player in the manner of the time." He was also astonishingly original.

No single work can give one any idea of the extraordinary range of Scarlatti's inventiveness, but the Sonata in C Major, K. 421, exemplifies some of his most characteristic musical habits (see Anthology 5). (K. 421 looks like one of the Köchel numbers that are traditionally assigned to Mozart's works; however, it refers to the catalogue of Scarlatti's music compiled in the mid-twentieth century by harpsichordist Ralph Kirkpatrick.) It also shows how much he owed to the galant style, despite the uniqueness of his musical voice and despite his being considerably older than Hasse, Pergolesi, and Latilla.

Like many great keyboard players and teachers, Scarlatti often conceived pieces, at least in part, as exercises for the development of particular keyboard skills. The title he gave his published sonatas resembles the one that J. S. Bach gave his series of published keyboard works: *Clavier-Übungen* ("keyboard exercises"). The quick repetition of notes was the most obvious challenge he offered his royal pupil in K. 421, which he laid out in a series of short, clearly differentiated segments, many of them articulated by half cadences. Typically galant are the repeated full cadences with which he announced the end of both parts of the binary structure; distinctively Scarlattian is the freshness and ingenuity with which he clothed even the most basic and repetitive harmonic progressions.

Scarlatti's special appeal to musicians much younger than he says something important about his place in galant musical culture. Charles Burney (born in 1726, thus 41 years younger than Scarlatti) remembered his own experiences in the 1740s, when he was a young man: "Scarlatti's were not only the pieces with which every young performer displayed his powers of execution, but were the wonder and delight of every hearer who had a spark of enthusiasm about him, and could feel new and bold effects intrepidly produced by the breach of almost all the old and established rules of composition." Scarlatti's music allowed Burney himself, at the keyboard, to show off his youthful bravura. The novelist Fanny Burney, in a biography of her father, wrote: "He fired away in a sonata of Scarlatti's, with an alternate excellence of execution and expression, so perfectly in accord with the fanciful flights of that wild but masterly composer."

BOCCHERINI AND THE MUSIC PUBLISHING BUSINESS

The young Burney, like most other European musicians, had access to relatively few of Scarlatti's sonatas because the composer allowed few of them to be published. He wrote them for Maria Barbara's private pleasure, and she valued them, in part, because of her exclusive ownership of them. Scarlatti lived on his salary; he probably conceived of the publication of the 30 *Essercizi per gravicembalo* more as a tribute to the dedicatee, his former employer King John of Portugal, than as a money-making enterprise. He preferred the prestige that came from being associated with a king and queen to the fame that he might have won through widespread publication of his works.

But as the population of European cities grew, with it grew the size of the middle class to which Burney belonged: merchants, bankers, secretaries, lawyers, craftsmen, artists, teachers, and their families. Music, especially music for keyboard and for small ensembles, gave members of the middle class pleasure and enhanced their status. Most of them could not afford to employ musicians or pay for the exclusive ownership of compositions, but they could buy printed music. Thus music publishing expanded far beyond the limits it had reached in previous centuries. Burney, playing Scarlatti's sonatas (almost certainly from printed sheet music), embodied Europe's middle class in its passion for music and its demand for printed scores and sets of parts.

One of many composers to contribute to and benefit from the eighteenth century's explosion of music publishing was Luigi Boccherini. Another Italian who settled in Spain, and another instrumental virtuoso, Boccherini enjoyed the patronage of a member of the Spanish royal family; but unlike Scarlatti, he also developed close relations with publishers, through whom he fed music lovers throughout Europe a steady supply of chamber music.

Boccherini, born in the small Italian city of Lucca, excelled equally as a cellist and a composer of instrumental music. The wanderlust that affected many Italian musicians pulled at Boccherini with particular urgency. Already as a teenager he spent several years in Vienna, playing in orchestras and winning applause as a soloist in concertos. He also composed, completing a set of string trios in 1760, when he was only 17. At the age of 24 he traveled to Paris, one of Europe's capitals of music publishing, and during a stay of only a few months he arranged for the publication of sets of his string trios, string quartets, and duets for two violins.

Publishers liked to issue instrumental music in sets of six pieces, to which they assigned a single opus number. (The absence of opus numbers from Scarlatti's sonatas resulted from their existing, with few exceptions, outside of print culture.) They published sets of instrumental pieces in the form of parts for each instrument. For example, they issued a set of six string quartets in four booklets: one containing the first violin part for all six quartets, another the second violin part, and so forth. Boccherini probably received a flat fee for each set of works, but no royalties. Publishers owned the music that Boccherini sold to them (probably in the form of a manuscript score) and they could print as many sets of parts as they thought they could sell. But they had to work fast to make a profit. Lack of enforceable copyright made it possible for other publishers to produce and sell pirated editions in other countries.

From Paris, Boccherini went to Spain, where he spent the rest of his life. He continued to compose with publication (at least partly) in mind, and he continued to rely on publishers in Paris to disseminate his music and to supplement his income. He joined the orchestra of an opera troupe that followed the Spanish court on its customary peregrinations from Madrid to the various royal palaces in the surrounding countryside. But he also must have made himself known to the music lovers of Madrid as a composer of chamber music. He sent away his six string quartets, Opus 9, to be published in Paris (1770), but dedicated them "to the amateur musicians of Madrid" (Fig. 5.3).

Figure 5.3: *The title page of the first violin part of the set of six string quartets to which Boccherini assigned the opus number 9 (although his publisher in Paris, Venier, called it Opus 10), published in 1770 and dedicated to the amateur musicians of Madrid. (Alto is an Italian word for "viola.")*

In the same year, Don Luis, a member of the Spanish royal family, engaged Boccherini as a musician and composer. They seem to have enjoyed relations as close and productive as those between Scarlatti and Maria Barbara, with the major difference that Boccherini published much of the music that he wrote for Don Luis. He managed to operate simultaneously in two different worlds of musical production, serving a royal master while selling his wares on the open market. For several years Boccherini's ambidexterity earned him a comfortable living and the admiration of music lovers all over Europe. Thus it may be appropriate to end this brief consideration of Boccherini with praise from a musician who lived far from Madrid, who probably never met the composer or heard him play, but came to know and love his music through the medium of print: "The admirable trios, quartets, quintets, and sextets of Boccherini will always be the most perfect models of instrumental music because, besides their inspiration, learning, invention, and precision, they have always joined with these qualities that of *cantabile*, which renders these notes not just a capricious jumble of sweet sounds, but a measured and harmonious poetic song."

That encomium to Luigi Boccherini came from an amateur musician in Naples, who included it in a book published in 1785. His statement constitutes the closing of a circle. Exactly 100 years earlier, Domenico Scarlatti was born in the same city, where he studied and began his career. Gaetano Latilla, whose overture to *La finta cameriera* exemplifies the early sinfonia (the model for the concert symphony that became one of the most important genres of eighteenth-century music), also studied in Naples. Latilla's overture uses an orchestra, including the pair of horns introduced to Neapolitan opera around 1715 by Scarlatti's father, very close to the one that predominated in much of Europe during the rest of the century.

Like Lodovico Giustini, another member of "the class of 1685" and an early promoter of the piano, Scarlatti eventually found his niche as a composer of keyboard sonatas. But unlike Giustini, Scarlatti left Italy, thus contributing to the spread of Italian musical culture to the rest of Europe. Boccherini, another Italian instrumental virtuoso born 58 years after Scarlatti, also left Italy. He composed as prolifically as Scarlatti but differed from him in partaking enthusiastically in Europe's burgeoning music publishing industry. Through the publication of his works Boccherini became known to music lovers throughout the continent, including those in Naples, the city that contributed more than any other, well before his birth, to the rise of the galant style.

FOR FURTHER READING

Adams, Sarah, "International Dissemination of Printed Music during the Second Half of the Eighteenth Century," in *The Dissemination of Music: Studies in the History of Music Publishing,* ed. Hans Lenneberg (Lausanne: Gordon and Breach, 1994), 21–42

Kirkpatrick, Ralph, *Domenico Scarlatti* (Princeton, NJ: Princeton University Press, 1953)

Koster, John, "Towards an Optimal Instrument: Domenico Scarlatti and the New Wave of Iberian Harpsichord Making," *Early Music* 35 (2007): 575–603

Le Guin, Elisabeth, *Boccherini's Body: An Essay in Carnal Musicology* (Berkeley: University of California Press, 2006)

Pollens, Stewart, *The Early Pianoforte* (Cambridge: Cambridge University Press, 1995)

Russell, Craig, "Spain in the Enlightenment," in *The Classical Era: From the 1740s to the End of the 18th Century,* ed. Neal Zaslaw (Englewood Cliffs, NJ: Prentice Hall, 1989), 350–67

Spitzer, John, and Neal Zaslaw, *The Birth of the Orchestra: History of an Institution, 1650–1815* (Oxford: Oxford University Press, 2004)

Sutcliffe, W. Dean, *The Keyboard Sonatas of Domenico Scarlatti and Eighteenth-Century Musical Style* (Cambridge: Cambridge University Press, 2003)

Ⓢ **Additional resources available at wwnorton.com/studyspace**

CHAPTER SIX

Paris of the Ancien Régime

Although Paris kept its rank throughout the eighteenth century as Europe's second-largest city, it grew little compared to London (which began the century with a population only slightly larger than Paris's but ended up almost twice as large) and some other cities, such as Vienna and St. Petersburg. But its relatively stable population did not cause it to lose its musical importance and influence even as other cities grew more quickly.

Paris lies on both sides of the Seine at the point where two islands, the Ile Saint Louis and Ile de la Cité, make it easier to bridge the river than elsewhere. It was already a major city (and a major musical center) in the Middle Ages; indeed, some of its most splendid Gothic buildings, such as the Cathedral of Notre Dame on the Ile de la Cité, still stand. Most of the rest of the medieval city disappeared in the nineteenth-century urban renewal projects that gave the French capital many of the wide, straight, tree-lined avenues that we now associate with it. But in the eighteenth century, Paris still maintained something of its medieval appearance: a walled city with hundreds of dark, narrow alleys. On the eastern edge of the old city, just north of the Seine, stood the Bastille, the massive fourteenth-century fortress that served as a state prison.

During his long reign (1643–1715), King Louis XIV, known as the Sun King, built France into a strong, centralized state that he ruled from the great palace of Versailles, his favorite residence, about nine miles from the center of Paris. Louis was an extravagant patron of the arts, as Wendy Heller shows

Figure 6.1: *Detail of the Plan Turgot, a bird's-eye view of Paris published in 1739, showing the Palais Royal (on the left), location of the Opéra, and the Tuileries Palace (on the right), location of the hall that hosted the Concert Spirituel. The Louvre is at top left.*

in the preceding volume in this series. The wealth and power concentrated at Versailles found visible and audible expression in the concentration of theatrical and musical talent at the French court. To maintain control over his playwrights, actors, dancers, and musicians, Louis founded organizations to which he assigned specific activities, giving each a subsidy and a monopoly over the activity assigned to it. The Académie Royale de Musique (informally known as the Opéra), established by Louis in 1669, presented opera in French; the Comédie Française presented spoken plays in French; and the Comédie Italienne presented Italian plays, especially commedia dell'arte. With the death of Louis XIV in 1715, his nephew Philip, the Duke of Orléans, ruled as regent for Louis's underage great-grandson. During the Regency (1715–23), Philip made the Palais Royal in the center of Paris his principal residence, thus establishing Paris as the country's new cultural capital (Fig. 6.1). Artistic leadership shifted to a new generation of patrons and artists with tastes different from the Sun King's. When Louis XV came to the throne in 1723, he made Versailles his main residence; but neither he nor his son Louis XVI—the last monarch of the pre-Revolutionary ancien régime (old regime)—ever won back for it the prestige it had enjoyed in the seventeenth century. Louis XIV had imposed his tastes on his court, and through it on France; after his death most cultural trends emerged from and circulated among the aristocratic mansions of Paris.

TRAGÉDIE LYRIQUE AT THE OPÉRA

The Opéra, consisting of vocal soloists, chorus, dancers, and an orchestra trained to perform the operas of Jean-Baptiste Lully and his successors, resided for most of our period at the Palais Royal. The first of its theaters, built in 1637, was redecorated in the early eighteenth century. It specialized in the performance of *tragédie lyrique* (lyric tragedy, also known as *tragédie en musique*, tragedy in music), a spectacle that, as Voltaire wrote, brought together poetry, ballet, instrumental and vocal music, and painting:

Il faut se rendre à ce palais magique	*You must go to this magic palace,*
Où les beaux vers, la danse, la musique,	*where beautiful verse, dance, music,*
L'art de tromper les yeux par les couleurs,	*the art of deceiving the eyes with color,*
L'art plus heureux de séduire les coeurs,	*and the even more fortunate art of seducing the heart,*
De cent plaisirs font un plaisir unique.	*transform a hundred pleasures into one unique pleasure.*

One of those "hundred pleasures" was Greek mythology, from which the plots of many French operas were derived (as opposed to the historical origins of the librettos of most Italian serious operas). Another distinctive element of *tragédie lyrique* was its style of singing, quite different from the Italian style cultivated in much of Europe. This singing helped to make an evening at the Opéra an unforgettable experience for those attending for the first time.

One of the ways in which the Opéra kept alive musical practices and tastes of the seventeenth century was the frequent revival of old operas. The works of Lully, who died in 1687, continued to be performed throughout much of the eighteenth century (Fig. 6.2). Even in its more modern repertory the Opéra tended to be retrospective. Its new theater opened in 1770 with a revival of Jean Philippe Rameau's *Zoroastre* of 1749.

In addition to revivals, the Opéra also presented new works; but it expected composers to respect stylistic traditions going back to Lully. Some of the pamphlet wars that raged in Paris (public controversies carried on mainly through the publication of pamphlets) were basically generational conflicts,

Figure 6.2: *Gabriel de Saint-Aubin's drawing of a performance of Lully's* Armide *at the Opéra, 1761*

with Rameau caught in the middle. In the fight between the "Lullists" and the "Ramists" during the 1730s, the partisans of Lully attacked Rameau for breaking with French traditions. A few years later, during the *querelle des bouffons* (quarrel of the comic actors), defenders of modern Italian opera attacked Rameau for upholding the traditions that he had earlier been accused of abandoning. (For one of the principal pamphlets in this debate over the respective merits of French and Italian opera, see Jean-Jacques Rousseau's pro-Italian *Lettre sur la musique française* [Letter on French Music], SR 133; 5/12.)

OPÉRA COMIQUE

While the Opéra guarded France's most venerable operatic traditions in its theater in the Palais Royal, a short distance away a new kind of musical theater appeared at the very end of the reign of Louis XIV. Two trade fairs took place on the outskirts of Paris each year. Like fairs everywhere, they included various kinds of shows. Especially popular in Paris were musical plays involving commedia dell'arte characters. The Opéra's monopoly on sung theater meant that it was literally against the law for anyone to sing on stage except in its productions. This prohibition inspired great ingenuity in the fair theaters. Around 1712 they started presenting dramas in pantomime in which the texts of songs were displayed above the stage on placards, and the audience sang these texts to the tunes of well-known songs, known as *vaudevilles*.

One of the first such pieces was *Arlequin roi de Sérendib* (Harlequin, King of Serendip), performed in 1713. Written by the witty and prolific Alain-René Lesage (1668–1747), it used more than 60 existing melodies—from street songs to an air from Lully's *Isis* (1677)—to enliven a series of commedia dell'arte sketches held together by a plot as slim as it is amusing. Two years later, in 1715, Lesage added spoken dialogue to the dramatic and musical techniques he had used so effectively in *Arlequin* to produce a parody of a recently premiered *tragédie lyrique*.

The death of Louis XIV and a subsequent relaxation of the rigidly hierarchical society he had led put the Opéra in a weak position when dealing with the energetic, popular, and inventive fair theaters. Negotiations led to an agreement in 1716 that gave the fairs permission to present "spectacles mixed with music, dance and *symphonies* [instrumental pieces] under the name of Opéra-Comique." The Opéra allowed the actors at the fairs to sing (thereby making the placards no longer necessary); but it kept for itself the lyrical recitative developed by Lully for the declamation of dialogue, thus forcing the fair theaters to use spoken dialogue. In reserving the right to present dramas sung throughout, the Opéra unwittingly gave *opéra comique* (comic opera) its most distinctive feature: the alternation of spoken dialogue and song.

Opéra comique thrived and developed, with Lesage and other librettists adding new stock characters to the commedia dell'arte types with which the genre began and increasing the amount of newly composed music. In the 1730s and 1740s the dramatist Charles-Simon Favart raised the literary and moral tone of opéra comique above its fairground origins; Voltaire congratulated him as "the first to have made a decent and ingenious amusement out of a form of production which before you did not concern polite society. Thanks to you it has become the delight of all decent folk."

Although the Opéra's monopoly on recitative kept Italian opera from being performed regularly in Paris, librettists and composers of opéra comique were well aware of developments in Italy and elsewhere in Europe where Italian opera delighted audiences. The Opéra itself gave Italian opera a big boost when, in 1752, it engaged a traveling opera buffa troupe to perform under its auspices in Paris. This company's performance of Giovanni Battista Pergolesi's *La serva padrona*, Gaetano Latilla's *La finta cameriera*, and other Italian comedies took the capital by storm, igniting the *querelle des bouffons*. The Opéra eventually returned to its regular repertory of *tragédies lyriques*; but the success of the Italian comic troupe that it brought to Paris hastened the Italianization of opéra comique.

Many opéras comiques of the 1750s were parodies or imitations of Italian comic operas, with the recitative replaced with spoken dialogue. French composers incorporated Italian arias into their operas, and they wrote their own arias in the Italian style. By the 1760s, under the influence of opera buffa, opéra comique had started to abandon the use of *vaudevilles* and other existing musical material. A new generation of composers found exciting possibilities in the newly Italianate opéra comique and inspiration in the finely crafted, vigorously imaginative librettos of a new theatrical figure, Michel-Jean Sedaine (1719–1797).

Opéra comique led to the development in other countries of similar genres, first ballad opera in England and then Singspiel in Germany (see Chapters 7 and 9). England returned the favor by providing librettists of opéra comique with ideas. Sedaine derived *Le diable à quatre* (All Hell Breaks Loose), his first libretto, from Charles Coffey's ballad opera *The Devil to Pay, or The Wives Metamorphos'd* (1731), in which a magician causes a noblewoman and a cobbler's wife to change identities. Sedaine's version, first performed in Paris in 1756, shows opéra comique in transition. It still contains many traditional songs (nearly 70 of them!), but it also has arias borrowed from Italian operas and newly composed arias, all bound together with spoken dialogue. Several musicians worked together as arrangers and composers, and it is not completely clear who did what. What is clear is that Paris loved *Le diable à quatre*. Its popularity was to have repercussions outside of France, as we will see in later chapters.

PHILIDOR'S *TOM JONES*

One of the musicians who collaborated with Sedaine on *Le diable à quatre* won more fame as a chess master (at least outside of France) than as a composer: François-André Philidor (1726–1795). Nine years after the triumph of *Le diable à quatre*, Philidor turned to a much more complicated English source, Henry Fielding's sprawling comic novel *Tom Jones* (1749). He transformed the first half of *Tom Jones* into an opéra comique. After an initially poor reception, he asked Sedaine for help in revising the opera, and in this second version it was a great success.

In three acts, *Tom Jones* does not try to dramatize more than a few episodes of Fielding's novel. Act 1 presents the story's main characters and the situation they find themselves in. Handsome young Tom, a foundling raised by Mr. Allworthy, loves Sophie (Sophia in the novel), the beautiful daughter of Allworthy's neighbor, Squire Weston, who wants Sophie to marry Allworthy's unappealing nephew Blifil. In Act 2, Tom and Sophie declare their love, but she tells him of her intention to obey her father's wishes. In the middle of an intimate farewell they are surprised by the arrival of the rest of the characters. Allworthy banishes Tom. The drama reaches its crisis and resolution in Act 3, which takes place at an inn. Sophie has run away from home, and now she finds herself surrounded by drunken strangers. Tom rescues her. When he discovers his own noble identity (evidence of which Blifil had tried to suppress), Weston welcomes him as his future son-in-law, and he and Sophie anticipate married happiness.

Philidor adorned his score with a wide variety of musical gems. He evoked the story's rural setting as well as Weston's vigorous personality in Act 1 by having him sing a brilliant aria, *D'un cerf dix cors* (A ten-point deer), describing a stag hunt. Since the Middle Ages hunters have used horns to communicate with one another and with their dogs. They developed a vocabulary of signals through which they summoned and encouraged their dogs and informed one another what kind of animal was being pursued and into what kind of vegetation the quarry was leading them. The big, coiled hunting horns developed in France during the reign of Louis XIV ("French horns") and the signals they broadcast through woods and across fields were adopted, like so many other aspects of seventeenth-century French culture, throughout much of Europe during our century. The illustrations in the article on hunting in Denis Diderot's *Encyclopédie* present French hunting signals as a language applicable wherever the *Encyclopédie* was read (Fig. 6.3). In the aria *D'un cerf dix cors* Philidor greatly enriched Weston's description of the hunt by incorporating hunting signals much like those that Diderot quoted.

Philidor evoked different emotions near the beginning of Act 3, where Sophie, alone on stage, expresses fear, shame, and despair in an orchestrally accompanied recitative and aria that border on the tragic. Sophie's mono-logue successfully integrates into opéra comique one of the most dramatically and musically effective devices of Italian opera seria, the orchestrally accom-panied recitative. (It was called *recitativo accompagnato* to distinguish it from the *recitativo semplice*, with a simple continuo accompaniment, that we encoun-tered in Chapter 4.) The scene begins with the orchestra alone; it includes not only the strings that, in an Italian opera, one would expect to accompany a scene in which an emotionally distraught heroine pours out her feelings, but also an oboe and a bassoon with important solo parts (Ex. 6.1). To them Philidor as-signed one of the recitative's most expressive passages: a sequence in which the oboe and bassoon in dialogue repeatedly play notes a dissonant minor ninth above the bass (mm. 5–8). Syncopations, abrupt changes of dynamics, and augmented-sixth harmony (mm. 9–10), and chains of suspensions (mm. 11–12), help to convey Sophie's emotional state. Short, repeated motives are in-terspersed with rests, as if to suggest that Sophie, in her distress, has trouble breathing. Indeed her first words, when she finally speaks, are "Let me catch my breath."

Among the high points of *Tom Jones* are its ensembles. Philidor treated the discovery of Tom and Sophie in each other's arms at the end of Act 2 as a moment frozen in time, in which each character expresses his or her feelings si-multaneously. The resulting septet is a delightfully chaotic musical joke. Equally innovative and amusing is the drinking chorus at the beginning of Act 3, which begins with an unaccompanied round, or what the English called a "catch."

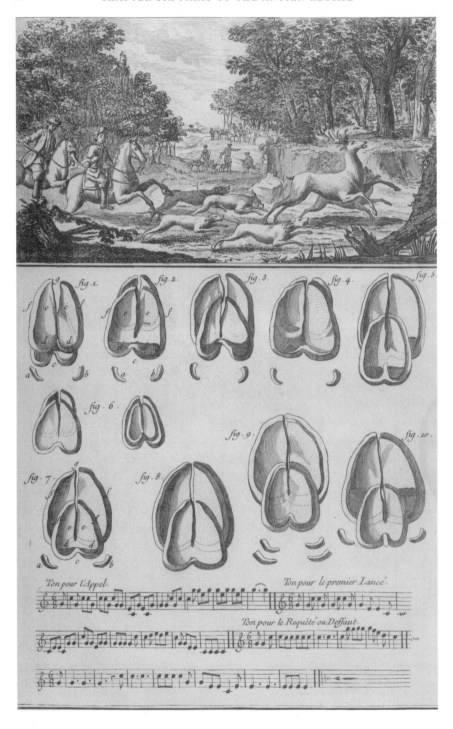

Figure 6.3: *One of several illustrations for the article on hunting in Diderot's* Encyclopédie. *It depicts a parforce hunt (a stag hunt using dogs and horses), animal tracks, and three horn signals.*

Example 6.1: *François-André Philidor,* Tom Jones, *Sophie's accompanied recitative* Respirons un moment, *mm. 1–19*

Let me catch my breath for a moment. Rest yourself, my heart. Where am I? What have I been doing? What a night! What horror!

INSTRUMENTAL MUSIC IN PARISIAN SALONS

François Couperin (1668–1733) played an important role at the court of Louis XIV as music teacher to the royal children at Versailles. But as the king's long reign drew to a close, Couperin, like many courtiers, looked with increasing fondness to Paris. He began publishing his keyboard music in 1713, and in 1716, at the beginning of the Regency, he published instructions on how his music ought to be played. Without turning his back on Versailles, he was clearly looking for a new and wider audience.

That new audience consisted largely of the French nobility and upper middle class, which patronized the arts in its Parisian residences. The living rooms of these mansions—the salons—became focal points of French culture, including music. Parisians favored qualities associated with what came to be known as the galant style: simplicity, grace, and naturalness. We have seen, in Chapter 2, how Couperin's *Les graces naturelles* (published in 1716) embodied these qualities in its title as well as in the music itself.

The Regency witnessed not only stylistic changes in French instrumental music, but also an increase in the amount of Italian music being performed in Paris. The Duke of Orléans himself endorsed Italian instrumental music by employing an Italian violin virtuoso, Michele Mascitti, for many years.

Figure 6.4: *A sunlit concert room, probably at the home of the Comtesse de Saint-Brisson. Engraving by Augustin de Saint-Aubin after a drawing by Antoine-Jean Duclos*

The nobility imitated the regent in collecting and performing Italian music and in cultivating the typically Italian genres of the three-movement concerto and sinfonia. They enjoyed this music in gatherings such as the one taking place in the concert room depicted in Figure 6.4, whose enormous windows, allowing the sunlight in, constitute a visual representation of enlightenment.

From the 1750s to his death in 1762, the most important of Paris's musical salons was that of Alexandre Le Riche de la Pouplinière, a rich tax farmer (a private tax collector entitled to keep a portion of whatever he raised for the government). La Pouplinière maintained an excellent orchestra of about 15 musicians and engaged several first-rate singers and instrumentalists to perform for him and his friends. Rameau, the leading opera composer in midcentury Paris, led the band. A writer who enjoyed La Pouplinière's hospitality remembered his music fondly:

> He had in his employ the best orchestra then known. The musicians lived in his house, and each morning rehearsed, with marvelous precision, the symphonies they were to play that evening. The leading theatrical talents, and especially the female singers and dancers of the Opéra, came to embellish his dinner parties. All the best musicians who came from Italy—violinists, singers—were welcomed, given lodging, and fed in his house, and they competed with one another to excel in his concerts.

GOSSEC'S SYMPHONIES

François-Joseph Gossec (1734–1829), one of the musicians who benefited from La Pouplinière's patronage, came to Paris from the Austrian Netherlands (part of what is now Belgium) as a young man in 1751 and found work and artistic inspiration as a violinist in the tax farmer's orchestra. On the death of La Pouplinière, Gossec found other noblemen eager for his services as music director and composer. By the mid-1760s he had established a reputation as France's leading composer of symphonies, of which he wrote nearly 60 during a career of more than five decades. Like Luigi Boccherini (see Chapter 5), he supplemented the income he received from noble patrons and made himself known to an expanding audience of middle-class music lovers through an intensive engagement in music publishing.

It was probably for La Pouplinière's concerts that Gossec wrote the symphonies published around 1762 as his Opus 6, though the title page shows him looking for a wider audience and hoping for performances by a variety of ensembles: *Six Symphonies, the first three with obbligato oboes and ad libitum horns, and the other three in four parts, for the convenience of large and small orchestras.* The obbligato oboes cannot be omitted without seriously damaging the music; the ad libitum horns contribute to the volume and richness of sound without being absolutely necessary. The symphonies "in four parts" are for strings alone. Although in some of his earlier symphonies Gossec had experimented, like Johann Stamitz at Mannheim, with a four-movement format, in Opus 6 he returned to three movements, which he favored (like most French symphonists) for the rest of the century.

The third symphony in the set, in C minor, exemplifies the skill Gossec achieved as a composer of symphonies during his first decade in Paris. Within the fast-slow-fast framework, he made unusual choices in the character of the second and third movements. A minuet serves as the central "slow" movement. Eighteenth-century composers usually wrote minuets in the same key and mode as the symphony's first movement; but here Gossec, in keeping with this minuet's unusual location and function, wrote it in the parallel major. In the finale, labeled Fugato, he combined the learned and galant styles by incorporating fugal expositions into binary form; Haydn, Mozart, and Beethoven would later write similar hybrid finales—a tradition that culminated in the fourth movement of Beethoven's String Quartet in C Major, Op. 59, No. 3 (see Anthology 29).

PUBLIC CONCERTS AND THE CHEVALIER DE SAINT-GEORGES

In 1725 a musician at the royal court received permission to give public concerts on religious holidays and during Lent, when the theaters were closed. The Concert Spirituel, one of Europe's first regular series of public concerts,

Figure 6.5: *Joseph Boulogne, Chevalier de Saint-Georges. Engraving by William Ward after a painting by Mather Brown*

played a major role in Parisian music during its 70 years of existence. In a large room in the Tuileries Palace (near the Louvre and the Palais Royal; see Fig. 6.1), it presented concerts consisting of symphonies, concertos, sacred vocal music, and Italian arias. The Concert Spirituel gave several performances of Pergolesi's *Stabat Mater*, contributing to its classic status. It also fostered the development of a distinctive instrumental subgenre: the misleadingly named *symphonie concertante* was not a symphony but a concerto for two or more solo instruments.

The composers of the orchestral music and the soloists in the concertos included Italian and German as well as French musicians, making the Concert Spirituel a cosmopolitan focal point in the cultivation of European instrumental music. In 1769, Parisian concert life became even richer, when Gossec founded a second series, the Concert des Amateurs. Yet a third series, the Concerts de la Loge Olympique, organized by one of Paris's Masonic lodges, was founded in 1779; for it Haydn wrote his six Paris Symphonies (Nos. 82–87) in 1785 and 1786.

One of the violinists in the Concert des Amateurs, Joseph Boulogne, Chevalier de Saint-Georges (1745–1799; Fig. 6.5) was born in the French West Indies, the son of a Frenchman and a slave woman who lived on the island of Guadeloupe. He may have spent part of his childhood in Saint-Domingue, the largest of the French West Indian sugar colonies, where wealth generated by slave labor made possible an urban life for white colonists that included opéra comique. (Such pleasant diversions ended suddenly in 1791 with the slave revolt that eventually led to the French withdrawal from Saint-Domingue and the establishment of the Republic of Haiti.)

Saint-Georges's father brought him to Paris and gave him a solid education that included riding and fencing, in which he became one of France's leading experts.

He probably studied composition with Gossec, with whom he enjoyed a long and fruitful association. In 1772, three years after Gossec engaged him as a violinist in the Concert des Amateurs, he appeared with the orchestra as soloist and composer, introducing his Violin Concertos Op. 2. He probably wrote the Concerto Op. 3, No. 1 shortly thereafter, and for performance with the same orchestra.

Saint-Georges scored the concerto for a big, colorful ensemble, with pairs of flutes, oboes, and horns in addition to strings. He laid it out in the normal three-movement, fast-slow-fast format that he had inherited from Antonio Vivaldi and concerto composers of the first half of the eighteenth century (see Wendy Heller's *Music in the Baroque*), and that Johann Joachim Quantz had carefully described in the early 1750s (SR 125: 800–4; 5/4: 66–70).

The first movement, in D major, uses a kind of binary form very similar to what we have encountered in the **A** section of da capo arias. There are two major solo passages, the first modulating from tonic to dominant, the second returning to and ending on the tonic. The opening ritornello (or orchestral introduction), in the tonic, introduces much of the movement's thematic material; the second ritornello, in the dominant, brings the first part of the binary structure to a conclusion; and the third and final ritornello concludes the second part of the binary structure and the movement as a whole. Mozart, the greatest composer of concertos in the second half of the eighteenth century, was to base the first movements of his concertos on this same plan.

The slow movement, an Adagio in D minor, also uses binary form, but for a completely different purpose (see Anthology 6). Here Saint-Georges offered his listeners a momentary glimpse at something dark and introspective, even tragic. After the festive, heroic virtuosity of the first movement, the Adagio tempts us to hear it as a statement of the private feelings of a young man whose mixed race would hinder the achievement of emotional and professional aspirations.

One of the functions of the slow movement of a concerto is to enhance the brilliance of the finale that follows. Saint-Georges's finale takes the form of a rondo, in which a theme in the tonic is presented several times, always in the tonic, in alternation with contrasting episodes. The principal theme here is an elegant, minuet-like melody in triple meter and in the balanced phrases (adding up to 16 measures) characteristic of dance music. Fermatas at the end of all three episodes invite the soloist to improvise cadenzas, thus playfully delaying the return of the rondo theme and enhancing the pleasure we feel at its return.

With the death of Louis XIV and the beginning of the Regency, France's artistic center of gravity shifted from Versailles to Paris: from the royal court to the mansions of the Parisian nobility. The salon became the focal point of cultural life. Private music-making led to the development of a thriving music publishing business, and together they produced conditions under which composers such as François-Joseph Gossec flourished. A new operatic genre, opéra comique, managed to insinuate itself into French musical life, giving rise to such works as François-André Philidor's *Tom Jones*. Equally novel and influential was the Concert Spirituel, a public concerts series founded in 1725, just after the end of the Regency.

Both opéra comique and the Concert Spirituel staked out unoccupied territory in the new cultural landscape, though not without protest from the Opéra. The precedents set by Louis XIV, in music as in other aspects of French culture, could not be easily ignored or undone. Lully's operas, like the splendors of Versailles, survived the Regency. So did the system of royal privileges that gave theatrical companies monopolies over the performance of works in particular genres, and kept Italian opera from being performed in Paris for most of our period. The story of French music in the eighteenth century is largely one of interaction between old court-sponsored institutions, which generally encouraged aesthetic conservatism, and new ideas and talents that emerged in Paris during the Regency and its aftermath.

FOR FURTHER READING

Banat, Gabriel, *The Chevalier de Saint-Georges: Virtuoso of the Sword and the Bow* (Hillsdale, NY: Pendragon, 2006)

Charlton, David, *Grétry and the Growth of Opéra-Comique* (Cambridge: Cambridge University Press, 1986)

Michel-Jean Sedaine (1719–1797): Theatre, Opera and Art, ed. David Charlton and Mark Ledbury (Aldershot, England: Ashgate, 2000)

Heartz, Daniel, *Music in European Capitals: The Galant Style, 1720–1780* (New York: W. W. Norton, 2003), 595–800

Mongrédien, Jean, "Paris: The End of the Ancien Régime," in *The Classical Era: From the 1740s to the End of the 18th Century,* Neal Zaslaw ed. (Englewood Cliffs, NJ: Prentice Hall, 1989), 61–98

Paris: Life and Luxury in the Eighteenth Century, ed. Charissa Bremer-David (Los Angeles: J. Paul Getty Museum, 2011)

Roche, Daniel, *France in the Enlightenment* (Cambridge, MA: Harvard University Press, 1998)

Spitzer, John, and Neal Zaslaw, *The Birth of the Orchestra: History of an Institution, 1650–1815* (Oxford: Oxford University Press, 2004), 180–212

Verba, Cynthia, "Music and the Enlightenment," in *The Enlightenment World*, ed. Martin Fitzpatrick (Abingdon: Routledge, 2004), 307–322

Ⓢ Additional resources available at wwnorton.com/studyspace

CHAPTER SEVEN

Georgian London

"Whoever wants to achieve something in music nowadays goes to England," wrote the German composer Johann Mattheson in 1713. "The Italians exalt music, the French enliven it, the Germans strive after it, the English pay well for it." Many of the musicians who came to London from the continent of Europe during our period would have agreed with Mattheson. Whether they visited the city or settled there permanently, they made it one of Europe's liveliest musical capitals.

METROPOLIS ON THE THAMES

Seventeenth-century England, with its access to the Atlantic Ocean, its colonies in North America and the Caribbean, and its strong navy and merchant fleet, became Europe's leader in international trade. England consolidated its domination of the rest of the British Isles in 1707, when the kingdoms of England and Scotland joined to become Great Britain—a political entity whose viability was strengthened with the establishment of a new ruling dynasty, the house of Hanover, in 1714. The Treaty of Utrecht that ended the War of the Spanish Succession in 1713 confirmed Britain's gains at the expense of its Continental rivals.

Britain's wealth and power were concentrated in London, the meeting place of trade routes that spanned the globe. London led the world in trade and manufacturing, and in the banking and insurance industries on which trade depended. Every year thousands of ships moved up and down the river Thames; huge quantities of raw materials and merchandise passed through London's docks and customs offices.

Ships involved in Britain's thriving slave trade sailed mostly out of ports on the west coast, but London's financiers invested in the business and reaped its rewards. Slavery also contributed to London's prosperity in other ways. Sugar from British colonies in the West Indies, the product of slave labor, became London's largest import. The sugar trade enriched not only the merchants who bought the raw sugar, refined it, and resold it, but also the owners of sugar plantations, some of whom lived in London.

With prosperity came expanding population: London grew from about 575,000 in 1700 to about 948,000 a century later, larger than any other city in Europe, and second in size worldwide only to Beijing. In the West End, developers laid out new neighborhoods, whose plans reflected the rationalism of the Enlightenment. Many of their wide, straight streets (different from the labyrinthine alleys of the medieval city) met at right angles or at rectangular plazas lined with elegant brick townhouses. One of the new urban plazas, Hanover Square, gave its name to London's most important concert hall.

The name of the concert hall and the square on which it was located paid tribute to the royal dynasty that presided over London's growth and prosperity. When Queen Anne died in 1714 without a direct heir, Parliament looked abroad for a prince to succeed her. George, elector of the German principality of Hanover and Anne's closest Protestant relative, was crowned king later the same year. His coronation marks the establishment of the Hanoverian dynasty. From his name and that of his successors, also called George, comes the adjective "Georgian," with which historians refer to distinctive elements of eighteenth-century British culture.

The Hanoverian kings did not control most aspects of cultural life in their capital. Their relatively small influence reflected both the limited power of the king in a parliamentary monarchy and London's size and wealth: many of its cultural institutions did not need the king's money. But in one respect London's music did mirror the court: many composers, instrumentalists, singers, and instrument makers came from abroad. Having imported a ruler, London thought nothing of importing the Continent's finest musical talent. The Germans George Frideric Handel and Johann Christian Bach settled in London; several of Italy's leading composers served as music directors; many of the best Italian singers appeared on the stage and in concert rooms; and English music lovers applauded both the child Mozart and the mature Haydn. (Wendy Heller discusses Handel and the Italian diaspora in *Music in the Baroque*.)

London's theaters, like those in other European capitals, operated under government control. The Licensing Act of 1737 reinforced existing patents that allowed only two large, permanent theaters to present dramas in English: the Theatre Royal, Drury Lane and the Theatre Royal, Covent Garden (which in the 1730s replaced, and took over the patent from, an older theater at Lincoln's Inn Fields). Another theater, the King's Theatre in the Haymarket, specialized in the production of Italian opera. Built in 1709, and quite small in comparison with Covent Garden and Italy's principal theaters, it seated about 940 people. Despite its name, the King's Theatre was not owned or run by the Crown. The building itself was in private hands, and the Italian opera companies that occupied it operated under a succession of different managers. The opera's most important patrons were its subscribers, mostly members of the nobility, who paid substantial sums to rent boxes throughout the season.

BALLAD OPERA

On January 29, 1728, the impresario John Rich presented *The Beggar's Opera* at Lincoln's Inn Fields. An immediate success, it was performed 62 times during its first run. It maintained a place in the London repertory for the rest of the century, presented far more frequently and widely (all over Britain and in the North American colonies as well) than any other English opera.

The Beggar's Opera defined and established a new genre of musical theater in English: ballad opera, a spoken play interspersed with existing songs sung to new words. John Gay (1685–1732) wrote the words for *The Beggar's Opera* and chose the songs. The 69 musical numbers came from a wide variety of sources: mostly folk songs, including English ballads and traditional tunes from Ireland, Scotland, and France, but also vocal pieces by major composers such as Henry Purcell and Handel.

Historians disagree about how *The Beggar's Opera* differed from the masques, "English operas," and other forms of musical theater that Wendy Heller describes. Some have suggested it had no real precedent; others have argued that it reflects the influence of opéra comique, which emerged in Paris around 1715. As we saw in Chapter 6, early opéra comique consisted largely of popular songs strung together by spoken dialogue. French troupes performed opéra comique in London in the early 1720s, and these productions probably inspired Gay to put the rich folk traditions of the British Isles to similar use.

Gay presented familiar songs in unexpected dramatic contexts and with words that often amusingly contradict the sense of the original words, in a drama that undermines and makes fun of theatrical conventions in general and operatic conventions in particular. The title refers to the drama's frame: a pair of scenes at the beginning and end. In the opening scene a beggar who has written an opera introduces his work to an actor, proudly declaring that his work conforms to operatic conventions: "I have introduced the similes that are in all your celebrated operas: the swallow, the moth, the bee, the ship, the flower, etc. Besides, I have a prison scene, which the ladies always reckon charmingly pathetic. As to the parts, I have observed such a nice impartiality to our two ladies, that it is impossible for either of them to take offence." But by making most of his characters thieves and prostitutes, and by making his hero a criminal and a libertine, Gay turned the world of Italian opera upside down.

In the final scene the beggar and actor reappear. The actor objects to the hero's impending death: such an ending would make "a downright deep tragedy. The catastrophe is manifestly wrong, for an opera must end happily." The beggar agrees, allowing his criminal hero to go free. Thus Gay ends his drama by making fun of Italian opera's fondness for happy endings.

Macheath is a daring outlaw and a womanizer as insatiable and charming as the legendary Don Juan, who not only enjoys the company and the sexual favors of a group of prostitutes but also marries the virtuous Polly Peachum. Polly's father, a seller of stolen goods, plans to turn Macheath in to the authorities, so that when he is hanged Polly will inherit his money. Macheath is arrested and imprisoned, but Lucy, daughter of the jailer and one of Macheath's girlfriends, frees him. Lockit the jailer, thinking his daughter freed Macheath in exchange for money, demands that she share it. She tells him that she did it for love and explains (to the tune of Purcell's *If love's a sweet passion*) how Macheath seduced her. Gay replaced the plaintively erotic love poetry of Purcell's song with something bawdier:

Anonymous poem set by Purcell (*The Fairy Queen*, 1692)	Gay's parody
If love's a sweet passion why does it torment?	When young at the bar you first taught me to score,
If a bitter, oh tell me whence comes my content?	And bid me be free with my lips, and no more;
Since I suffer with pleasure, why should I complain,	I was kiss'd by the parson, the squire, and the sot.
Or grieve at my fate, when I know 'tis in vain?	When the guest was departed, the kiss was forgot.
Yet so pleasing the pain is, so soft is the dart,	But his kiss was so sweet, and so closely he press'd,
That at once it both wounds me, and tickles my heart.	That I languish'd and pin'd till I granted the rest.

Macheath, betrayed again, does not remain free for long, and Polly and Lucy plead for his life (Fig. 7.1). He is about to be taken to the gallows when the beggar and the actor suddenly intervene.

Figure 7.1: *A ticket for a benefit performance of* The Beggar's Opera, *showing the climactic scene in which Polly (on the left) and Lucy (on the right) plead for Macheath's life. Engraving by Sympson after a drawing by William Hogarth*

The phenomenal success of *The Beggar's Opera* led to the production of other ballad operas, few of them as daringly subversive as Gay's. Stricter enforcement of censorship laws pushed ballad opera toward more innocuous and less memorable fare. Like opéra comique, it borrowed its music increasingly from Italian opera, to the point where, by the 1760s, whole Italian comic operas were translated into English, with the recitative transformed into spoken dialogue. But the traditions of ballad opera prevailed in English dramas in which songs from a wide variety of sources were linked with spoken dialogue. One of the most popular of such operas was *Love in a Village*, which replaced the biting satire and gritty urban setting of *The Beggar's Opera* with a gently comic and sentimental picture of the English countryside. Thomas Arne (1710–1778) supplied the music, composing several numbers and collecting the rest from the works of other composers and from folk music. First performed at Covent Garden in 1762, *Love in a Village* delighted audiences for many years.

ITALIAN OPERA

Many of London's operagoers had developed their musical tastes during travels in Italy. They had heard the greatest Italian singers and were willing to pay what it took to bring them to England. The list of singers who appeared in the Haymarket is a who's who of Italian stars.

Composers of Italian opera also came to London in droves. Handel was the first of a splendid succession of composers from the Continent who served the King's Theatre as music directors or composers or in a more informal capacity (Table 7.1). Most came from Italy or had extensive experience there. Several spent the rest of their lives in England and contributed to music far beyond the Haymarket. Almost all (with the exception of Handel) were Catholic; their presence in Protestant London constitutes a compelling example of our period's division of musical roles (proposed in Chapter 1) between Catholic producers and Protestant consumers.

These musicians presented both their own works and operas from Italy. They also oversaw the production of *pasticci* (as defined in Chapter 4), as popular in London (accustomed to ballad operas and other dramas containing music from many different sources) as in Italy. The value Londoners placed on virtuoso singing, and the prestige leading singers consequently enjoyed, put them in a strong position in discussions with music directors about what arias they were to sing. The most important duty of a music director in the Haymarket was to display singers as brilliantly as possible. If this meant cobbling together the music of several composers, so be it.

The kinds of Italian operas performed in the King's Theatre varied according to the tastes and strategies of the impresario in charge and the abilities of singers under contract. Opera seria dominated the repertory into the 1760s. When the Mozart family visited London in 1764–66, the Haymarket presented only opera seria and the operatic season was organized around a single celebrated and highly paid *musico*, Giovanni Manzoli. The 9-year-old prodigy studied Manzoli's singing intently. A few months later, accompanying himself at the keyboard, Mozart improvised Italian arias in Manzoli's style. In the late 1760s Italian comedy began winning more attention from London audiences.

PICCINNI'S *LA BUONA FIGLIUOLA*

The great success of *La buona figliuola* (The Good Girl), a comic opera by Niccolò Piccinni (1728–1800) that reached London in 1767, did more than anything else to put opera buffa on a footing more or less equal to that of opera seria. "The music of this favourite opera appears always new," a critic wrote of *La buona figliuola* in 1774; "and we may venture to affirm that it will for ever remain the standard of true harmonical taste. The first motion of the overture never fails to call on the

Table 7.1: *Some foreign-born composers active at the King's Theatre in the eighteenth century*

NAME	COUNTRY (OR COUNTRIES) OF ORIGIN AND OF PREVIOUS OPERATIC EXPERIENCE	YEARS OF RESIDENCE IN BRITAIN
George Frideric Handel	Germany, Italy	1710–1759
Atillio Ariosti	Italy	1720–1728
Giovanni Battista Bononcini	Italy	1720–1732
Nicola Porpora	Italy	1729–1736
Giovanni Battista Pescetti	Italy	1737–1745
Baldassare Galuppi	Italy	1741–1743
Giovanni Battista Lampugnani	Italy	1743–1744
Christoph Gluck	Bohemia, Italy	1745–1746
Vincenzo Ciampi	Italy	1748–1756
Felice Giardini	Italy	1750–1784
Gioacchino Cocchi	Italy	1757–1772
Johann Christian Bach	Germany, Italy	1762–1782
Mattia Vento	Italy	1763–1776
Pietro Alessandro Guglielmi	Italy	1767–1772
Felice Alessandri	Italy	1767–1770
Antonio Sacchini	Italy	1772–1781
Venanzio Rauzzini	Italy	1774–1810
Ferdinando Bertoni	Italy	1778–1783
Pasquale Anfossi	Italy	1782–1786
Luigi Cherubini	Italy	1785–1786
Angelo Tarchi	Italy	1787–1789
Vincenzo Federici	Italy	1790–1793
Joseph Haydn	Austria	1791–1792, 1794–1795
Vicente Martín y Soler	Spain, Italy, Austria	1794–1796
Francesco Bianchi	Italy	1795–1810

countenance of the audience the most radiant symptoms of chearfulness and heart-felt satisfaction; and it continues so to the end of the opera." No Italian opera came closer to achieving the status of a classic than *La buona figliuola*. First performed in Rome in 1760 (with a *musico* in the title role), Piccinni's opera was heard in many European cities. But it was especially popular in London, partly because it was based (loosely) on an English literary source, Samuel Richardson's

Figure 7.2: *Anna Zamperini in the role of Cecchina, which she sang in the first London production of* La buona figliuola *in 1767. Mezzotint by Finlayson (ca. 1771) after a painting by Nathaniel Hone*

novel *Pamela*. The King's Theatre revived it often: between 1767 and 1810 it received 112 performances, more than twice as many as any other Italian opera.

In *La buona figliuola* Piccinni achieved a perfect balance of comedy and pathos, of musical simplicity and grandeur. An array of character types extends from servant girls to aristocrats. In the middle is Cecchina (soprano; Fig. 7.2), a beautiful, virtuous young noblewoman unaware (like Tom Jones of Henry Fielding's novel and François-André Philidor's opéra comique) of her noble birth, who works as a gardener on the estate of a young nobleman (tenor). Although he loves Cecchina, the apparent difference in their social status keeps him from marrying her, while Cecchina's innate nobility keeps her from forming close bonds with the servants and peasants. We laugh at the snobbery of the nobleman's sister and her lover, who wants to break off their engagement because his future brother-in-law loves his gardener, and at the petty maliciousness of the servant girls, jealous of Cecchina. But we take Cecchina seriously, pitying her because of her misfortune and rejoicing with her when she finally discovers her identity and finds happiness in a noble marriage. Piccinni excelled in the portrayal of Cecchina's sweetness and sincerity, bringing to opera buffa a sentimentality that it had, until then, largely lacked.

Cecchina sings one of the opera's musical high points, *Vieni il mio seno* (Come, sweet rest), as she falls asleep (Ex. 7.1). Piccinni's prominent use of flutes, which

Example 7.1: *Niccolò Piccinni,* La buona figliuola, *aria:* Vieni il mio seno, *mm. 6–10*

Come, sweet rest, to console my grief-filled breast

sound rarely in the opera, together with muted violins and pizzicato cellos and basses, enhances the aria's sweetness. The simple harmonic language gives unexpected power to a sudden move to the parallel minor just before the end.

A few days after the premiere of *La buona figliuola* in the Haymarket, Covent Garden presented an English version of it, with spoken dialogue, under the title *The Accomplish'd Maid.* In *The Beggar's Opera,* English musical theater distanced itself as far as possible from Italian opera; in *The Accomplish'd Maid,* Italian opera and English opera came close to being one and the same.

J. C. BACH AND *LA CLEMENZA DI SCIPIONE*

Despite the popularity of opera buffa and opera in English, London's music lovers continued to demand opera seria and the vocal virtuosity that brought it to life. The diaries of Susannah Burney testify vividly to the fascination that opera seria exerted in London; she was especially enamored of the great *musico* Gasparo Pacchierotti (for excerpts, see SR 145; 5/24). During the season that ran from November 1777 to May 1778, the Haymarket presented seven comic operas and four serious operas. If that suggests that opera buffa dominated the repertory, the number of times each opera was performed tells a different story. Antonio Sacchini's opera seria *Creso* (Croesus) reached 16 performances, twice as many as any other opera. Among the four operas given eight times were two more *opere serie*, including Bach's *La clemenza di Scipione* (Scipio's Clemency).

Johann Christian Bach (1735–1782), the youngest of Johann Sebastian Bach's children, was born in Leipzig and received some basic musical education from his father. After Sebastian's death in 1750 he moved to Berlin, where his half brother Carl Philipp Emanuel guided his development as a musician. But Christian's personality and ambitions differed from Emanuel's. Opera, from which the Lutheran Bach family had always kept its distance, fascinated him, and so did the singers who created it. In 1755, at the age of 20, he fell in love with an Italian soprano and followed her to Italy—a country that neither his father nor his older brothers had visited. In yet another rejection of the traditions into which he was born, he converted to Catholicism. After further musical studies, J. C. Bach entered the world of opera seria. The success of his first opera, *Artaserse* (Artaxerxes; Turin, 1761), led to commissions from the Teatro San Carlo in Naples, for which he wrote *Catone in Utica* (Cato in Utica) and *Alessandro nell'Indie* (Alexander in the Indies).

The manager of the King's Theatre heard of the exciting young operatic talent emerging in Italy and engaged Bach to compose and direct operas in London. He arrived in England in the summer of 1762 and lived there for the rest of his life, writing operas for the Haymarket, serving as music teacher to Queen Charlotte (wife of George III), and organizing, composing music for, and directing concerts. His career—as a musician born in Lutheran Germany who became an opera composer in Italy, came to London to write operas, but contributed to music outside the opera house—resembled Handel's (as Wendy Heller describes it in *Music in the Baroque*). But having been born exactly 50 years after Handel, he brought to London a very different musical language.

La clemenza di Scipione is one of five full-length serious operas that Bach wrote for the Haymarket during the 1760s and 1770s. The libretto, by an unknown poet, is Metastasian in style and content (see Chapter 4), but with less dialogue than in Metastasio's librettos. (Bach recognized the reluctance of English audiences to sit through long stretches of recitative, especially in Italian.) The opera takes place in 209 B.C.E., during a war between Rome and Carthage. The Roman general Scipio (Scipione in the opera; tenor) has conquered Cartagena, a Carthaginian city on the Mediterranean coast of Spain. Among his captives is Arsinda, a princess of a tribe allied with Carthage (high coloratura soprano). Arsinda's lover Prince Luceio (male soprano) comes to Scipione disguised as an ambassador and offers a ransom for Arsinda, but Scipione refuses. Luceio and Arsinda, trying to escape, are captured, and Luceio, having revealed his identity, is sentenced to death. But at the last minute Scipione, moved by his prisoners' devotion and courage, grants them life and freedom; Luceio and Arsinda, in return, promise allegiance to Rome.

La clemenza di Scipione testifies to Bach's eagerness to generate and maintain a lively dramatic pace. Instead of the three-movement (fast-slow-fast) overtures of his earlier operas, he wrote an overture in a single fast movement, which he integrated into the opera by bringing some of its music back in Scipione's opening recitative and in the opera's final chorus. In place of the da capo and dal segno arias that dominated opera seria into the 1770s (see Chapter 2), Bach set most of the arias in La clemenza di Scipione in various permutations of binary form, corresponding in length and structure to the **A** section of the da capo aria.

Perhaps inspired by the music with which Cecchina in La buona figliuola goes to sleep on stage, Bach gave Arsinda an equally fine sleep aria, Dal dolor cotanto oppressa. It begins with a melody that beautifully manipulates melodic conventions of the galant style (Ex. 7.2). The text begins:

Dal dolor cotanto oppressa   *My soul is oppressed*
È quest'alma, o giusti numi   *by such sadness, oh just gods*

Example 7.2: *Johann Christian Bach,* La clemenza di Scipione, *aria:* Dal dolor cotanto oppressa, *mm. 8–13*

My soul is oppressed by such sadness, oh just gods

After Bach's prima donna Francesca Danzi sang these lines as two two-measure phrases, her listeners must have expected her to complete a six-measure **ABB'** melody by repeating the second phrase and bringing it to a full cadence. But she surprised them by replacing one galant device with another. Her lovely $\hat{6}$–$\hat{5}$–$\hat{4}$–$\hat{3}$ melodic descent on the words "o giusti numi" over a bass descending $\hat{4}$–$\hat{3}$–$\hat{2}$–$\hat{1}$ elaborated the voice-leading schema that Gjerdingen has named the Prinner, as discussed in Chapter 3. Danzi revealed a different side of Arsinda's personality in Act 2, where the Iberian princess expresses despair in a grand coloratura aria with concerto-like solos for flute, oboe, violin, and cello.

PUBLIC CONCERTS

A large and prosperous population made public concerts economically viable earlier in London than in Europe's other cities. Already in the second half of the seventeenth century musicians charged admission to their performances in taverns and coffeehouses. Handel's first oratorio, *Esther,* had its premiere in the Crown and Anchor Tavern in 1732.

Taverns remained an important site for concerts throughout the eighteenth century, but as audiences grew, musicians found other venues. In the 1740s Handel presented his oratorios in concerts during Lent (when other theatrical activity was restricted) at Covent Garden. Subscription concerts were given at Hickford's Room in James Street from 1728. During the 1760s and 1770s Teresa Cornelys, a former actress, gave a series of subscription concerts in richly decorated rooms at Carlisle House in Soho Square.

To direct her concerts Cornelys engaged Friedrich Abel and Christian Bach. Abel (1723–1787), a German composer of instrumental music who had studied with Bach's father in Leipzig, joined Bach in presenting, from 1765, London's finest concert series. The concerts included, among other works, symphonies by Bach, who in April 1765 announced the publication of six symphonies, Opus 3, "as they were performed at the Wednesday Subscription Concert, in Soho-square."

Having established their reputation in Cornelys's concerts, Bach and Abel looked for a larger space. In 1774 they converted a building in Hanover Square into a hall designed specifically for concerts. The Hanover Square Rooms quickly became London's most important concert venue: the site not only of the Bach-Abel concerts and other subscription series but of concerts that individual musicians organized for their own benefit.

One of the musicians who contributed to Hanover Square's reputation as the focus of London's concert life was Ludwig Dülon (1767–1826), a blind flutist from Germany who visited England in 1786. He recalled in his autobiography that within a few days of his arrival he had been welcomed at the court of George III and had played for the king and queen. That reception made him a minor celebrity, and a week or so later he played a concerto on the stage of the King's Theatre during the intermission of an oratorio. But the high point of his visit was

Figure 7.3: *William Boyce's song "The Adieu to the Spring-Gardens," with an engraving that depicts the grove and orchestra at Vauxhall Gardens at night in an image evoking the artistic values of Watteau. From George Bickham's* The Musical Entertainer *(1737).*

his benefit concert at Hanover Square, where he assembled some of the finest musicians in a city that attracted musical talent from all over Europe. He remembered the concert as "one of the most excellent, if not the best, that I ever gave."

Londoners often visited pleasure gardens on the outskirts of the city, where they enjoyed food and drink, walked, socialized, and listened to music. Among the most popular of the gardens were Vauxhall (Fig. 7.3) and Ranelagh, the latter offering, in addition to tree-shaded walks and sunny lawns, a large indoor space: a magnificent rotunda where guests promenaded. In both of these gardens, platforms high above the ground allowed orchestras to be seen as well as heard by hundreds of visitors (Fig. 7.4). The concerts offered a mixture—normal in this period—of instrumental and vocal music, but differed from the concert rooms of the West End, such as Hanover Square, in presenting music mainly by British composers, performed mainly by British singers and instrumental soloists.

"ANCIENT" AND MODERN INSTRUMENTAL MUSIC

When the flutist Dülon played before King George III and Queen Charlotte in 1786, he was prepared for the court's cultivation of old music as well as new: "His Majesty the king loved old music exclusively; but the queen preferred newer music. This I knew already, and I had brought both with me in order to win the applause of both Their Majesties." The king's tastes reflected and reinforced London's fondness for what it called "ancient music," a predilection that led to the rise of several organizations devoted to its performance in private and public. London shared its taste for ancient music with Paris, but with this important difference: London had no equivalent of Jean-Baptiste Lully. The older music that British audiences enjoyed was rarely operatic. With the exception of a few classics such as *The Beggar's Opera* and *La buona figliuola*, London's opera lovers wanted contemporary music.

VAUXHALL GARDENS shewing the *Grand Walk* at the entrance of the Garden, & the Orchestra with the Musick Playing.

Figure 7.4: *The music pavilion at Vauxhall Gardens. Etching and engraving by Johann Sebastian Muller, after a drawing by Samuel Wale, ca. 1751.*

One of several musical groups that had their origins in London's taverns was the Academy of Ancient Music, founded (as the Academy of Vocal Music) in 1726. In keeping with its original name, at first it presented only vocal music, especially madrigals and sacred music of the sixteenth century. The Academy of Ancient Music faded in the 1750s, but its name came back into prominence in the 1780s, now attached to a more formal concert organization that offered a series of subscription concerts featuring a combination of vocal and instrumental music of the late seventeenth and early eighteenth centuries and contemporary music—a repertory that appealed to a wider audience than its earlier, more esoteric fare.

GALLO'S TRIO SONATAS

In 1780 the London publisher Bremner issued a set of trio sonatas under the title *Twelve Sonatas for two Violins and a Bass or an Orchestra compos'd by Gio. Batt.ᵃ Pergolese.* The attribution was doubted already in the eighteenth century and was definitely rejected in the twentieth, but not before Igor Stravinsky, in his ballet score *Pulcinella* (1920), reworked several movements and, in doing so, identified them indelibly with Giovanni Battista Pergolesi and himself. Subsequently, some of the sonatas surfaced in manuscripts with attributions to one Domenico Gallo, and on the basis of those manuscripts the whole set has been tentatively attributed to Gallo. But more interesting for our purposes is the way in which the set and its publication document London's taste for ancient music.

The publication was a product of the Grand Tour (see Chapter 1), an institution that the British especially relished. The music they heard abroad helped to shape their taste and thus affected their musical patronage at home. The British Library owns hundreds of Italian musical manuscripts, many of which British travelers bought on the Grand Tour. In the case of the "Pergolesi" sonatas, Bremner's title page informed prospective buyers: "The Manuscript of these Sonatas were [sic] procured by a curious gentleman of fortune, during his travels through Italy."

English music lovers welcomed the sonatas: they were reprinted at least twice. Their appeal went beyond the attraction of Pergolesi's name. Although they contain some features of the galant style, the learned predominates. The trio sonata as a genre was favored by composers born before 1700, as was the particular combination of two violins and basso continuo. But those composers often laid out their sonatas in four movements, slow-fast-slow-fast; Gallo used the more modern fast-slow-fast format. His opening melodies occasionally sound galant (for example, several movements begin with **ABB′** melodies), but several fugal movements display the composer's solid contrapuntal skills.

Partisans of ancient music had much to admire in the Trio Sonata No. 1 in G Major, which begins with a movement (one of those that Stravinsky adapted) that combines the learned and galant, with an emphasis on the former (see Anthology 7). The initial phrase (mm. 1–2) elaborates the galant romanesca and the Prinner (compare the beginning of Leonardo Vinci's aria *Non ha quell' augelletto*, Ex. 3.4, which uses the same two schemata in the same order). But Gallo's music continues with a sequence in the learned style. Notice how rarely the violins play in parallel thirds or sixths; the second violin is only slightly subordinate in melodic interest. The sonata ends with a fugue. That such music could have been successfully published in the 1780s shows how strongly British musicians and audiences favored the learned style.

If we can imagine George III, "who loved old music exclusively," listening to Gallo's trio sonata with delight, what kind of sonata did Queen Charlotte—and other British music lovers who "preferred newer music"—enjoy? For an answer we can turn again to the music of the queen's music teacher, Christian Bach. In his keyboard sonatas, just as in symphonies for his public concerts and operas for the Haymarket, he gave British music lovers the most modern incarnations of the galant style.

J. C. BACH'S OP. 5, NO. 2, AS AN EXAMPLE OF SONATA FORM

Bach published his Opus 5, a set of six keyboard sonatas, in 1766. Although they appeared in print 14 years before Gallo's sonatas, Bach's are in every respect more modern. As a genre, the keyboard sonata appealed to musicians born in the eighteenth century as strongly as the trio sonata appealed to older musicians. The title page of Opus 5 describes the sonatas as being written for harpsichord or piano, but frequent changes in dynamics show that Bach wrote them with the piano in mind. (His appearance in a concert in 1767 playing a piano solo is one of the earliest documented instances of a piano being played in a public concert.)

The first movement of the Sonata in D Major, Op. 5, No. 2, conveys the excitement and grandeur of an operatic overture (see Anthology 8). Whereas Gallo's Moderato alternates between homophonic and polyphonic textures, Bach's Allegro di molto is consistently homophonic. It shows Bach expertly manipulating contrast and balance on several levels, using binary form as a framework for a panoply of contrasting ideas. He divided both parts of the binary structure into several sections that differ in character and function. In doing so, he produced an example of a form that would challenge and fascinate composers for the rest of the century and beyond.

Theorists in the nineteenth century referred to this kind of internally articulated binary form as "sonata form." They labeled the first part "exposition," the second part "development" and "recapitulation." In Bach's Allegro di molto (and in many other sonata-form movements) the recapitulation begins with a double return: the simultaneous return of the tonic key and of melodic material from the beginning of the first part.

During the next several decades, sonata form dominated European music. Movements in the major mode follow the same general tonal plan as Bach, with a similar succession of melodic, connecting, and cadential passages (with the development becoming increasingly long and elaborate); movements in the minor mode generally modulate to the relative major in the first part. Just as each of the two parts of binary movements (in instrumental music) is usually repeated, so the exposition and the development/recapitulation are usually repeated (exceptions include operatic overtures and movements in concertos). Repetition of both parts of the binary structure encourages listeners to hear sonata form as a two-part form, ‖: A : ‖‖ : BA′ : ‖, with A the exposition, B the development, and A′ the recapitulation. Sonata-form movements without repetition, especially when the development section is long, can sometimes be heard as being in three parts: **ABA′**. Often, composers expected listeners to perceive binary and ternary patterns simultaneously and to enjoy the resulting structural ambiguity.

The nineteenth-century theorists who named sonata form and its constituent parts described it with much more specificity and attributed to it more rigidity than it deserves. Such terms as "first theme" and "second theme" (in reference to the first and second melodic areas, respectively) fail to explain the melodic content of many movements in sonata form, a wonderfully flexible framework that allowed eighteenth-century composers practically limitless possibilities for the organization of large-scale movements. Sonata form gave composers significant freedom in the number, character, and location of tunes in the first part of the binary structure and in the way they carried out the modulation from the tonic to the key of the second melodic area. They gave composers even greater freedom—and demanded correspondingly greater creativity and craftsmanship—in the second half of the binary structure, which had to return to the tonic, but left to composers a wide choice in how they achieved that return. Sonata form fascinated composers of the eighteenth and nineteenth centuries. The study of how they met its challenges is a source of endless interest to musicians and music lovers alike.

Ballad opera, Italian opera both comic and serious, oratorio, "ancient" and modern instrumental music: eighteenth-century London served its residents a musical banquet of unprecedented variety and offered unparalleled opportunities for composers and performers, British and foreign. Although it used its enormous wealth to import much of its musical talent, the city also nurtured one of the greatest musical geniuses of the century at a crucial point in his artistic development. Mozart lived in London for more than a year (1764–66) and celebrated his ninth birthday there.

London offered Mozart his first sustained contact with opera seria, a genre that dominated the first half of his career as a composer for the stage. The *musico* Giovanni Manzoli aroused Leopold Mozart's envy because of the high salary he earned at the King's Theatre; but in young Wolfgang he excited a passion for Italian opera. J. C. Bach befriended Mozart, who probably played Bach's Opus 5 sonatas when they were brand new, admiring, as we have admired, the beautifully crafted opening movement of the Sonata in D Major. Around 1771 Mozart transformed this sonata into a concerto (K. 107, No. 1) by adding orchestral ritornellos based on material in the sonata. The arrangement shows him appropriating Bach's mastery of sonata form—a process that probably began already in London. In using the galant style to create music of great elegance, charm, and structural coherence, Bach laid the foundation for Mozart's even greater achievements, which we will examine in Chapters 13 and 14.

FOR FURTHER READING

Brewer, John, *The Pleasures of the Imagination: English Culture in the Eighteenth Century* (New York: Farrar, Straus, Giroux, 1997)

Burden, Michael, "The Lure of Aria, Procession and Spectacle: Opera in Eighteenth-Century London," in *Cambridge History of Eighteenth-Century Music*, ed. Simon P. Keefe (Cambridge: Cambridge University Press, 2009), 385–401

Caplin, William E., *Classical Form: A Theory of Formal Functions for the Instrumental Music of Haydn, Mozart, and Beethoven* (New York: Oxford University Press, 1998)

Heartz, Daniel, "The Beggar's Opera and Opéra-Comique en Vaudevilles," *Early Music* 27 (1999), 42–53, 178–87; reprinted in Daniel Heartz, *From Garrick to Gluck: Essays on Opera in the Age of Enlightenment*, ed. John A. Rice (Hillsdale, NY: Pendragon, 2004)

———, *Music in European Capitals: The Galant Style: 1720–1780* (New York: W. W. Norton, 2003), 883–929

Hepokoski, James, and Warren Darcy, *Elements of Sonata Theory: Norms, Types, and Deformations in the Late-Eighteenth-Century Sonata* (New York: Oxford University Press, 2006)

Inwood, Stephen, *A History of London* (New York: Carrol & Graf, 1998)

Weber, William, "London: A City of Unrivalled Riches," in *The Classical Era: From the 1740s to the End of the 18th Century*, ed. Neal Zaslaw (Englewood Cliffs, NJ: Prentice Hall, 1989), 293–326

Ⓢ **Additional resources available at wwnorton.com/studyspace**

CHAPTER EIGHT

Vienna under Empress Maria Theresa

Built on the site of a Roman outpost guarding the southern bank of the Danube, Vienna occupied a position of strategic importance between the river and the Alps, whose forested foothills (known as the Vienna Woods) descended to within a few miles of the city walls. Although as recently as 1685 these walls had served their original purpose of protecting Vienna from invaders, when a Turkish army unsuccessfully laid siege, by the beginning of our period the walls served mostly to divide it into two parts: the inner city (Vienna proper) and the rapidly growing suburbs. The villages outside the walls coalesced into one metropolitan area that by 1800 dwarfed the inner city in population, but most of the musical activity with which this chapter is concerned took place within the walls.

Vienna became a great capital city by virtue of its being the chief residence of the Habsburg family. The Habsburgs ruled two overlapping domains: the Holy Roman Empire and the monarchy (Fig. 8.1). The empire was a loose confederacy that covered much of northern and central Europe. The emperor was subject to election (by rulers of some of the main principalities within the empire, known as electors); but a centuries-old tradition made it all but inevitable that a member of the Habsburg dynasty would be elected. The monarchy, in contrast,

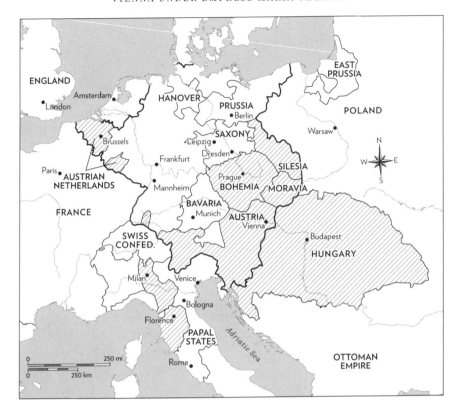

Figure 8.1: *The Habsburg monarchy and the Holy Roman Empire in 1740.* The heavy black line is the border of the empire; cross-hatching marks the territories of the monarchy.

consisted of the provinces and kingdoms the Habsburgs claimed as their family estate, passed from father to oldest son (and, in one special case, from father to daughter). Habsburg emperors earned that prestigious title by being elected the head of the empire, but most of their actual power came from being hereditary rulers of the monarchy.

The monarchy included the cluster of small principalities that made up much of the territory of what is now Austria, the kingdoms of Bohemia and Hungary, parts of Italy, and most of what is now Belgium. Under the Habsburgs, Vienna became the capital of the monarchy, and already by the beginning of the eighteenth century the largest city in the German-speaking part of Europe by far (see Table 1.1). It was also one of Europe's most cosmopolitan cities: the residence of noble families whose mother tongues, reflecting the multinational character of the monarchy, included French, Czech, Hungarian, and Italian, as well as German.

THE COURT THEATER AND THE THEATER AT THE KÄRNTNERTOR

The years around 1715, when so many epochal events happened in France and England (see Chapter 1), constituted less of a turning point in Vienna. Although it too felt the effects of the end of the War of the Spanish Succession, Vienna did not mourn the death of a ruler or celebrate the establishment of a new dynasty. Emperor Charles VI, born in 1685, modeled his cultural policies on those of his rival Louis XIV. As a patron of architecture he dreamed of building a palace outside Vienna that would match Versailles. As a patron of music he supported Johann Joseph Fux and Antonio Caldara, both considerably older than he; Fux was born in 1660, Caldara in 1670 or 1671. They presented operas, in lavish productions celebrating the emperor's name day, in the court theater. Built in 1700, its vast size and rich decoration embodied seventeenth-century values.

For most of the first half of the eighteenth century the massive court theater remained the focus of Vienna's operatic life. But another theater was to enjoy a much longer operatic history. In 1709 Vienna's municipal government built a theater outside the imperial palace, next to the Kärntnertor (one of the city gates). The Kärntnertor Theater operated with the permission and under the supervision of the court; indeed, the court eventually took it over completely. Yet from the beginning it differed from the court theater in being open to a public that paid for admission, and in presenting a wide variety of theatrical entertainments, mostly in German, including improvised comedy. Much later, in the nineteenth century, it became Vienna's principal opera house.

As Wendy Heller explains in *Music in the Baroque*, Emperor Charles's most forward-looking act of operatic patronage was to bring the fashionable young librettist Pietro Metastasio to Vienna as court poet in 1730. Metastasio had come to public notice in the 1720s (see Chapter 4) as some of the most adventurous and talented young composers and singers of the age discovered his beautifully crafted librettos to be perfect vehicles for their music. But he found no such composers in Vienna, dismissing Caldara, who made the first settings of several of his librettos in the early 1730s, as "a worthy master of counterpoint but excessively negligent with respect both to expression and to his attention to the delightful"—a judgment that succinctly places the composer and poet on opposite sides of the learned/ galant divide. The music with which Caldara brought Metastasio's librettos to theatrical life was more in keeping with the old-fashioned court theater in which these operas were performed than with the galant spirit of Metastasio's poetry.

CRISIS, REFORM, AND A NEW COURT THEATER

With the 1730s began a long period of crisis and retreat in the Habsburg monarchy, much of it related to Emperor Charles's having no son, and consequently no obvious heir. His efforts to ensure that on his death the monarchy would pass in its entirety to his daughter Maria Theresa, and that her husband Francis would become emperor, brought the monarchy into war with France and Spain. When Charles died in 1740, Maria Theresa did indeed succeed him as ruler of the monarchy, but by this time it was so weak that its neighbors Prussia and Bavaria were tempted to seize parts of its territory.

Under Maria Theresa's skillful and courageous leadership, the monarchy slowly recuperated. She began a series of reforms with the aim of transforming the monarchy into a modern state capable of competing, economically as well as militarily, with Britain, France, and Prussia. In its foreign relations, the monarchy rejected an old policy of hostility to France, initiating a rapprochement that eventually led to the marriage of Maria Theresa's daughter Marie Antoinette to the French prince who was to become King Louis XVI. Out of crisis, reform, and diplomatic realignment emerged, in the 1750s and 1760s, a monarchy very different from the one Charles VI had ruled, with a more productive economy and a stronger army.

Caldara died in 1736, Fux in 1741; they left the way clear for a transformation of the musical landscape as dramatic as Maria Theresa's political and economic reforms. One crucial part of that transformation could be seen as well as heard. Maria Theresa had the great court theater—closely associated with her father and his musical tastes—demolished. In deference to her husband's French tastes, she had the young French architect Nicolas Jadot turn an indoor tennis court in the imperial palace into a new court theater, much smaller than the old one; it came to be known as the Burgtheater, or Castle Theater. Whereas the old theater had been open just a few nights a year for performances by which the emperor and his courtiers celebrated his name day and other dynastic events, the new court theater, imitating the Kärntnertor Theater, was open to the public on a more or less regular schedule. Whoever could afford the substantial prices for admission could enjoy ballets, operas, plays, and concerts.

The Burgtheater stood next to the old riding school, whose massive corner dwarfed the theater; the contrast between these buildings dramatized the novelty of the architectural tastes of Theresian Vienna (Fig. 8.2). The Burgtheater's relatively small size and simple yet graceful façade signaled that the aesthetic values of the French Regency had finally arrived in Vienna.

The façade shown in Figure 8.2 was actually a false front, behind which was the back of the stage; the audience entered through the other end of the building. The five big windows were mostly for decoration (in the nineteenth century those on the ground floor were removed, revealing the walls behind them); yet they communicated the same passion for light and clarity expressed in the illustration of a sunlit Parisian concert room in Chapter 6. By favoring the galant style in her musical patronage, Maria Theresa established conditions under which her Burgtheater, during the next half-century,

Figure 8.2: *A photograph of the Burgtheater (on the right) in 1885, shortly before its demolition*

witnessed the creation of more vocal and instrumental masterpieces than any other theater in Europe.

MARIA THERESA AS MUSICIAN AND PATRON

Maria Theresa (1717–1780) went through childhood in the 1720s, just as the galant style emerged from Naples. In keeping with Habsburg family tradition, she received solid music training and already at the age of five took part in family theatricals. Her performance in a musical celebration of the emperor's birthday in 1740 caused a member of the audience to write: "In all my life I have experienced nothing more beautiful, touching, or perfect than Her Majesty's performance, whether in regard to singing or acting."

Johann Adolf Hasse, the foremost German proponent of the early galant style (see Chapter 4), spent several months in Vienna in 1734–35. His music spoke more persuasively to the teenage princess than that of Caldara and Fux. He gave her music lessons, and she remembered the experience for the rest of her life. As empress she often invited him to Vienna and commissioned from him many of the operas that celebrated important family events, such as weddings. In 1771 she praised him in words that allude to the shift in musical taste that occurred during her childhood: "He is old and was my music teacher 38 years ago. I have always treasured his compositions above all others. He was the first one who made music more delightful and less heavy."

Maria Theresa gave her children a musical education as rich as her own. For her girls' keyboard instruction she engaged Georg Christoph Wagenseil (1715–1777), whose teaching of composition was discussed briefly in Chapter 2. He dedicated to his royal pupils several sets of divertimentos for keyboard. These are in fact sonatas, but Wagenseil's generic term—which emphasizes the pleasure and entertainment to be derived from his music—projects galant values.

The first movement of Wagenseil's Divertimento Op. 3, No. 2 (published in 1761) begins with music whose delicate, transparent texture, frequent half cadences, triplets and Lombard rhythms, and reliance on IV_4^6 harmony are all galant. So is the **ABB'** melodic shape (Ex. 8.1). Yet the spaciousness of this melody represents a significant novelty. Whereas young composers of the 1720s and 1730s often wrote **ABB'** melodies in three or six measures, Wagenseil slowed down the harmonic rhythm in phrases **B** and **B'** to create a tune that unfolds at a more leisurely pace. Note also the structural ambiguity of this opening—related to the theme's ending on a half cadence—within the sonata-form movement's exposition. The initial melody, in C major, continues to measure 16 and is followed directly by a tune in the dominant, G major. Only when this second melody begins do we realize that the second and third phrases of the opening theme (mm. 5–16) serve a modulatory as well as a melodic function. In other words, the music in measures 5–16 is both the end of the first theme and the bridge.

Marie Antoinette (1755–1793), Maria Theresa's youngest daughter, passed her childhood hearing and playing such music. A portrait made shortly before she left Vienna to marry the crown prince of France in 1770 shows her at the keyboard of what is probably a square piano (a rectangular instrument in which the strings are perpendicular to the keys; Fig. 8.3). Although the music she is playing has not been identified, it could well be by her teacher Wagenseil. As queen of France (wife of King Louis XVI), Marie Antoinette helped shape musical taste in Paris during the 1770s and 1780s (as we will see in Chapter 13), basing her patronage on an aesthetic foundation laid largely by Wagenseil in his teaching and compositions.

It was also with Wagenseil's music that Wolfgang Amadeus Mozart, on his first visit to Vienna in 1762, delighted Maria Theresa and her family. A few months younger than Marie Antoinette, the six-year-old boy was full of excitement and affection. His father Leopold wrote: "Wolferl leapt up into the empress's lap, put his arms around her neck, and kissed her heartily." Sitting down at the keyboard, he asked the emperor: "Is Herr Wagenseil not here? He should come here. He understands."

Example 8.1: *Georg Christoph Wagenseil, Divertimento for Keyboard, Op. 3, No. 2, movement 1, mm. 1–18*

Figure 8.3: *Archduchess Marie Antoinette at the keyboard. Anonymous painting traditionally attributed to Franz Xaver Wagenschön.*

The emperor had Wagenseil take his place by the instrument, and Mozart said to him: "I'm playing a concerto of yours. You must turn the pages for me."

GLUCK AND VIENNESE OPÉRA COMIQUE

The reversal of alliances that brought Marie Antoinette to Paris also made Vienna receptive to artistic products of France, and in particular the musical products of the Regency and the reign of Louis XV. One such product was opéra comique, a genre whose origins coincided almost exactly with the beginning of the Regency, as we saw in Chapter 6. A troupe of French singer-actors resided in Vienna from 1752 to 1764, presenting a mixture of opéras comiques from Paris and new works written for Vienna by a composer who served as the troupe's music director, Christoph Gluck (1714–1787; Fig. 8.4).

Born in a small village near the border of Bohemia and Bavaria, Gluck embodied the cosmopolitanism of eighteenth-century music. He probably benefited from the rich musical education offered by Bohemian schools (to be discussed in Chapter 15). In his twenties, like so many other young, ambitious musicians, he went to Italy. In Milan he quickly broke into the opera business, presenting his *Artaserse* (Artaxerxes) in 1741. By the mid-1740s he had achieved such success in Italy that he was invited to London to compose operas for the King's Theatre. From the early 1750s to the early 1770s he spent most of his time in Vienna, before the last major phase of his career brought him to Paris (see Chapter 13).

Figure 8.4: *Christoph Gluck at the keyboard of what is probably a square piano. Portrait by Duplessis dated 1775.*

In keeping with his single-minded devotion to musical theater, Gluck easily and fully absorbed the galant style and paid correspondingly little attention to the learned style, as George Frideric Handel (in his characteristically fractured English) noted in response to the operas Gluck presented in London: "He knows no more of contrapunto, as mein cook, Waltz." Yet he brought to his theatrical music a distinctive artistic personality. For comedies he wrote music that sparkles with wit and charm; in serious opera he displayed a flair for violence and tragedy and a willingness to depart from convention for dramatic effect. Gluck's work with opéra comique in Vienna involved the composition not only of complete operas but also of arias for existing operas from Paris. One of these new numbers, a song about snuff, may serve as an example of his contribution to the genre.

We briefly encountered *Le diable à quatre* in Chapter 6: an opéra comique adapted by Michael-Jean Sedaine from a ballad opera and first performed in Paris in 1756. Three years later Gluck adapted it for Vienna. To the mixture of vaudevilles, Italian arias, and freshly composed arias in Sedaine's opera, he added new music of his own, including *Je n'aimais pas le tabac beaucoup* (I didn't like tobacco much), a charming song that Haydn was soon to immortalize in his symphony *Le soir* (see Anthology 14; a keyboard-vocal score of Gluck's song accompanies the symphonic movement by Haydn that it inspired).

OPERATIC REFORM AND *ORFEO ED EURIDICE*

During the years between 1750 and 1770 many of the arts were subject to enthusiastic, high-minded, and self-conscious reform, as part of a movement that later came to be called "Classicism" or "Neoclassicism" (not to be confused with the twentieth-century Neoclassicism that Joseph Auner discusses in his volume in this series). French painters, encouraged by theorists to believe that painting should be a school of morals, rejected the perceived frivolities of Watteau (see Fig. 2.2) and his followers, preferring to glorify the great men and noble deeds of Greco-Roman antiquity. The critic Johann Joachim Winckelmann inspired artists to imitate the "noble simplicity" of Greek sculpture and architecture. The actor David Garrick astonished audiences in London with a new style of acting that valued realism and sought, especially by means of gesture, to express emotions as intensely as possible.

Opera and ballet too felt the urge to reform themselves, to become more natural and noble. The critic Francesco Algarotti, in his widely read *Saggio sopra l'opera in musica* (An Essay on the Opera, 1755; for an excerpt, see SR 134; 5/13), proposed a reform of Italian opera that would replace Metastasian drama with a more varied spectacle bringing together Italian arias with the choral music and dance characteristic of French opera. The choreographer Jean-Georges

Noverre, in his *Lettres sur la dance* (Letters on Dance, 1760), argued that steps, leaps, and gestures should not only please the eye; they should express a character's emotions as vividly as they could be expressed in word or song. In what he called *ballet d'action*, audiences admired heroic pantomime ballets in which the dancers acted out a serious drama, instead of the decorative entertainments then prevalent.

The seeds of theatrical innovation fell on fertile ground in Vienna, where in the early 1760s several ambitious and talented artists collaborated in the creation of an opera that marks a turning point in the history of the genre. Gluck, the librettist Ranieri de' Calzabigi, the choreographer Gasparo Angiolini, and the *musico* Gaetano Guadagni all contributed to the conception and the production of *Orfeo ed Euridice* (Orpheus and Eurydice), first performed in the Burgtheater on October 5, 1762.

Calzabigi laid out the drama in three short acts. Based on the Greek myth of Orpheus, it begins with a scene in which Orfeo (portrayed by Guadagni) mourns Euridice, who has recently died. Gluck and his collaborators put together a splendid tableau in which Orfeo's expressions of grief are combined with choral song and instrumentally accompanied dance. In the second act Orfeo, having descended to the underworld in the hope of bringing his wife back from the dead, finds his way blocked by the Furies. Orfeo/Guadagni represented all the beauty and power of Italian operatic singing (including the elaborate improvised ornamentation that every *musico* was expected to bring to his part); the dancers and choristers that Orfeo faced represented the most exciting and dramatic elements of French musical theater (see Anthology 9; Opera Sampler). Orfeo eventually persuades the Furies to yield, and the moment in which music and scenery simultaneously depict his arrival in the Elysian Fields is an unforgettable theatrical stroke.

In Act 3 Orfeo leads Euridice back to the world of the living, loses her again when he turns to look at her, and expresses his grief in the opera's most celebrated aria, *Che farò senza Euridice* (What will I do without Euridice?). In composing this aria, Gluck rejected the traditional da capo form in favor of a more modern rondo, in which a recurring theme alternates with contrasting sections. Our sensibilities and ears might expect, in such a tragic situation, music in the minor mode. But Gluck (like Hasse in *Per questo dolce amplesso*; see Anthology 3), chose the major mode instead, expressing Orfeo's grief with sweetness and lyricism rather than violence and pain. Likewise, eighteenth-century musicians and audiences were reluctant to follow Greek myths to their tragic conclusions; Calzabigi and Gluck, true to their time, invented a way for Orfeo to win Euridice a second time, and the opera ends with a celebration of love's power.

Seven years after the performance of *Orfeo*, Gluck put into printed words, in the dedication of his opera *Alceste* (SR 136; 5/15), a specifically Viennese expression of reformist ideals that had been simmering in several of Europe's theatrical centers during the previous two decades. But he had brought many of those ideals to the stage much earlier, and nowhere more memorably than in the second act of *Orfeo*.

CHURCH MUSIC: VANHAL'S *MISSA PASTORALIS*

The efflorescence of Catholic architecture that produced magnificent churches all over southern Germany and Austria found an artistic counterpart in sacred music. The illustration of the Church of St. Peter and St. Paul at Steinhausen (see Fig. 2.3) suggests that those who designed and decorated such buildings experienced religion as something intensely theatrical and celebratory. This church inspires feelings less of guilt and fear than of exuberance and delight. The music that filled such spaces expressed the same kind of religiosity.

Maria Theresa's Vienna cultivated church music with great energy. Charles Burney discovered in 1772 that "there is scarce a church or convent in Vienna, which has not every morning its *mass in music*: that is, a great portion of the church service of the day, set in parts, and performed with voices, accompanied by at least three or four violins, a tenor [viola] and base [cello or double bass], besides the organ." Services on Sundays and holidays sometimes used larger forces, including oboes, trumpets, and timpani. An article on Viennese music published in 1766 praised the church music of Georg Reutter (1708–1772), the court music director, in terms that convey what Vienna looked for in sacred music: "Who knows better than he how to express—when the music requires it—magnificence, happiness, and rejoicing, without falling into the profane and the theatrical? Who is more pathetic, richer in harmony, when the music calls for sadness, a prayer, pain? The music of his masses always attracts a throng of listeners, and each goes away edified, convinced, and wiser."

Another skillful and prolific composer of church music was the Bohemian Johann Baptist Vanhal (1739–1813). Although born into serfdom, Vanhal benefited from Bohemia's excellent system of musical education. By 1760 he found work as an organist and choir director. His master held the reins of servitude loosely, allowing him to go to Vienna, where he continued his studies, played violin, and composed. With money earned from his music-making he purchased his freedom. Then, believing (in the words of an early biographer) "that in order to perfect himself in his profession he needed to master the Italian language as well as to develop further his aesthetic understanding of the Italian masters," he embarked on a Grand Tour. During visits to Venice, Florence, Rome, and Naples, "he studied composition after the best models."

Vanhal returned to Vienna in 1770 and lived there as a freelance musician for the rest of his life. Burney met him in 1772; he later praised the Bohemian's "spirited, natural, and unaffected symphonies" and quartets and other chamber music for strings that "deserve a place among the first productions, in which unity of melody, pleasing harmony, and a free and manly style are constantly preserved." Vanhal's enormous output included about 50 settings of the Mass. He wrote his *Missa pastoralis* (Pastoral Mass) in G Major no later than 1782, the date of one of the manuscripts in which it is preserved.

This mass is pastoral in making use of musical elements that had been associated since the seventeenth century with shepherds, and hence with the Christmas story (Luke 2:8: "And there were in the same country shepherds abiding in the field, keeping watch over their flock by night"). The marriage of pastoral music and the Christmas liturgy was characteristic of rural Bohemia. In composing the *Missa pastoralis*, Vanhal returned to the countryside of his childhood. Just as Christmas has always involved a mixture of pagan and Christian celebration, so the drones of the shepherds' bagpipes give this music a secular, rustic flavor. Also pastoral are the triadic, repetitive melodic fragments reminiscent of the four-note horn call (scale degree $\hat{1}$, down to $\hat{5}$, up to $\hat{3}$, and back down to $\hat{1}$) that central European cowherds used to summon their animals, which recur in several movements of Vanhal's mass, including the opening Kyrie (Ex. 8.2).

Example 8.2: *Johann Baptist Vanhal,* Missa pastoralis, *Kyrie, mm. 65–68*

The minor mode has a small role in such a festive mass. Vanhal used the key of G minor (the parallel minor) strategically, at the beginning of the last movement, Agnus Dei, to provide a somber moment of introspection and to enhance the effect of G major on its return later in the movement (see Anthology 10). The trumpets and oboes heard frequently earlier in the mass are silent; strings alone accompany the chorus in its tender supplication. Then, like sunshine suddenly filling the church with light and color, the chorus begins the final Allegro moderato with a folk-like melody that shepherds might have sung; indeed, a music historian has called it "a catchy syncopated motif somewhat reminiscent of the American folk song *Shoo fly, don't bother me*."

WOMEN AT THE KEYBOARD

The enthusiasm with which Maria Theresa and her daughters cultivated keyboard music inspired other women in Vienna's upper classes to study the harpsichord and piano with seriousness and success. Most of them kept their musical activities private, playing and composing for the pleasure of family and friends. Their music-making has consequently remained largely unexplored by historians.

Maria Theresia von Paradis (1759–1824) was perhaps the best all-around female musician of Maria Theresa's Vienna. The daughter of an official at court, and named after the empress, she overcame blindness to become a fine singer, pianist, and composer. In the 1780s she toured Europe, performing in London, Hamburg, Berlin, Prague, and Paris, where she appeared at the Concert Spirituel and won praise for "the touch, precision, fluidity, and vividness of her playing." Her compositions, many of which have unfortunately been lost, included operas, cantatas, songs, and concertos.

The sisters Caterina Auenbrugger (1756–1825) and Marianna Auenbrugger (1759–1782) also came to prominence as keyboard players during the 1770s. Their performances impressed Leopold Mozart: "Both of them, and in particular the elder, play extraordinarily well and are thoroughly musical." Marianna's ambitions as a composer led her to study composition with the Viennese court composer Antonio Salieri. When she died, at the age of 23, he published her only piano sonata together with a cantata of his own composition that mourns her death.

Another keyboardist, Josepha Auernhammer (1758–1820), was already an accomplished player when she began studying with Mozart in 1781. In a letter to his father, he told of her ambition to become a professional musician:

> The young lady is a fright, but plays enchantingly. . . . She has told me (as a great secret) of her plan, which is to work hard for two or three years more and then go to Paris and make music her profession. She said: "I am no beauty—*au contraire*, I am ugly. I have no desire to marry some chancery official with an income of three or four hundred Gulden and I have no chance of getting anyone else. So I prefer to remain as I am and to live by my talent." And there she is right.

Auernhammer never realized her dream of settling in Paris, but she did enjoy an active career as a performer in Vienna. During the 1780s she appeared frequently in public and private concerts. From 1793 until 1806 she gave a concert almost every year in the Burgtheater, playing piano concertos by Mozart, Beethoven, and other Viennese composers, and her own variations on popular melodies.

Some of Vienna's female keyboard players wrote music; they also commissioned works and accepted dedications from the city's leading composers. In 1773 Salieri wrote an organ concerto for Paradis and two keyboard concertos, according to an early biography of the composer, "for two ladies" (the Auenbrugger sisters?). Mozart also wrote a concerto (possibly the Concerto in B♭ Major, K. 456) for Paradis, and two (including one of his greatest, the Concerto No. 17 in G Major, K. 453, to be discussed in Chapter 14) for his student Barbara Ployer. For Auernhammer he wrote the Sonata for Two Pianos in D Major, K. 448. Haydn in 1780 dedicated six sonatas to the Auenbrugger sisters. Collaboration between female pianists and male composers produced some of Vienna's finest keyboard music.

VICTOIRE JENAMY AND MOZART'S PIANO CONCERTO IN E♭, K. 271

The recent discovery of another important female pianist active in Vienna during the reign of Maria Theresa—and yet another recipient of a concerto by Mozart—shows how an accomplished female musician, by remaining in the private sphere, could hide her abilities not only from most of her contemporaries but also from historians. But the music Mozart wrote for her testifies to her musical skills.

In January 1777 Mozart finished his celebrated Piano Concerto in E♭ Major, K. 271, which he later referred to has having been written for a woman named Jenomy. In the early twentieth century a Mozart biographer speculated that he had misspelled the name of an otherwise unknown French pianist, Mademoiselle Jeunehomme, and since then the work has been known as the "Jeunehomme" Concerto. It was only in 2003 that a musicologist working in Viennese archives identified Mozart's "Jenomy" as Victoire Jenamy, the daughter of the choreographer Jean Georges Noverre.

If she accompanied her father on his professional travels, Victoire grew up in exceptionally cosmopolitan surroundings, living in Lyon, Paris, London, and Stuttgart, which under Noverre's direction became one of Europe's leading centers of theatrical dance. Noverre moved to Vienna in 1767, and his daughter came too. In 1768 she married Joseph Jenamy, a Viennese merchant, but remained close to her father. After Noverre went to Paris in 1776, she spent part of her time in France. Of Jenamy's musical activities we know almost nothing beyond the fact that during February 1773 she appeared in public in Vienna as a keyboard player. Noverre presented a ballet during a carnival ball, and his daughter also contributed to the program; according to a Viennese newspaper, she "played a concerto on the keyboard with much artistry and facility."

The concerto that Mozart wrote for Jenamy four years later, when he was 21 years old and she was 28, gives us a glimpse of her "artistry and facility" and conveys something of the sophistication and cosmopolitanism of her artistic background. Writing for a musician whose maiden name was synonymous with theatrical novelty and dramatic integrity, Mozart began with a completely original idea: having the soloist share in the presentation of the opening melody, in dialogue with the orchestra (Ex. 8.3). In the slow movement, the language of

Example 8.3: *Wolfgang Amadeus Mozart, Piano Concerto in E♭ K. 271, movement 1, mm. 1–7*

recitative made the soloist into an operatic heroine, whose tragic situation is suggested by the similarity of this music to that of a *scena* (a combination of recitative and aria intended for performance in a concert) that Mozart wrote two years later, *Popoli di Tessaglia* (People of Thessaly, K. 316). The text of that *scena* comes from Gluck's *Alceste*, performed in Vienna in 1768 with choreography by Noverre. The finale of K. 271 is a rondo in which Mozart, in another innovation, delayed the return of the main theme by inserting a complete minuet—perhaps an allusion to the Terpsichorean world from which his soloist had emerged.

Table 1.1 shows that several Protestant cities (such as London and Berlin) grew rapidly in the eighteenth century, while several Catholic cities (Paris, Madrid, Milan, Venice) grew much more slowly or in some cases even shrank. The rising population of predominantly Catholic Vienna ran counter to these trends, and by the end of the eighteenth century it was the fifth-largest city in Europe.

Vienna's vigorous growth was but one of several factors encouraging its musical life to flourish. The multiplicity of languages spoken in the Habsburg monarchy (hence in Vienna) made music attractive to the city's elites as an artistic language understood and appreciated by all. The court and the nobility used French in conversation and correspondence, but it was often music that they talked and wrote about. The fact that the monarchy included Bohemia and parts of Italy, both great exporters of musical talent, meant that Vienna had easy access to many fine musicians. Immigrants and visitors to Vienna included composers, singers, instrumentalists, and instrument builders, who found patronage among the city's growing aristocracy and upper middle class.

Of the musicians mentioned in this chapter, very few were natives of Vienna. They included Italians, although Italians did not predominate as much as they did in London and St. Petersburg. At various times in the eighteenth century Vienna played host to musicians from Spain, France, Ireland, the Netherlands, Germany, and Bohemia, as well as Italy. This exceptional diversity of musical talent, corresponding to the cosmopolitanism of the city's upper classes, helps to explain the extraordinary richness of its musical life. It continued to flourish into the nineteenth century, as we will see in Chapters 14 and 17, providing the conditions under which Mozart, Haydn, and Beethoven thrived.

FOR FURTHER READING

Beales, Derek, *Joseph II: In the Shadow of Maria Theresa, 1741–1780* (Cambridge: Cambridge University Press), 1987

Brown, Bruce Alan, "Maria Theresa's Vienna," in *The Classical Era: From the 1740s to the End of the 18th Century*, ed. Neal Zaslaw (Englewood Cliffs, NJ; Prentice Hall, 1989), 99–125

———, *Gluck and French Theatre in Vienna* (Oxford: Clarendon, 1991)

Heartz, Daniel, *Haydn, Mozart, and the Viennese School, 1740–1780* (New York: W. W. Norton, 1995)

MacIntyre, Bruce C., *The Viennese Concerted Mass of the Early Classic Period* (Ann Arbor, MI: UMI Research Press, 1986)

Rice, John A., *Antonio Salieri and Viennese Opera* (Chicago: University of Chicago Press, 1998), 32–60

Wangermann, Ernst, *The Austrian Achievement, 1700–1800* (London: Thames and Hudson, 1973)

Yonan, Michael, *Empress Maria Theresa and the Politics of Habsburg Imperial Art* (University Park, PA: Penn State Press, 2011)

ⓒ Additional resources available at wwnorton.com/studyspace

CHAPTER NINE

Leipzig and Berlin

Two German cities, both predominantly Protestant and both with great musical achievements in the eighteenth century, offer a study in contrasts. Leipzig, in Saxony, was a small city with a relatively stable population (about 30,000 during most of our period, not big enough to appear in Table 1.1; see Chapter 1) and a long history, going back to the Middle Ages. Berlin, 90 miles to the northeast, was the capital of Prussia. It entered the century with a population of about 55,000 and by 1800 had become a metropolis five times bigger than Leipzig and one of Europe's most dynamic cities. Leipzig was a commercial center, governed by a city council that consisted largely of wealthy merchants; Berlin was a city of royal administration dominated by a court. Leipzig's musical history is inextricably bound up with the lives of two musicians, Johann Sebastian Bach and Johann Adam Hiller; Berlin's is inseparable from the life of a king, Frederick the Great.

LEIPZIG IN 1750

The year 1750 has emerged as a turning point in the history of Western music not only because it divides the century in half, but also because J. S. Bach died in that year. The date has relatively little importance in this book: Bach's death passed unnoticed by most of Europe's musicians, many of whom would have dismissed him as largely irrelevant in a musical culture dominated by the galant style and Italian

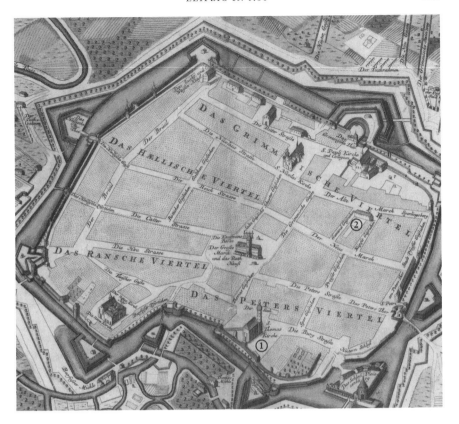

Figure 9.1: *Bird's-eye view of eighteenth-century Leipzig, by Mattäus Seutter, ca. 1730, showing the location of the Thomaskirche, where Johann Sebastian Bach worked (1), and the Gewandhaus, where Johann Adam Hiller organized concerts (2)*

opera. In Leipzig, however, 1750 was indeed a turning point: it separated the age of Bach from that of Hiller.

Leipzig (Fig. 9.1) was a more important city than its small population might suggest. The center of German publishing, the site of trade fairs, and the home of a university, it attracted money and well-educated and ambitious people. Its affluent residents could afford good music and its university students enjoyed making it. Only its operatic efforts sometimes failed; from 1720 until 1764 it had no resident opera company. Probably its population was too small to support it.

Hiller (1728–1804) arrived in Leipzig about a year after Bach's death. Champions respectively of the learned and the galant, Bach and Hiller differed about as much as two composers active in the same city and the same century could have differed. That both of them ended up with the same prestigious title, as cantor of Leipzig's Thomasschule (St. Thomas School), dramatizes the diversity of musical style that our period encompassed.

HILLER AS ORGANIZER OF CONCERTS AND COMPOSER OF SINGSPIELE

In 1751 Hiller enrolled as a law student at the University of Leipzig. He brought musical experience with him from Dresden, one of Germany's leading centers of Italian opera, where he had studied keyboard and where exposure to the operas of Johann Adolf Hasse (see Chapter 4) had made his tastes thoroughly galant. Interest in law soon gave way to love of music, and he participated in Leipzig's concerts as a flutist and singer. With administrative skills that equaled his musical abilities, he reinvigorated Leipzig's concert life after it languished during the Seven Years' War (1756–63). In 1776 he founded a concert organization, the Musikübende Gesellschaft (Music-Making Society). This group found a new home in 1781, when a concert hall was built within the Gewandhaus, the cloth merchants' assembly hall. The Gewandhaus gave a series of concerts on Thursday evenings from October to Easter; it also welcomed visiting musicians, as when Mozart led a concert of his music in 1789.

While Hiller was making Leipzig famous for its concerts, he also helped to shape its operatic life. In 1766 it became home to a theatrical troupe whose repertory included German-language comedies that, imitating opéra comique and ballad opera, combined spoken dialogue with songs. Hiller became the troupe's music director, composing music for a German version of *Le diable à quatre* that Michel-Jean Sedaine had adapted ten years earlier from *The Devil to Pay* (see Chapter 6). Its success led him to write several more operas during the following decade, mostly on German translations of opéra comique librettos. Although Germans used the word *Singspiel* (literally, "song play") to mean any kind of opera, in any language, historians find it a convenient term for the kind of German-language opera with spoken dialogue that Hiller championed in Leipzig and that soon became popular throughout the German-speaking part of Europe.

The actors with whom Hiller worked had only modest ability as singers, and this limited the length, the number, and the complexity of musical pieces in his operas. He thrived under these limitations, composing short, charming, and memorable songs and ensembles. The composer Johann Friedrich Reichardt summed up Hiller's achievement in 1774: "He knew French and Italian comic operas; he took from them what pleased him, rejected what he found unfit, and created a form closer to Nature and to our language, but more especially one that was necessary owing to our miserable singers. He discarded long-winded arias because he knew they were not suited to comedy."

HILLER'S *DIE JAGD*

Hiller's *Die Jagd* (The Hunt, 1770), though first performed in Weimar, reflects the operatic aesthetic that Hiller inculcated in Leipzig in the second half of the 1760s. It takes place in the country, presenting an idealized picture of the simple plea-sures of rustic life and the virtues of country people; in this it resembled many opéras comiques and such English operas as *Love in a Village* (see Chapter 7). The action revolves around the family of Michel, a village judge. His son Christel is engaged to Hannchen, daughter of a farmer. Count Schmetterling (Butterfly), a wicked nobleman, abducts Hannchen, but Christel believes that she went will-ingly and is about to break off their engagement. She escapes Schmetterling and returns to the village; with difficulty she persuades Christel that she has been faithful to him. Their reconciliation is interrupted by a storm, during which Mi-chel rescues a man who has been separated from his hunting party and is lost in the woods. Unaware that the man is his king, Michel offers him shelter in his simple home, where Hannchen accuses Schmetterling of having imprisoned her. The king, moved by the virtue of Michel and his family, reveals his identity, banishes Schmetterling, and blesses the wedding of Hannchen and Christel.

Hiller's score contains two different two kinds of solo numbers. Lieder—songs, often strophic in form, with folk-like melodies and light accompani-ments—alternate with arias in the Italian style to which he became accustomed in his early years in Dresden.

In the opera's most famous number, *Als ich auf meiner Bleiche* (As I was at my washing), Hannchen narrates her abduction and imprisonment (Ex. 9.1).

Example 9.1: *Johann Adam Hiller,* Die Jagd, *Lied:* Als ich auf meiner Bleiche, *mm. 3–14*

As I was at my washing, moistening a piece of wool, out of the woods came a breathless maiden. She said: Ah, have pity, come help my father. An accident has broken his leg in two.

With the simplest possible means Hiller produced what soon became a kind of German national folk song. Four years after the premiere of *Die Jagd*, Reichardt marveled at the popularity of this Lied: "Every person from the highest to the lowest sings it, plays it, and whistles it, and I should almost say drums it, so much is it used, in every conceivable way, all over Germany." For Hannchen, Hiller also wrote some fine Italianate music, including the aria that she sings in Act 1, just after she flees from Schmetterling, expressing joy at being back home. *Du süsser Wohnplatz* (Home, sweet home), unlike the narrative Lied she sings later, begins with a long orchestral introduction (strings, horns, and flutes) that uses the galant style to depict her sweetness and sincerity (Ex. 9.2).

Example 9.2: *Johann Adam Hiller*, Die Jagd, *aria:* Du süsser Wohnplatz, *mm. 1–12*

A MUSICIAN-KING'S VIOLENT COMING OF AGE

Historians who like to explore the psychology of celebrated figures of the past may find no more fascinating subject than Frederick the Great (1712–1786), who embodied many of the contradictions of his age. He subscribed to the Enlightenment's ideals, but ruled with an iron fist and used his army as his principal tool of foreign relations. He loved French literature and Italian opera, but never traveled to France or Italy. He disliked to speak or write in German, but worked throughout his reign to increase the strength and size of his German-speaking kingdom. He was a fine musician, yet with few exceptions he played only music by his teacher, the flutist Johann Joachim Quantz, and himself.

We saw Frederick's father in the double portrait reproduced as Figure 2.1. Obsessed with military affairs, King Frederick William spent his leisure in hunting and carousing at his "Tobacco College," a kind of club where he and his military officers drank and smoked. He had little interest in art or music, but hypocritically professed a pious brand of Protestantism. Uncouth, cruel, and unable to control his anger, he was hated and feared by his wife, who thought herself cheated of the luxuries and pleasures to which she felt entitled as queen.

Between King Frederick William and Queen Sophie Dorothea were their children, whose psychological development was at the mercy of the toxic parental struggle into which they were born. The two oldest, Wilhelmina and Frederick, found solace in music. She played the lute, calling it her "Principe" (Prince); he played the flute, calling it his "Principessa" (Princess). The pet names suggest the depth of the emotional needs that music satisfied in them. Frederick studied keyboard from the age of seven. He also found emotional sustenance in passionate friendships with other boys.

Frederick's same-sex friendships, love of music and the other arts, passion for fine clothes and other luxuries, and lack of interest in religion enraged Frederick William, who reprimanded him for "unmanly, lascivious, female occupations, highly unsuited to a man," and hoped that a stint in the army would cure him. The king's brutality, which included beatings, reached a point where, in 1730, at the age of 18, Frederick decided to flee with two army friends, one of whom, Lieutenant Katte, was probably his lover. Frederick and Katte were arrested for desertion; the king sentenced Frederick to imprisonment and Katte to death. He forced Frederick to watch his friend's beheading.

After about a year in prison and house arrest, Frederick reentered the army, agreed to marry, and learned to use discretion to stay out of trouble. On his father's death in 1740 he became king. He ruled for 46 years, but never forgot the traumatic events of 1730. In his emotional life, as in his musical taste, he did not progress much beyond them. Those events probably helped to make him the strange, contradictory person he was.

FREDERICK'S MUSICAL FAMILY

With his marriage, Frederick set up his own household. Avoiding the normal marital business of starting a biological family, he fathered a musical family instead: a group of musicians who adapted their style of composition and performance to his tastes and stood constantly ready to accompany his performances of flute sonatas and concertos.

When he came to the throne he divided his musical family into two separate establishments. He founded an Italian opera company and placed it under the direction of Carl Heinrich Graun (1704–1759). The royal chamber group assembled daily whenever he was present, whether at one of his palaces in Berlin or nearby Potsdam, where he lived most of the time. Frederick engaged Quantz as director of the chamber ensemble at a princely salary, with extra fees to be paid for new compositions. The terms of his employment, Quantz wrote proudly in his memoirs, included "the privilege of not having to play in the [opera] orchestra, but only in the royal chamber music, and not having to take orders from anyone but the king." His role as chamber musician and composer, producing vast amounts of music that was to remain in manuscript as the exclusive property of the sovereign, closely resembled the role that Domenico Scarlatti played, at more or less the same time, as Queen Maria Barbara's personal musician at the Spanish court (see Chapter 5).

One of Frederick's generals wrote of the chamber concerts in Potsdam that the ensemble "consisted of a first and one second violin (rarely doubled), a viola, a cello, and as keyboard a fortepiano by Silbermann, one flute, or two flutes when the king played trio sonatas with Quantz. One or two castratos and occasionally one of the best female singers of the opera received orders and a royal coach for their journey to Potsdam. Only voices or flutes were heard in these concerts; the other instruments were there only for the accompaniment." This description corresponds quite closely to a visual representation of one of Frederick's concerts (Fig. 9.2), which shows an orchestra of ten, in addition to Frederick himself: six violins and violas (four violins, two violas?), one flute (Quantz?), one cello, one double bass, and a grand piano or harpsichord.

Figure 9.2: *Frederick the Great playing the flute at a private concert*

By limiting the participation of singers in his concerts to altos and sopranos, both male and female, Frederick revealed a fondness for the treble register that he also showed in choosing singers for his opera troupe, which consisted almost entirely of sopranos and altos, including several *musici*. Here again we may be able to perceive the effects of Frederick's tumultuous youth and its tragic climax. The flute gave him a soprano voice, even as an adult. When he compared the voice of his prima donna Giovanna Astrua to the sound of a flute, he not only revealed his love of vocal coloratura but alluded to what he valued in his own instrument: "This singer is really amazing: she produces arpeggios like the violin, she sings everything the flute can play, with infinite facility and quickness. Of all the voices ever created by nature, none like this one has ever before existed." But Frederick's flute brought him even closer to a *musico*, whose voice was the product of a childhood operation analogous to the psychological trauma that Frederick had endured. In the king's devotion to the treble voice—instrumental as well as vocal, male as well as female—and in his allegiance to the musical style of his youth, we may be tempted to see a man whose violent and painful upbringing kept him from progressing in a normal, healthy way into adulthood.

The music that gave young Prince Frederick pleasure and comfort during his emotionally bruising teenage years was the galant music of the 1720s and 1730s; he remained loyal to that style throughout his life. It predominates in the music he played, whether of his own composition or by Quantz. Frederick's Sonata in A Major, No. 117, for flute and basso continuo illustrates his skills as a composer. Like many of his sonatas, it has the modern three-movement format; but by beginning with a slow movement it acknowledges the older tradition of the sonata da chiesa (church sonata). In the opening Grave ed affettuoso, Frederick used repeated sixteenth and thirty-second notes to practice and display his tonguing. The second movement, Allegro ma non molto (Ex. 9.3), shows Frederick as impeccably galant. In the opening **ABB′** melody, the first two phrases together elaborate a melodic framework to which galant composers had frequent recourse: a phrase ending on

Example 9.3: *Frederick the Great, Sonata No. 117 in A Major, movement 2, mm. 1–5*

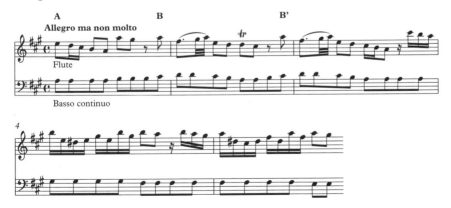

the scale degrees $\hat{1}$–$\hat{7}$ is answered by a phrase ending $\hat{4}$–$\hat{3}$. Because the phrase ending $\hat{4}$–$\hat{3}$ is a Prinner, we have here a case of one galant schema embedded within another. After two movements in duple meter, the triple meter and moderate tempo of the third, Tempo giusto, help us to hear it as an elegant minuet.

Neither Frederick nor his teacher rejected the learned style completely. Quantz had solid training in counterpoint. The flutist and historian Mary Oleskiewicz finds in Frederick's collection of music by Quantz "a wide range of textures, tonalities, and harmonic procedures," including "canon and fugue, as well as double fugue, in all of which the bass usually participates as an equal partner." Frederick's experience with the learned style helps to explain his excitement when he heard that J. S. Bach was in Potsdam in 1747. "Gentlemen," he exclaimed to his musicians, "old Bach has come!" He canceled his concert for that evening, ordered that Bach be summoned, showed him his pianos, and invited him to improvise on them. Bach, using a theme that Frederick gave him, improvised the fugue that he later developed into *Musikalisches Opfer* (Musical Offering).

Frederick's playing impressed Charles Burney, who visited Potsdam in 1772 and heard him perform three difficult concertos in succession, "all with equal perfection." But Burney found Frederick's repertory decidedly odd. It consisted only of concertos by Quantz and of sonatas by Quantz and by the king himself. Frederick went through manuscript collections of these works—roughly 300 concertos and 200 sonatas by Quantz, and 120 sonatas by the king—from beginning to end, over and over. Burney's report has unfairly shaped perceptions of Frederick as a musician and patron. We need to keep in mind that he was 60 years old when Burney heard him play. The comfortable routine into which he had settled did not necessarily characterize his earlier music-making.

FREDERICK'S OPERA COMPANY AND GRAUN'S *MONTEZUMA*

Among Frederick's first actions as king was to commission his architect Georg von Knobelsdorf to build a theater and to send Graun to Italy to engage singers for a new opera troupe. During the first 15 years of his reign he gave opera the same intense attention that he gave to playing the flute, building up his army, and leading it in the field. He supervised the engagement of singers and the preparation of librettos (in several cases preparing a draft of the libretto himself), rehearsals, scenery, and costumes.

The Royal Theater opened in Berlin in December 1742. (Twice destroyed, once by fire and once by wartime bombing, it survives today as a modern replica.) Unlike most earlier opera houses, which formed parts of larger buildings, this magnificent edifice stood alone (Fig. 9.3). With the inscription on the façade, Frederick took full credit for the building: FRIDERICUS REX APOLLINI ET MUSIS ([dedicated by] King Frederick to Apollo and the Muses). The opera

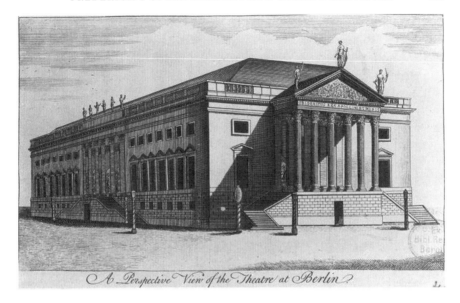

A Perspective View of the Theatre at Berlin

Figure 9.3: *The Royal Theater in Berlin. Anonymous eighteenth-century print.*

season generally ran from late November to late March, with two performances a week. The repertory consisted entirely of opera seria. Each year the troupe typically presented two new operas and one revival.

Graun composed almost all of the new operas. Frederick depended so completely on him because he gave the king what he wanted: dramatic music in the style he had absorbed in his youth. Graun, moreover, was willing to work with Frederick, to incorporate his musical suggestions, to rewrite or replace arias, even to replace his own arias with those written by the king. Many of Graun's operas are settings of librettos closely based on French plays and librettos, reflecting Frederick's interest in and knowledge of French literature. The king fought against his contemporaries' love of happy endings; several of Graun's operas end tragically.

Montezuma, first performed in the Royal Theater in January 1755, is neither the first nor the last opera to depict Hernán Cortés's conquest of Mexico in 1520. But it presents a particularly striking interpretation of the events. The librettist Giampietro Tagliazucchi based the book on a sketch by Frederick himself. The king used the account of the conquest by the seventeenth-century historian Antonio de Solís and Voltaire's play *Alzire* as sources for a largely fictional plot, onto which he projected his own ideas—especially about religion—and his own family history.

One current of Enlightenment thought to which Frederick was particularly susceptible was hostility to the more dogmatic and intolerant aspects of Christianity. He saw the story of Cortés and Montezuma, ruler of the Aztecs, as an opportunity to depict Christianity as a system of belief used only to steal and to enslave. More than a year before *Montezuma* reached the stage he wrote to a friend in Italy: "I chose this subject and I am working on it at the present moment. As you can well imagine, I take the part of Montezuma. Cortés will be the tyrant, and consequently [the opera] will likely discharge, in the music as well, some good jibes against the barbarity of the Ch[ristian] r[eligion]."

Frederick did not call attention to another aspect of the opera: the similarity of its central dramatic conflict to the terrible conflict of his own youth. Using violence, trickery, and Christian cant, the tyrant Cortés imposes his will on the peace-loving and virtuous Montezuma (Fig. 9.4a), who is led off in chains to be executed, and his bride Eupaforice (Fig. 9.4b), having set fire to the city, stabs herself to death. Likewise Frederick's father had tried to impose Calvinism on his son, imprisoned him, and ordered the execution of his closest friend. In the opera's tragic ending the king could relive the terrible events of 1730.

Montezuma also reflects Frederick's musical tastes. Although five of its seven characters are male, Frederick's love of the treble register resulted in a cast that includes not a single bass or tenor. He directed Graun to make most of the arias much shorter than normal da capo arias. Graun responded with arias in binary form, equivalent in length and structure to a da capo aria's **A** section. Arias of this kind, known as cavatinas, were not new, but an opera consisting mostly of cavatinas did constitute a novelty.

Eupaforice's aria *Barbaro che mi sei* (Barbarian, cruel object of horror), in which she berates Cortés in response to his proposal of marriage, exemplifies the mixture of innovation and tradition that characterizes *Montezuma*. It begins with an

Figure 9.4: *Costume design, possibly for Carl Heinrich Graun's* Montezuma: *Montezuma (left) and Eupaforice (right)*

Example 9.4: *Carl Heinrich Graun,* Montezuma, *aria:* Barbaro che mi sei, *mm. 1–12*

Barbarian! Cruel object of horror for me, you want to speak of love?

idea shamelessly lifted from Hasse's celebrated aria *Pallido il sole* (1730; see Fig. 4.2): a melodic line that rises against a chromatic descent in the bass, reaching a climax by way of an augmented-sixth chord (Ex. 9.4). Yet the aria as a whole differs greatly from *Pallido il sole*. With hardly any repetition of text, it depicts Eupaforice's rapidly changing emotions (rage against Cortés, tenderness for Montezuma) with an alternation of fast music in duple meter and slow music in triple.

The final act offers several examples of Graun's inventive responses to Frederick's darkly tragic vision. The composer wove recitative, aria, and duet into a musical fabric that carries the action inexorably forward. The act begins with a prison scene. Montezuma, alone, expresses despair and resignation in an orchestrally accompanied recitative and an aria. The aria ends on (or is interrupted by) a half cadence, as Montezuma hears the sound of the prison gate opening. It is Eupaforice, and the lovers sing a duet. Just before being taken away to be killed, the king tells Cortés, in the aria *Sì, corona i tuoi trofei* (Yes, crown your triumph), that he will face death without fear. An Allegro that begins in F minor and modulates to A♭ major sets up expectations of a conventional movement in binary form. But Graun withheld the return of the tonic until after an unexpected and dramatic change of tempo. In the aria's concluding Adagio, Montezuma bids farewell to Eupaforice. Seeing him being led to his death, she expresses her anguish in a long, tumultuous monologue that ends with her suicide.

Only in the opera's final number did Graun lose his nerve, setting the tragic chorus of Aztecs ("Oh heaven! Alas, what a horrible day of damnable crimes") to music that is conspicuously bright and cheerful. Graun, in writing this music, and Frederick, in allowing it to stand, gave in to their century's strong preference for happy endings.

More than a month before the first performance of *Montezuma*, Frederick boasted to his sister Wilhelmina: "I have heard the rehearsal of *Montezuma*, at which I directed the actors as to the sense of the drama. I believe this opera would give you pleasure. Graun has created a masterpiece." In *Montezuma* Graun, Tagliazucchi, and Frederick produced a musical drama quite unlike those performed in the other cities that cultivated opera seria. It vividly reflects Frederick's enigmatic personality and the musical culture he created in Berlin.

CARL PHILIPP EMANUEL BACH

When Frederick became king, he made Carl Philipp Emanuel Bach, who had played chamber music with him since 1738, a permanent member of the chamber ensemble. But the conditions under which he engaged Bach show how much less he valued him than Quantz. Instead of the flutist's yearly salary of 2,000 thalers, Bach made only 300. He must have felt the prestige of being in royal service compensated at least in part for the low salary. "It was my honor at Charlottenburg [Frederick's palace on the outskirts of Berlin] to accompany, quite alone at the *Flügel* [harpsichord or grand piano], the first flute solo that His Majesty played as king," wrote Bach in a short autobiography. "From this time onwards until November 1767 I was continuously in the service of the king of Prussia." For 27 years Bach played the keyboard in Frederick's chamber music sessions, accompanying the king as he worked his way through the royal repertory of flute music.

The work—and the relatively small reward he received for it—might have killed Bach's love of music; instead it encouraged him to find other outlets for his creativity. Frederick, normally dictatorial when it came to artists in his employ, allowed Bach to spend his free time as he wished. He earned extra money by teaching and directed whatever energy he had left to composition and to writing what turned out to be the century's most important book on performance at the keyboard, *Versuch über die wahre Art das Clavier zu spielen* (Essay on the True Way of Playing the Keyboard), published in two parts in 1753 and 1762.

By 1745 Bach had written more than 20 keyboard sonatas and 10 keyboard concertos. He had published two sets of keyboard sonatas, both under the title *Sei sonate per cembalo*: one in 1742 (the Prussian Sonatas, dedicated to Frederick), the other in 1744 (the Württemberg Sonatas, dedicated to Count Carl Eugen of Württemberg, who studied with Bach between 1742 and 1744). Together these 12 sonatas constitute an important monument in the early history of the genre.

The sonatas explore a wide range of styles and keyboard techniques. Bach occasionally displayed his father's learned style: for example, the three-part counterpoint in the slow movement of the Sonata in E Major, the third Prussian Sonata. More often he adopted a galant idiom, as in the first movement of the first Württemberg Sonata, in A minor, which begins with a three-measure **ABB′** melody punctuated with a three-note slide. In the first Prussian Sonata, the slow movement's galant gestures—a drum bass and a iv$^6_4$ harmony resolving to i in measure 1—lead to an instrumental recitative (Ex. 9. 5). Bach, to give the player the feeling of actually accompanying a recitative, supplied the bass line with figures (which have been supplemented with chords in the example).

This recitative is one of many instances in which Bach—who composed no operas—used the keyboard to evoke the singing voice and, through it, to excite emotions in his audience. In his autobiography he wrote:

Example 9.5: *Carl Philipp Emanuel Bach, Prussian Sonatas, No. 1, movement 2, mm. 1–10*

My chief effort, especially in recent years, has been directed towards playing and composing as songfully as possible for the Clavier, notwithstanding its lack of sustaining power. This is not at all easy if the ear is not to be left too empty and the noble simplicity of the melody is not to be disturbed by too much bustle. It seems to me that music must primarily touch the heart, and the clavierist never can accomplish that through mere bluster, drumming, and arpeggiating, at least not in my opinion.

THE *EMPFINDSAMER STIL*

All three of the keyboard passages cited above are in the minor mode, which Bach probably used more than most of his contemporaries; it contributes to the melancholy, introspective quality of much of his music. Bach often combined the minor mode with various gestures—appoggiaturas that evoke sighs, moments of silence, dissonant melodic leaps, sudden changes of dynamics—to create a musical language that musicians have called the *empfindsamer Stil* (the sensitive style).

Music in the *empfindsamer Stil* sounds especially good on the clavichord, Bach's favorite instrument. The clavichord (Fig. 9.5) has a very simple action, involving a single moving part for the production of each pitch: the key. This long, thin piece of wood is attached to the instrument by a pivot. By depressing one end of the key, the player causes a tangent (a thin metal tongue) attached to the other end to rise and strike a string, making it vibrate. Dynamic gradations depend on the force with which the tangent hits the string: the player produces a

Figure 9.5: *A clavichord built in Germany in 1763. Faintly visible, at the far end of the keys (under the strings), are the tangents that, when the player depresses the front of the keys, rise and cause the strings to vibrate.*

kind of vibrato by holding the key down and varying the pressure of the tangent against the string. Bach accompanied Frederick on the piano and harpsichord to make a living; he played the quieter, subtler clavichord at home to make music by himself and to communicate with attentive listeners in an otherwise silent room.

One particularly attentive and appreciative listener was Burney, who visited Bach in Hamburg several years after he left Berlin. His description of Bach at the clavichord conveys something of the values embodied in the keyboard music:

> He played three or four of his choicest and most difficult compositions, with the delicacy, precision, and spirit, for which he is so justly celebrated among his countrymen. In the pathetic [emotional] and slow movements, whenever he had a long note to express, he absolutely contrived to produce, from his instrument, a cry of sorrow and complaint, such as can only be effected upon the clavichord, and perhaps [only] by himself.
>
> After dinner . . . I prevailed upon him to sit down again to a clavichord, and he played, with little intermission, till near eleven o'clock at night. During this time, he grew so animated and *possessed*, that he not only played, but looked like one inspired. His eyes were fixed, his under lip fell, and drops of effervescence distilled from his countenance.

Bach took the *empfindsamer Stil* to its extreme in several fantasies that evoke many different emotional states by means of extraordinary flights of musical imagination. The Fantasia in C Minor (see Anthology 11) consists of two tonally unstable improvisatory passages, notated without barlines, that serve as a frame for a Largo in E♭ major and triple meter—a tender minuet unfolding in parallel thirds in the right hand, triple meter, and four-measure phrases. After the minuet reaches a cadence in E♭, its triple meter continues in a beautifully crafted transition leading back to the unmeasured musings with which the fantasy ends. The interaction of unmeasured and measured music, of declamatory and lyrical, calls to mind the operatic interaction of recitative and aria. Here again, as in the slow movement of the Prussian Sonata No. 1, we sense Bach's desire to evoke on the keyboard the passionate emotions of tragic heroes and heroines.

Some of Bach's contemporaries felt the theatrical ambitions of such music. The Fantasy in C Minor caused the poet Heinrich von Gerstenberg to think of men on the brink of death, expressing their feelings as if on an operatic stage. He published an arrangement of Bach's fantasy with two added texts: Hamlet's soliloquy ("To be or not to be") and a meditation on death by the Greek philosopher Socrates in the moments before he took his own life. Picking out the melodic fragments from Bach's fantasy that correspond most closely in style to the vocal line in an orchestrally accompanied recitative, Gerstenberg transformed these melodic fragments into recitative by applying words to them.

Johann Adam Hiller and Frederick the Great both played the flute and promoted the galant style, but beyond that their tastes and interests differed. To the largely middle-class audiences of Leipzig, Hiller brought a new operatic genre, Singspiel, while establishing a strong tradition of public concerts. Frederick made Berlin a center of Italian opera. His interest in instrumental music was limited mostly to private concerts in which he played the flute, and he did not fully appreciate the greatest composer in his employ, C. P. E. Bach, who wrote much of his best music in Berlin but eventually left the city.

Bach's Fantasia in C Minor gives us a glimpse of a musical personality quite different from the one that he displayed during his day job, accompanying the king. Yet both Bach the impassioned, introspective improviser and Bach the polished courtier were products of the musical culture that Frederick fostered in Berlin. Frederick's promotion of galant music was partly a reaction to the tyranny and cruelty of his father; Bach, in embracing the galant style, distanced himself just as firmly from the intensely learned musical culture that his father had so brilliantly promoted in Leipzig.

FOR FURTHER READING

Bauman, Thomas, "Courts and Municipalities in North Germany," in *The Classical Era: From the 1740s to the End of the 18th Century,* ed. Neal Zaslaw (Englewood Cliffs, NJ: Prentice Hall, 1989), 240–67

Heartz, Daniel, *Music in European Capitals: The Galant Style, 1720–1780* (New York: W. W. Norton, 2003), 354–439

Helm, Eugene, *Music at the Court of Frederick the Great* (Norman: University of Oklahoma Press, 1960)

MacDonogh, Giles, *Frederick the Great* (London: Weidenfeld & Nicolson, 2001)

Oleskiewicz, Mary. "The Trio in Bach's Musical Offering: A Salute to Frederick's Tastes and Quantz's Flutes?" in *The Music of J. S. Bach: Analysis and Interpretation,* ed. David Schulenberg (Lincoln: University of Nebraska Press, 1999), 79–110

———, "The Court of Brandenburg-Prussia," in *Music at German Courts, 1715–1760: Changing Artistic Priorities,* ed. Samantha Owens et al. (Woodbridge: Boydell, 2011), 79–130

Ottenberg, Hans-Günter, *Carl Philipp Emanuel Bach* (Oxford: Oxford University Press, 1987)

Ⓢ Additional resources available at wwnorton.com/studyspace

CHAPTER TEN

Courts of Central Europe

Mannheim, Bayreuth, and Eisenstadt/Eszterháza

The German-speaking part of Europe consisted in the eighteenth century of hundreds of political units of various sizes, ranging from a kingdom (Prussia) to archbishoprics (small principalities, such as Salzburg and Cologne, ruled by archbishops) to independent cities such as Hamburg and Nuremberg. According to traditions going back to the Middle Ages, the rulers of some of these territories were known as electors, because they were responsible for electing the leader of the Holy Roman Empire. But since the sixteenth century that election had been no more than a formality, the title of emperor being the exclusive possession (as we noted in Chapter 8) of the Habsburg dynasty.

Regardless of the size of their domains, central European rulers tended to look to France for examples of how to project their wealth and power. Inspired by the massive construction projects of Louis XIV, they built great palaces. And inspired by the splendid musical festivities with which the Sun King celebrated the important events of his reign, they vied with one another to build the grandest theaters and to assemble the finest orchestras and opera troupes.

CARL THEODOR AND STAMITZ AT MANNHEIM

In 1742 Carl Theodor became ruler of the Electoral Palatinate, a tiny state with bits of territory scattered over what is now western Germany. Carl Theodor was a man of the Enlightenment: an admirer of Voltaire and a founder of learned academies devoted to fine arts, sciences, economics, and German literature. In his musical patronage he fostered the galant style in Italian opera and in instrumental music, in which he had a special interest. He engaged several Bohemian musicians who specialized in the composition and performance of instrumental music and who developed at Mannheim, the capital of Carl Theodor's little principality, one of the best orchestras in Europe.

The most important of Carl Theodor's Bohemian musicians was Johann Stamitz (1717–1757). Like so many of his countrymen, Stamitz received musical training at school, as part of his basic education. After university studies in Prague, he decided to devote himself to music. He went to Germany, where at the age of 25 he was already able to call himself, in announcing a concert, "the famous virtuoso Stamitz." He promised that the concert would include "a concerto with two orchestras newly composed by him" and that he would play solos on violin, viola d'amore (a viol-like instrument with extra strings that vibrated sympathetically—that is, in response to the vibrations caused by the bowing of the regular strings), cello, and double bass. By the following year, 1743, he had entered Carl Theodor's service. While the Italian Carlo Grua supervised church music and opera, Stamitz took over the production of concerts, which under his direction became an increasingly important part of musical life at Mannheim.

Coordinating his activities as composer and conductor, Stamitz simultaneously provided his orchestra with a new and challenging concert repertory and developed its ability to play it with absolute mastery. As a composer of instrumental music, wrote Charles Burney, Stamitz "pushed art further than any one had done before him; his genius was truly original, bold, and nervous; invention, fire, and contrast, in the quick movements; a tender, graceful, and insinuating melody, in the slow; together with the ingenuity and richness of the accompaniments, characterize his productions; all replete with great effects, produced by an enthusiasm of genius, refined, but not repressed by cultivation."

Writing in 1772, Burney suggested that "the present style of *Sinfonies*, so full of great effects, of light and shade," was largely derived from Stamitz's "fire and genius." But Burney, like several historians since then, attributed more historical importance to Stamitz than he deserved. Some of the most typical aspects of his symphonic style, including his frequent and celebrated use of the crescendo, have been traced to Italian opera of the 1730s and 1740s, of the kind that Stamitz probably heard in Mannheim's court theater. Burney himself acknowledged the influence on Stamitz of Italian opera, citing the music of the brilliant composer Niccolò Jommelli as a particularly important model.

One innovation for which Stamitz has justifiably received credit is the four-movement symphony. But the claim sometimes made that he added a minuet and trio to the original three-movement, fast-slow-fast plan (see Chapter 5) is still subject to debate. Composers of three-movement symphonies faced a choice as to the tempo and character of the finale. They could write a minuet, or a minuet-like movement, often labeled "Tempo di minuetto," or a faster movement in duple or triple meter. Stamitz simply avoided this choice by writing a minuet *and* a fast movement. (That eighteenth-century composers of four-movement symphonies, even long after Stamitz, almost always wrote the minuet in the same key as the first movement, while they usually wrote the slow movement in a foreign key, is a relic of the minuet's original role as a closing movement.)

STAMITZ'S ORCHESTRA AND THE MANNHEIM CRESCENDO

Although we do not know the exact size and composition of the orchestra that Stamitz assembled for any particular concert, lists of instrumentalists employed by Carl Theodor suggest that on some occasions the orchestra had more than 40 players—slightly larger than the 32-piece opera orchestra shown in Figure 4.1. In 1756, for example, Stamitz could draw on a staff of 20 violinists, four violists, four cellists, two double bass players, pairs of oboists, flutists, and bassoonists, four horn players, and two keyboard players, together with trumpeters and drummers from the elector's trumpet corps. From 1758, a year after Stamitz's death, two clarinetists were available as well.

Several eighteenth-century writers attested to the outstanding quality of the concert orchestra that Stamitz carved from this larger group of players, and that after his death maintained the tradition of excellence that he instilled. One listener recalled vividly his experience at a concert in Mannheim: "No orchestra in the world ever surpassed that of Mannheim in performance. Its *forte* is like thunder, its *crescendo* a cataract, its *diminuendo* a crystal stream burbling into the distance, its *piano* a breath of spring. The winds are all used just as they should be; they lift and support, or fill out and animate, the storm of the strings." Burney admired the talent of individual players and the discipline with which they were welded into a single whole: "I found [the orchestra] to be indeed all that its fame had made me expect: power will naturally arise from a great number of hands; but the judicious use of this power, on all occasions, must be the consequence of good discipline; indeed there are more solo players, and good composers in this, than perhaps in any other orchestra in Europe; it is an army of generals, equally fit to plan a battle, as to fight it." In the many exposed parts for winds and brass in Stamitz's symphonies, the commander-in-chief gave his generals ample opportunity to display their skills.

Figure 10.1: *The Rittersaal in the electoral palace at Mannheim*

This, then, was the orchestra that assembled, usually twice a week at six o'clock in the evening, for the academy (as concerts were often called in our period) that under Stamitz's direction became one of Mannheim's most celebrated musical institutions. Typically consisting of vocal pieces (operatic arias, for example) and concertos as well as symphonies, the academy took place in the Rittersaal, a large, beautifully decorated hall in the electoral palace (Fig. 10.1). Carl Theodor used the occasion to entertain distinguished guests not only with music but with card playing, conversation, and refreshments. The "art-religion" of the nineteenth century (discussed by Walter Frisch in Chapter 2 of the next volume in this series) had not yet transformed the concert into the solemn spectacle that we recognize still today, silently heard and respectfully applauded.

Stamitz's Symphony in D Major, Op. 3, No. 2, may serve to illustrate the skill, compositional as well as directorial, that he displayed on such occasions. Published in 1757 and probably written in the early 1750s, this symphony shows Stamitz at the height of his powers, and strongly under the influence of Italian music. The first movement, in sonata form, begins with massive chords that allowed Stamitz to show off the precision of his ensemble, then an example of the crescendo for which the orchestra was famous (see Anthology 12). The symphony continues with a slow movement in binary form in which the oboes and horns play a prominent role. The third movement is a minuet whose closing material resembles the analogous passage in the third and final movement of an operatic sinfonia that Giovanni Battista Pergolesi wrote in the early 1730s. The parallel not only illustrates Stamitz's debt to Italian composers, it also helps us think of this minuet as a movement that could have easily served (like Pergolesi's) as the conclusion of a symphony. The fourth movement, a colorfully orchestrated Prestissimo, is an "extra movement" that Stamitz added to what many musicians of the time would have considered a fully worked-out three-movement overture or concert symphony.

MARGRAVINE WILHELMINA AND ANNA BON AT BAYREUTH

Princess Wilhelmina of Prussia (1709–1758), introduced in Chapter 9 as the older sister of King Frederick the Great, shared with her brother a passionate interest in music and theater. In 1735 she married Margrave Frederick of Bayreuth, a small principality in southeastern Germany. She devoted much of her energy to transforming Bayreuth into a significant musical center. Until her death in 1758 she rarely ceased her activities as performer, composer, and patron. She brought to Bayreuth an operatic troupe under the direction of the Kapellmeister Johann Pfeiffer; she wrote opera librettos, at least one of which she set to music herself (*L'Argenore*, performed in 1740); and she assembled around her a group of musicians for private music-making. Between 1745 and 1748 the French architect Joseph Saint-Pierre built for Wilhelmina and her husband a magnificent theater. Its interior, like those of most eighteenth-century theaters, consisted largely of painted wood, illuminated by candles—a combustible combination that eventually burned down many of these buildings. The bombs of World War II destroyed some of the theaters that fire had spared, but miraculously, Wilhelmina's has survived (Fig. 10.2).

Among the many musicians who enjoyed Wilhelmina's patronage was Anna Bon, whom we met in Chapter 2 as an exemplar of the galant. Bon was born in Venice around 1740, according to the title page of her first publication, which is dated 1756 and states that she was 16 years old. Her mother (a singer) and father (a stage designer, librettist, and actor) spent most of the 1740s in St. Petersburg, Dresden, and Potsdam. They enrolled their daughter at the Ospedale della Pietà, one of the Venetian charitable institutions that had evolved, under the leadership of such musicians as Vivaldi, into important musical schools (see Chapter 4). By the mid-1750s Anna was old enough to accompany her parents as they earned a living among the courts of northern Europe. When they came to Bayreuth, sometime before 1756, Anna joined them there. If she composed the six sonatas for flute and basso continuo, published as Opus 1, in the hope that they might lead to a position at court, she attained her goal. On the title page of

Figure 10.2: *The Margravine Theater at Bayreuth; view of the auditorium*

her next publication, six keyboard sonatas, she identified herself as "virtuosa di musica di camera" (chamber music virtuoso) at the court of Bayreuth. Her third and final set of published works, the six divertimenti for two flutes and bass, came out in 1759.

We have already pointed to Bon's Keyboard Sonata in F Major (see Anthology 13) as an example of the galant style; it shows the high level of craftsmanship that she achieved so quickly. It shares with the five other keyboard sonatas a three-movement, fast-slow-fast format that she probably borrowed from C. P. E. Bach's Prussian and Württemberg Sonatas (both likewise sets of six sonatas). We might expect that Bon, as the protégée of the sister of Bach's employer, had access to Bach's music and learned from it. Within the Bachian framework, Bon's sonatas display a good deal of variety. Among the finales, for example, are four movements in binary form, a minuet with trio, and a minuet with variations.

Bon probably modeled her Sonata No. 5 in B Minor on the sixth sonata in Bach's Württemberg set, in the same rarely used key. Dotted rhythms and fast scalar runs dominate the first movements of both sonatas (Bach: Moderato; Bon: Allegro moderato). The slow movements have the same tempo (Adagio non molto) and key (B major); but Bon's individuality and expertise show through

Example 10.1: *Anna Bon, Sonata No. 5 in B Minor, movement 2, mm. 1–20*

as well, for example in the enchanting, dreamlike alternation of tonic and subdominant harmony over a tonic pedal in the first three measures, and in the skill with which she used a Fonte (as explained in Chapter 3) as part of a modulation to the dominant, tonicizing first G♯ minor and then F♯ major (Ex. 10.1, mm. 13–16).

This music leaves no doubt that the teenager who wrote it, with all the elements of the galant style at her command, had the talent and training to become a first-rate composer. All Bon lacked, like many other young female musicians of the eighteenth century, was opportunity. If she had been able to establish long-term musical relations with Wilhelmina like those that linked Domenico Scarlatti and Queen Maria Barbara, who knows what musical riches might have resulted? But the margravine died when Anna was only 18, and most of the court's musical establishment was dissolved. The Bons resumed their travels; in 1762 they gave a concert in Vienna's Burgtheater that included Anna's performance of a keyboard concerto. They eventually found employment at the court of Prince Nicolaus Esterházy at Eisenstadt, near Vienna. By 1767 Anna had married a tenor, and with that marriage she ceased to leave traces (including even her date of death) in the historical record.

JOSEPH HAYDN IN VIENNA AND EISENSTADT

Until about 1770, the Esterházy princes, among the wealthiest noblemen of Europe, divided their time between their palace at Eisenstadt, near their huge Hungarian estates, and their palace in Vienna. (Hungary being part of the monarchy ruled from Vienna, it was important for the Hungarian nobility to have residences in the Habsburg capital.) Prince Paul Esterházy employed as his music director Gregor Werner, who by 1761 was too old to carry out all of his duties. So the prince hired Joseph Haydn (1732–1809), a young, energetic, and remarkably talented musician who agreed to take over most of Werner's responsibilities in the hope that, if his work pleased the prince, he would soon become music director.

Haydn was an experienced composer approaching 30 years of age when he entered the service of Prince Esterházy as associate music director (vice-Kapellmeister). Born in a small village near Vienna, he had learned to read music and to play the keyboard and violin as a choirboy in St. Stephen's Cathedral. When his voice broke, around 1750, he left the choir school and—without money from his family—lived in poverty, making barely enough to survive by playing in churches, giving lessons, and providing the accompaniment at singing lessons given by a famous Italian musician, Nicola Porpora.

From Porpora, Haydn received not only money but musical insight that shaped his development as a composer. Porpora had played an important role in the emergence of the galant style in Naples in the 1720s, both as a composer and as the vocal coach who guided the *musico* Farinelli to stardom. He brought his firsthand understanding of galant musical aesthetics with him to Vienna. Haydn remembered: "There was no lack of *asino* [ass], *coglione* [idiot], *birbante* [rogue], and pokes in the ribs, but I put up with it all, for I profited greatly with Porpora in singing, in composition, and in the Italian language."

At more or less the same time Haydn underwent another kind of education that was self-imposed. According to his early biographer Georg Griesinger, he got hold of a copy of Johann Joseph Fux's *Gradus ad Parnassum* (see Chapters 1 and 2): "Haydn took infinite pains to assimilate the theory of Fux; he went through the whole work laboriously, writing out the exercises, then laying them aside for a few weeks, to look them over again later and polish them until he was satisfied he had done everything exactly right." Thus to the galant, Italianate musical language that Haydn absorbed from Porpora he added the weight and rigor of the learned style. Much later, in the 1790s, his particular way of combining the galant and the learned earned praise in a biographical dictionary of musicians: "Every harmonic device is at his command, even those of the gothic age of grey contrapuntists. But instead of their former stiffness, they assume a pleasing manner as soon as he prepares them for our ears. He has a great gift for making a piece sound familiar. In this way, despite all their contrapuntal artifices, he achieves a popular style and is agreeable to every amateur."

No document conveys more vividly than Haydn's contract with Paul Esterházy the conditions under which many able musicians worked in noble houses and princely palaces of central Europe. Here are some of the provisions to which Haydn agreed:

2. The said Joseph Heyden [sic] shall be considered and treated as a house officer. Therefore his Serene Highness is graciously pleased to place confidence in his conducting himself as becomes an honorable officer of a princely court. He must be temperate, not showing himself overbearing toward his musicians, but mild and lenient, straightforward and composed. It is especially to be observed that when the orchestra shall be summoned to perform before company, the vice-Kapellmeister and all the musicians shall appear in uniform, and the said Joseph Heyden shall take care that he and all his subordinates follow the instructions given, and appear in white stockings, white linen, powdered, and either with pigtail or hairbag: all, however, of identical appearance.

4. The said vice-Kapellmeister shall be under obligation to compose such music as His Serene Highness may command, and neither to communicate such compositions to any other person, nor to allow them to be copied, but he shall retain them for the exclusive use of His Highness, and not compose for any other person without the knowledge and gracious permission of His Highness.

5. The said Joseph Heyden shall appear daily (whether here in Vienna or on the estates) in the antechamber before and after midday, and inquire whether His Highness is pleased to order a performance of the orchestra. On receipt of his orders he shall communicate them to the other musicians, and take care to be punctual at the appointed time, and to ensure punctuality in his subordinates, making a note of those who arrive late or absent themselves altogether.

7. The said vice-Kapellmeister shall take careful charge of all music and musical instruments, and be responsible for any injury that may occur to them from carelessness or neglect.

8. The said Joseph Heyden shall be obliged to instruct the female vocalists, in order that they may not forget in the country what they have been taught with much trouble and expense in Vienna, and, as the said vice-Kapellmeister is proficient in various instruments, he shall take care himself to practice on all those with which he is acquainted.

HAYDN'S EARLY SYMPHONIES

Still relatively inexperienced as a music director when he entered his new position in 1761, Haydn may have read Johann Joachim Quantz's advice to orchestral directors, which included the following: "The brilliance of an orchestra will also be greatly enhanced if it contains good solo players on various instruments. Hence the leader must seek to encourage good solo players. To this end he must give those equipped to play alone frequent opportunities to distinguish themselves, not only privately but also in public concerts." Shortly after taking over the Esterházy orchestra, as if in response to such advice, Haydn wrote a series of three symphonies remarkable for the number and variety of solo passages. With these symphonies, entitled *Le matin* (Morning, No. 6), *Le midi* (Noon, No. 7), and *Le soir* (Evening, No. 8), Haydn made a spectacular debut in both of his primary duties as princely music director: directing the orchestra and composing for it.

Only one of the 12 movements of Haydn's symphonic trilogy has an individual title (the finale of *Le soir* is called *La tempesta*, or The Storm). He left no other written indications of the content of individual movements, some of which are more explicitly programmatic than others. One of the most obviously descriptive parts of these symphonies is the slow introduction to the first movement of *Le matin*, which depicts a sunrise with a gradual crescendo, beautifully orchestrated with the various instruments entering one after the other, and a gradual rise in the violins from near the bottom of their range (Ex. 10.2). From this sunrise we might guess that the morning with which this symphony is concerned takes place out of doors, and in the country. That guess is confirmed

Example 10.2: *Joseph Haydn, Symphony No. 6,* Le matin, *movement 1, mm. 1–10*

at the beginning of the Allegro, which presents a theme derived from a triadic horn call that central European cowherds used to summon their animals, and that Johann Baptist Vanhal also used in his *Missa pastoralis* (see Ex. 8.2).

The first movement of *Le soir* (see Anthology 14), in contrast, establishes a sophisticated, urban setting by quoting a song written by Christoph Gluck for a production in Vienna of the opéra comique *Le diable à quatre* (1759). In the song, a young woman confesses to a fondness for snuff, which she enjoys precisely because her husband forbids her to use it. Haydn's appropriation of this tune reminds us that Eisenstadt was close to Vienna culturally as well as physically.

Prince Paul Esterházy died in 1762 and was succeeded by his brother Nicolaus (1714–1790), an enthusiastic musician and a generous patron. One of his first acts was to increase Haydn's salary from 400 to 600 Gulden. Nicolaus played the baryton—a kind of viol, about the size of a cello, with extra strings that vibrated sympathetically (like those of the viola d'amore) and could also be plucked with the left thumb while the player was bowing the main strings. Haydn wrote a vast amount of chamber music with baryton for Nicolaus to play (mostly trios for baryton, viola, and cello), while continuing to add symphonies to the Esterházy orchestra's repertory.

On Werner's death in 1766 Haydn became Kapellmeister and took over the responsibility for church music that had been Werner's last remaining duty. In that same year he wrote his first great sacred work, the huge and splendid *Missa Cellensis* (also known as the *Cecilia Mass*).

HAYDN AT ESZTERHÁZA AND THE *FAREWELL* SYMPHONY

Versailles—and the idea that a great prince should build a magnificent palace in the country—haunted Prince Nicolaus Esterházy no less than other eighteenth-century rulers and noblemen. He loved building as much as making music. From the mid-1760s he supervised the construction of a great palace in the Hungarian countryside, Eszterháza (Fig. 10.3), which became his main residence during much of the year, even before its completion. Among the buildings at Eszterháza was a theater for which Haydn was to write most of his operas. The construction of the opera house in 1768 coincided with a change in Nicolaus's musical interests, away from the baryton and chamber music and toward opera. That led, unsurprisingly, to an analogous change in Haydn's compositional priorities. From 1768 he devoted much of his musical energy to the composition, rehearsing, and performing of opera.

The construction of the other buildings at Eszterháza dragged on for some years, and this led, in 1772, to dissatisfaction among Nicolaus's musicians and to Haydn's writing one of his finest, most unusual, and most enigmatic symphonies.

Figure 10.3: *Eszterháza*

Because the unfinished buildings had no place to accommodate the musicians'
wives, they had to stay at Eisenstadt, according to Griesinger:

> Contrary to his custom, the prince once wished to extend his stay in Esz-
> terháza by several weeks. The fond husbands, especially dismayed at this
> news, turned to Haydn and pleaded with him to do something. Haydn had
> the notion of writing a symphony (known as the *Farewell* Symphony) in
> which one instrument after the other is silent. This symphony was per-
> formed at the first opportunity in the presence of the prince, and each of
> the musicians was directed, as soon as his part was finished, to put out his
> candle, pack up his music and, with his instrument under his arm, to go
> away. The prince and the audience understood the meaning of this panto-
> mime at once, and the next day came the order to depart from Eszterháza.

Thus, in the account of someone who knew Haydn personally, the origins of
the Symphony No. 45 in F♯ Minor—a work whose finale of diminishing forces is
by no means its only remarkable feature. The stormy first movement is full of
the theatrical excitement and flair that Haydn had absorbed in his operatic work
since 1768—but rendered novel and bizarre by the unprecedented choice of key,
and by the strange major-mode interlude in the development section in which
Haydn introduced a theme unlike anything else in the movement. The second
movement, an Adagio in A, the relative major, has a galant character—like a
slow minuet—while recalling the darkness and violence of the first movement
in its many syncopations and its frequent excursions into the minor mode. The

minuet proper is in F♯ major, rather than the tonic minor that convention would lead us to expect; again syncopation is prominent.

With the beginning of the finale we hear the symphony's first music in duple meter. It begins conventionally enough, in the same key and mode as the first movement, with a sonata-form exposition that moves to the relative major. But the repeat of the exposition and a tumultuous development are followed not by the expected recapitulation but by a sudden pause, and by an Adagio that begins not only in the same tempo but in the same meter and key as the second movement. The minuet-like quality of the previous Adagio returns, now without the syncopation that enlivened the slow movement. The lack of syncopation gives this second Adagio a curiously placid, even listless character—as if to suggest that the musicians playing it, and taking part in the pantomime that it accompanies, are acting under a spell. The spirit of strangeness expressed by this symphony's opening syncopations in F♯ minor stays with it until its final, F♯-major *pianissimo* fadeout.

As an old man Haydn attributed some of his musical originality to the isolation of Eszterháza and to the fact that he wrote much of his music for one man: "My prince was content with all my works, I received approval, I could, as head of an orchestra, make experiments, observe what enhanced an effect, and what weakened it, thus improving, adding to, cutting away, and running risks. I was set apart from the world, there was nobody in my vicinity to confuse and annoy me in my course, and so I had to be original."

Haydn exaggerated his isolation. Earlier we cited his quotation of a popular Viennese tune as evidence of close musical ties between Haydn and Vienna. He visited Vienna often and stayed in contact with Viennese musicians and publishers. At the same time, it is hard to believe that he could have conceived of—let alone composed and performed—a work like the *Farewell* Symphony in circumstances other than those that produced it. A half-completed palace on the plains of Hungary echoed with the sounds of an orchestra led by one of Europe's greatest composers, playing music quite unlike anything that had ever been heard before.

This chapter has examined some aspects of musical life at three central European courts, each remarkable in its own way. Mannheim produced an orchestra of unprecedented discipline, brilliance, and power—qualities that its director Johann Stamitz instilled in it and that inspired him in his pioneering work as a composer of symphonies. Bayreuth offered unusually favorable conditions for musical patronage and composition by women. Margravine Wilhelmina supervised the construction of a lavish opera house, composed an opera for it, and encouraged the compositional ambitions of a young woman, Anna Bon. The Hungarian palaces of the Esterházy princes at Eisenstadt and Eszterháza witnessed the development of one of our period's greatest musicians, Joseph Haydn.

Endowed with extraordinary intellectual energy and a strong body, Haydn outlived Prince Nicolaus and the system of patronage that prevailed at the courts of central Europe. In 1790, at the age of 58, he traded his sheltered but restrictive position as a private music director for the more exciting and risky life of a free-lance musician. He thus opened a new and exciting phase of his life, of which we will read in Chapters 16 and 17.

FOR FURTHER READING

Geiringer, Karl, *Haydn: A Creative Life in Music*, 3rd ed. (Berkeley: University of California Press, 1982)

Heartz, Daniel, *Haydn, Mozart, and the Viennese School, 1740–1780* (New York: W. W. Norton, 1995), 235–406

——, *Music in European Capitals: The Galant Style, 1720–1780* (New York: W. W. Norton, 2003), 494–594

Jones, David Wyn, *The Life of Haydn* (Cambridge: Cambridge University Press, 2009)

Music at German Courts, 1715–1760: Changing Artistic Priorities, ed. Samantha Owens et al. (Woodbridge: Boydell, 2011)

Webster, James, *Haydn's "Farewell" Symphony and the Idea of Classical Style* (Cambridge: Cambridge University Press, 1991)

Wolf, Eugene K., "The Mannheim Court," in *The Classical Era: From the 1740s to the End of the 18th Century,* ed. Neal Zaslaw, (Englewood Cliffs, NJ: Prentice Hall, 1989), 213–39

——, *The Symphonies of Johann Stamitz: A Study in the Formation of the Classic Style* (Utrecht: Bohn, 1981)

Ⓢ **Additional resources available at wwnorton.com/studyspace**

CHAPTER ELEVEN

Galant Music
in the New World

Music and dance from other parts of the world occasionally found their way to eighteenth-century Europe, in printed transcriptions and in performances. In 1725 a pair of American Indians danced at the Théâtre Italien in Paris, as described in a newspaper:

> Two savages recently arrived from Louisiana, tall and well built, about twenty-five years of age, danced three kinds of dances, together and separately, and in a style that left no doubt they learned the steps and leaps a long way from Paris. . . . The first dancer represented the chief of his nation, dressed a bit more modestly than in Louisiana, but still with sufficient nudity. . . . He presented the peace pipe that one offered to one's enemy. Then together they danced the dance of peace. The second dance, called "War," expresses a gathering of savages. . . . They dance together the dance of victory.

About four years later Jean-Philippe Rameau published in his *Nouvelles suites de pièces de clavecin* (New Suites of Harpsichord Pieces) a piece called *Les sauvages*,

Example 11.1: *Jean-Philippe Rameau,* Les sauvages, *mm. 1–9*

in which he attempted to depict the performance of the "savages" (Ex. 11.1). But to what extent his music reproduces what was actually played at the Théâtre Italien is unknown.

Another kind of non-European music was evidently less favorably received in Berlin in 1733. During a dinner at court, the famously unmusical King Frederick William II, the father of Frederick the Great, presented a janissary ensemble (a Turkish military band) consisting of more than 50 black musicians playing trumpets, drums, and cymbals. The king's music-loving daughter Wilhelmina was appalled: "Together they made a frightful noise."

By the late eighteenth century European explorers had reached some of the most remote parts of the world, and they brought their music with them. When a French expedition landed on the southern coast of Tasmania, a large island south of Australia, in 1793, music helped to establish trust between the aboriginal people and the Europeans. A sailor's fiddle playing did not please the natives, but an exchange of songs was more successful, according to the expedition's naturalist, whose account suggests that the aborigines had developed, independent of Europe, the technique of singing in parallel thirds: "Several times two of them sang the same tune at once, but always one third above the other, forming a concord with the greatest justness." (Within 50 years the Tasmanians had been all but exterminated—and their music silenced—by European weapons and diseases.)

Colonists followed the explorers. Britain, France, Portugal, Spain, and Holland, Europe's main maritime states, had all established colonies in North or South America, and on the islands of the Caribbean, by the beginning of our period. They initiated a second wave of westward migration by importing millions of African slaves to work in agriculture and mining.

Most colonists were less open than the French explorers in Tasmania to the beauties of the music of native peoples. Nor were they willing to appreciate or to

Figure 11.1: *Slaves making music and dancing. Watercolor by an unknown artist, ca. 1800.*

learn from the music of their African slaves, although they occasionally recorded their impressions of it in pictures (Fig. 11.1) and in writing, often complain-
ing that the music kept them awake. Of the Afro-Brazilian *calundus*, a religious
ceremony accompanied by music, a Portuguese chronicler wrote: "I could not
sleep the whole night because of the blasts of the *atabaques*, *pandeiros*, *ganzas*,
bottles, and castanets, with such horrible outcries that they sounded to me like
the confusion of hell." Thomas Thistlewood, an English plantation manager
in Jamaica, wrote in his diary on the day after Christmas, 1751: "The Negroes
drumming and dancing all night along." Richard Ligon, an English musician
who visited Barbados more than a century earlier, left a better informed and
more positive account of African music-making (excerpt in SR 118: 714– 15;
4/38: 206–7).

European colonists preferred to reproduce, as far as local conditions
allowed, the musical culture they had left behind in Europe. For those who came
to the Americas during most of our period, that musical culture (insofar as it
was recorded in notation) was largely dominated by galant music. Yet the great
distances that separated the colonies from Europe meant that the colonists soon
developed distinctive musical dialects. This chapter briefly samples musical
life in four very different parts of the New World: Portuguese Brazil, Spanish
Mexico, British Jamaica, and the Moravian settlements in North Carolina and
Pennsylvania.

THE GOLD CITIES OF MINAS GERAIS

The Portuguese had colonized the coast of Brazil for almost two centuries before they discovered gold in 1695 in the mountainous inland region that came to be known as Minas Gerais (General Mines). In the gold rush that followed, the population of whites in the gold fields increased quickly (to 30,000 in 1709), though Indian and African slaves did most of the mining. They also did most of the diamond mining after large diamond deposits were discovered in the 1720s.

The Portuguese Crown claimed 20 percent of all the gold found in Brazil (the so-called royal fifth) and established a monopoly in the diamond fields. Although smuggling and fraud kept King John V from receiving anywhere near as much as he claimed, he did receive vast riches nevertheless, spending most of it in Portugal on such projects as the big monastery and palace complex at Mafra, and also on ambitious programs of church music and Italian opera. It was thanks in part to the gold of Minas Gerais that Domenico Scarlatti came to Lisbon in 1719, forming relations with the king's keyboard-playing daughter Maria Barbara that (as we saw in Chapter 5) resulted in the composition of his sonatas.

Revenues from the mines also paid for the construction of cities nearby, some of which survive today as remarkable monuments of eighteenth-century architecture. Ouro Preto (Black Gold), the most famous of the colonial cities of Minas Gerais, rises against a background of green tropical hillsides (Fig. 11.2). A description of Ouro Preto published in 1734 explained the reasons for its sudden rise to prominence:

> In this town live the chief merchants, whose trade and importance incomparably exceed the most thriving of the leading merchants of Portugal. Hither, as to a port, are directed and collected in the Royal Mint the grandiose amounts of gold from all the Mines. Here dwell the best-educated men, both lay and ecclesiastic. Here is the seat of all the nobility and the strength of the military. It is, by virtue of its natural position, the head of the whole of America; and by the wealth of its riches it is the precious pearl of Brazil.

The splendid churches needed music. Some of it came directly from Europe, in the form of an organ built between 1700 and 1720 for a church in Portugal by the great instrument maker Arp Schnitger of Hamburg or his student Heinrich Hulenkampf (the attribution is still in dispute). King Joseph I, shortly after coming to the throne in 1750, gave the organ to the newly created diocese of Mariana (a city near Ouro Preto). Taken apart and shipped by sea and muleback to Minas Gerais, it was carefully described on its arrival: "a large organ with its case and the carvings belonging to it that arrived in eighteen large numbered crates with

Figure 11.2: *Ouro Preto, Minas Gerais, Brazil*

specific instructions for assembling it, and ten large and small numbered parcels."
The organ, installed in the Cathedral of Mariana in 1753, stands there still today
(Fig. 11.3)—delightful evidence of the richness and sophistication of musical life
in eighteenth-century Minas Gerais.

Few European musicians were willing to make the same trip. Most of the
professional musicians in eighteenth-century Minas Gerais were mulattos—
free men of mixed race, probably in most cases the sons of Portuguese men and
African women. Working within *irmandades* (brotherhoods)—organizations
loosely associated with the Catholic Church that served as musical guilds—the

Figure 11.3: *The eighteenth-century organ at Mariana, Minas Gerais*

mulatto composers of Minas Gerais supplied music for ceremonies and celebrations that sometimes spilled out into the streets of the gold cities.

At the dedication of the Church of Nossa Senhora do Pilar in 1733, a procession through the streets of Ouro Preto anticipated the colorful carnival parades of modern-day Rio de Janeiro. According to a contemporary account, it included "a dance of Turks and Christians in military costumes, composed of thirty-two figures" and accompanied by "musicians with sweet voices and various instruments"; then "a dance of the pilgrims, richly costumed"; and "a stately dance of the musicians." Much later "a German mounted on a charger came by, breaking the silence with the sound of a trumpet," followed by "eight blacks on foot, dressed in fashionable style; they all played chalumeau [a reed instrument related to the clarinet], alternating their voices with those of the trumpet." In a part of the procession representing the planets, Mars was accompanied by three elaborately dressed musicians playing a military drum, a fife, and a trumpet.

The composers of Minas Gerais also wrote liturgical music that corresponds perfectly to the festive beauty of the buildings in which it was performed—choral music accompanied by an orchestra of strings, horns, and occasionally pairs of flutes or oboes. For that distinctively European ensemble, musicians who had never been to Europe wrote music whose predominantly homophonic textures, balanced phrases, and limited harmonic vocabulary conform to the ideals of the galant style.

A good example of the music of eighteenth-century Minas Gerais is the *Magnificat* of Manoel Dias de Oliveira (ca. 1735–1813), who spent most of his life in the mining town of Tiradentes. He may have been the son and pupil of Lourenço Dias de Oliveira, a white organist. That Manoel was of mixed race we know from his entry, in 1752, into the Irmandade de São João Evangelista dos Homems Pardos (Brotherhood of St. John the Evangelist for Mulattos).

Comparing Oliveira's *Magnificat* to well-known settings of the same text by European composers of the eighteenth century, such as Johann Sebastian and Carl Philipp Emanuel Bach, one is immediately impressed by the conciseness of the Brazilian's music—in part the result of the function of this *Magnificat* as the final movement of Oliveira's much longer setting of the Vespers for Holy Saturday (the day before Easter). A single Allegro in duple meter is interrupted near the end with a Largo in $\frac{6}{8}$ (for the Doxology) that sets the stage for a return to the movement's prevailing tempo, tonic key, and opening theme in the final acclamations of "Amen." Oliveira went through the text quickly, shifting from short duets in parallel thirds (soprano–alto; alto–tenor; soprano–tenor; tenor–bass) and chordal passages for all four voices. Only in the Largo did he allow himself time to develop his musical ideas fully.

It is partly for that reason that this passage from the Largo (Ex. 11.2) stands out as a particularly attractive example of Oliveira's art. Exclamations of the full chorus, repeating the word "Gloria," alternate with sweetly lyrical passages in parallel thirds and sixths. To dramatize the phrase "Et nunc et semper et in saecula saeculorum" (it is now and will be forever, world without end), Oliveira had the sopranos sustain a note for a measure and a half, and then, joined by the rest of the chorus, descend in a melismatic Prinner (see Chapter 3). Familiar with the conventions of galant music, he began the *Gloria* with a melody built on the scale degrees $\hat{1}$–$\hat{7}$–$\hat{4}$–$\hat{3}$, a melodic framework that European composers also favored (compare with the opening of the second movement of Frederick the Great's Sonata in A Major in Ex. 9.3). The Prinner with which Oliveira set the word "saecula," in contrast, uses voice-leading (the $\hat{6}$–$\hat{5}$–$\hat{4}$–$\hat{3}$ melodic descent in the tenor, the soprano doubling the bass) that a European composer would almost certainly have rejected as "incorrect." But we are free to enjoy it as an example of the way the galant style evolved as it spread far from its European origins.

Example 11.2: *Manoel Dias de Oliveira*, Magnificat, Gloria, *mm. 1–23*

Glory be to the Father, the Son, and the Holy Spirit; as it was in the beginning, it is now and shall be forever, world without end. Amen.

AN ITALIAN MUSICIAN IN MEXICO CITY

While Ouro Preto bought its fame, its architectural and musical riches, and
even its name with gold alone, Mexico City became the greatest urban center of
eighteenth-century Spanish America for many reasons, of which silver mining
in the surrounding area was only one. The city, on Mexico's high central plateau at an
altitude of some 7,200 feet, grew up on the site of the Aztec metropolis Tenochtitlán
that Hernán Cortés had conquered from Montezuma in 1520. On an island in
Lake Texcoco, Mexico City was subject to frequent flooding. As the lake was gradually drained and filled in during the early colonial period, the city developed as
a political and religious capital, a university town, and a commercial hub with a
vibrant artistic and theatrical life.

At the center of musical activity was the cathedral, the largest in Latin America,
built on the ruins of an Aztec temple (Fig. 11.4), and the Coliseo, the city's main
theater. The great Manuel de Sumaya, *maestro de capilla* in the cathedral from 1715
to 1738, brought musical standards to a very high level. But under Sumaya's successor, Domingo Dutra, music in the cathedral languished. The Coliseo as well
required an influx of musical talent, and in 1742 its director traveled to Spain to
recruit musicians. In the most important musician he brought to Mexico City we
find a direct link between the music of the Old World and the New.

Figure 11.4: *Mexico City Cathedral*

The violinist and composer who came to be known as Ignacio de Jerusalem (1707–1769) was born in Lecce, in the southern Italian region of Apulia. That made him a compatriot and a near contemporary of Farinelli, born in another Apulian town two years earlier. Like Farinelli, Jerusalem joined the Italian musical diaspora, which brought him (again like the *musico*) to Spain, where he played violin in a theater in Cádiz. In 1742 he joined other musicians on the voyage to Mexico.

Jerusalem spent most of his first years in Mexico City playing in the orchestra of the Coliseo and composing music for its productions. But at the same time the cathedral, suffering from Dutra's ineffectual musical leadership, drew his attention. In 1746 he entered its service and in 1750 he became *maestro de capilla*. Although he continued to work for the Coliseo, he eventually focused almost all his musical efforts on the composition and conducting of church music. A fine example of Jerusalem's large-scale works is the setting of the *Matins for the Virgin of Guadalupe* that he made in 1764 (see Anthology 15).

THE SLAVE COLONY OF JAMAICA AND SAMUEL FELSTED'S *JONAH*

Nowhere were the inequities, the ugliness, and the brutality of eighteenth-century society more obvious than on the island of Jamaica, where Africans and their descendents labored in the sugarcane fields under the constant threat of beatings and other more inventive and humiliating punishments from British landowners and plantation managers.

The diary of Thomas Thistlewood (1721–1786), an English plantation manager and slave owner, presents a detailed account of daily life in rural Jamaica, in all its sadistic violence and exploitation. Thistlewood, who lived on the island from 1750 until his death, was very much a man of his time and place—a hideous caricature of the enlightened gentleman. Like Thomas Jefferson, he was a bibliophile and a passionate and expert gardener, and he showed encyclopedic inclinations in the careful and systematic records he kept of Jamaican weather. He also recorded in his diary hundreds of sexual acts with his female slaves— revealing himself as a kind of distant relative of the Don Juan whose legendary exploits fascinated audiences in eighteenth-century European theaters and inspired Mozart to write one of his greatest operas, *Don Giovanni* (see Chapter 15).

As a young man in London, in 1748, Thistlewood had attended a performance of *The Beggar's Opera*. But in Jamaica he made very few references in his diary to European music of any sort. He apparently played no instrument. Living near the western end of the island, far from Spanish Town (the capital) and Kingston (the main port and commercial center), and without other whites in his household, he had little opportunity to hear music-making other than that of his slaves.

Thistlewood showed some interest in African music, at least at first. On his arrival in Kingston he went to see the "Negro diversions—odd music, motions, &c." And shortly before he left the plantation where he first served as overseer, the slaves under his control, including Marina, with whom he was sharing his bed, put on a party: "They was very merry all night. Mr. Markman's Caesar sang and drummed, Guy and Charles, Phibbah and Wanicker danced Congo, &c. Some top performances was had. Marina herself got very drunk as well as many others. I sat up good part of the night seeing their tricks." But in later years he referred to African music mostly when it kept him awake or otherwise annoyed him. January 3, 1764: "At night, about 11 o'clock, broke Job's banjar [banjo] to pieces in the mill house." November 20, 1773: "About 10 o'clock this night, got up and went to my Negro houses, where found Mrs. North's George playing upon the Banjar to Lincoln. I chopped all up in pieces with my cutlass, & reprimanded them." March 10, 1783: "Flogged Joe & Pompey for drumming last night."

The same social system that suppressed African music on the plantation encouraged European music in Jamaica's main towns. According to a description of the island published in 1774, the Governor's House in Spanish Town had a "grand saloon" used for entertainments and balls, with a movable platform for musicians at one end. Kingston boasted "a very pretty theatre, exceedingly well contrived, and neatly finished." But it was apparently empty most of the time; the town was "not able, or not disposed, to support so costly an amusement." For public music-making, Kingston's residents had recourse to its two largest taverns, named after the London pleasure gardens Ranelagh and Vauxhall; they contained long rooms used for "concerts, balls, and public entertainments." Several of the island's churches had organs. In Spanish Town an "exceeding fine organ" was installed in the parish church in 1755 at a cost of 440 pounds. "The organist has a salary of 120 l. [pounds] *per annum* currency, paid by the parishioners, and receives other emoluments, his assistance being generally required even of the free Negroes and Mulattoes buried in this parish."

Another organist, Samuel Felsted (1743–1802), served in the parish church of St. Andrew, just north of Kingston. He has a significant claim to fame as the composer of what appears to be the first oratorio written in the New World. We know little of Felsted beyond his service at St. Andrew's, which lasted at least eight years, until 1783. The title page of his *Six Voluntarys* [sic] *for the Organ or Harpsichord*, published in London between 1793 and 1795, identifies him as "Organist in Kingston, Jamaica." A letter of recommendation by one James Smith of Jamaica, written in 1771, called him "an ingenious young Gentleman" of "merit in the three Sister Sciences, Poetry, Painting, and Music." He had other admirers as well. Nearly 250 subscribers, in Britain and the New World, bought copies of his oratorio *Jonah*, published by subscription as a keyboard–vocal score in London in 1775.

Smith's allusion to Felsted's abilities as a poet makes it likely that the composer set to music his own libretto, based on a biblical text that must have resonated with special force in a seaport like Kingston, where the oratorio was probably performed in 1779. Many of Felsted's listeners in Jamaica, and many of those who heard *Jonah* in New York in 1788—possibly the first performance of a complete oratorio in the United States—had memories of at least one voyage across the Atlantic.

Consisting of 12 numbers (an overture, four airs, two choruses, and five recitatives), *Jonah* (Fig. 11.5) mixes Handelian grandeur with galant charm, with an emphasis on the latter. Instead of the two-part French overture that Handel

Figure 11.5: *The title page of Samuel Felsted's* Jonah

favored, it begins with an Italianate sinfonia in three movements, the first of which makes good use of dynamic contrast and crescendo. On Jonah's entrance, singing the da capo aria *Billows form around my head*, an old-fashioned running bass (with basso continuo figures) suggests the rolling of waves. Although the score gives no indication of orchestration, the sound of the orchestral unison depicting a stormy sea is easy enough to imagine. In the **B** section, an ardent prayer ("Save me, O Lord, revoke my doom"), Felsted used carefully notated dynamics to dramatize the rising vocal line.

MUSIC FOR THE MORAVIAN LOVEFEAST

Since the time of Jan Hus, the Bohemian religious reformer burned at the stake as a heretic in 1415 (a century before Martin Luther), the Czech-speaking lands of Bohemia and Moravia had given rise to reformist movements that both the Catholic Church and the main Protestant denominations tried, most of the time successfully, to stamp out. But in the eighteenth century the religious tolerance and pluralism fostered by the Enlightenment allowed the spiritual descendents of the Hussites, known as Unitas Fratrum (United Brethren) or, more informally, the Moravians, to organize a church without fear of being put to death. In 1722 the German nobleman Nicholas von Zinzendorf invited the Moravians to settle on his estate in Saxony, where they founded the utopian community of Herrnhut.

Music played an important role in the religious and secular life of the United Brethren, serving them as a kind of metaphor for social harmony. The music-making in Herrnhut impressed a visitor in 1730: "The Brothers were one heart and one soul. In their worship and in their private gatherings, one felt an unaffected simplicity, truly a godly wisdom. Their *Singstunden* were harmonies not only of voices, but also of the heart and the spirit. For all eternity, I will never forget what I saw in their company."

The *Singstunde*, or singing hour, was an early form of Moravian service based on the partly improvisatory singing of memorized hymns. But the Moravians also valued the ability to read music and to play instruments. Like their Catholic countrymen in Bohemia, they made music a part of basic education and considered choral and solo vocal music, accompanied by organ and other instruments, to be an essential element of the liturgy. Moravians also resembled certain Catholic organizations, especially the Jesuits, in the enthusiasm with which they organized missionary expeditions. And like the Jesuits they brought their rich musical traditions with them when they left Europe.

The first permanent Moravian settlement in the New World was Bethlehem, Pennsylvania (1741). Its success led to further settlements in nearby Nazareth and Lititz, Pennsylvania, and in Salem, North Carolina. Among the Moravians who moved to these new towns were several well-trained musicians, who brought with them not only musical skills but also large quantities of European music. Under their leadership the Moravian settlements quickly emerged as important centers of musical education, instrument building, composition, and music copying. The archives of the Moravian Music Foundation in Bethlehem and Winston-Salem preserve hundreds of manuscripts that document the Moravians' astonishing musical productivity.

Although the Moravians who settled in North Carolina initially tried to do without slaves, the cheap labor that slavery offered was a temptation that they could not resist for long. They began by renting slaves from non-Moravian neighbors. Later, when the financial benefits of owning slaves became clear, the church leaders decided that the church itself, rather than individual members, should own slaves. During the eighteenth century the number of slaves owned by the Moravians remained small. Although these slaves took part in the religious life of the community (it was not until the beginning of the nineteenth century that the Moravians forced their slaves into separate services), they seem to have had no influence on the strongly European orientation of its musical practices.

One of the finest of the eighteenth-century Moravian musicians was Johann Friedrich Peter (1746–1813). Born in Holland to German-Moravian parents, Peter studied in Holland and Germany and came to Pennsylvania in 1770. He served as music director at Salem from 1780 to 1790, when he went back north to Moravian communities in Maryland and Pennsylvania. Except for a set of six string quintets (1789; possibly the first chamber music for strings composed in North America), Peter's surviving output of about 100 compositions consists entirely of sacred music. He also copied many works by European composers, some of which apparently survive only in the copies he made. Thus he contributed to a thriving musical culture in which newly composed works, by him and several others, coexisted with a wide repertory of European music.

Peter's music shows him working skillfully within the galant idiom to which he must have been exposed in his youth in Holland and Germany. In his church music he adapted that style to a liturgical requirement for extreme brevity; many Moravian anthems of the period are less than three minutes in length. One service for which Peter provided music was the *Liebesmahl*, or Lovefeast, in which the congregation sang hymns, listened to instrumentally accompanied sacred vocal music, and shared simple food and drink. Peter's *Ich will dir ein Freudenopfer thun* (I wish to make you a sacrifice of joy) was probably sung on such occasions. The text, a line from Psalm 54, served as the theme for a service in Salem on December 26, 1787; it was most likely for that service that Peter wrote this piece. Its survival in at least four manuscript copies in Bethlehem and Winston-Salem attests to its popularity both north and south of the Mason-Dixon Line.

Peter scored this gently joyful anthem of thanksgiving for an orchestra of strings, pairs of flutes and horns, bassoon, and organ (Ex. 11.3; the tempo indication "Munter" means cheerful or lively). The organ part is largely a transcription of the orchestral accompaniment, allowing the chorus to be accompanied by organ alone in churches without an orchestra. The manuscript sources refer to the lowest string part as violoncello, not basso; this is consistent with other evidence suggesting that during most of the 1780s the orchestra in Salem did not include double basses.

Example 11.3: *Johann Friedrich Peter,* Ich will dir ein Freudenopfer thun, *mm. 13–18*

Flutes, bassoon, horns, strings, organ

I wish to make you a sacrifice of joy

Ich will dir ein Freudenopfer thun is in binary form, with the first part modulating from tonic E♭ to the dominant, and the second part moving first to the relative minor and then back to the tonic. One can perhaps sense at the end of this lovely miniature that Peter would have liked to allow his music to go on a little longer. After the return to E♭, the end seems to arrive too soon. Liturgical constraints evidently kept Peter from writing a full recapitulation of the first part, which he could have partly recomposed so as to stay in the tonic.

The flow of musical culture between the Old World and the New went in both directions, but predominantly from east to west. Performances of European music in the Americas far outnumbered performances of American music (whether by Indians, Africans, or Europeans) in Europe (such as that of the Indians from the Louisiana territory who danced in Paris in 1725).

Several European musicians (such as Johann Friedrich Peter and Ignacio de Jerusalem) brought their talents and experience with them to North and South America. Musical instruments, like the great organ in Mariana, made the same trip. Music shipped from Europe and music composed in the New World by European composers inspired compositional efforts by native-born musicians such as Manoel Dias de Oliveira and Samuel Felsted. Several of the most talented of these musicians, including Oliveira, were the offspring of European fathers and African mothers, and thus a product of the slavery that existed in most of the colonies.

Another mixed-race musician, whom we met in Chapter 6, exemplifies some of the ways in which European music profited from slavery and from the exportation of the galant style to the New World. Joseph Boulogne, Chevalier de Saint-Georges, became a leading violinist and composer in France during the second half of the eighteenth century. The beautifully crafted music he wrote for Paris's concert rooms and theaters betrays little of his African roots and Caribbean childhood. Like the music that resounded in the gorgeous churches of Ouro Preto, the cathedral and theaters of Mexico City, the parish churches and taverns of Jamaica, and the Moravian chapels of Salem, North Carolina, and Bethlehem, Pennsylvania, Saint-Georges's concertos and string quartets testified to Europe's cultural dominance over its possessions on the other side of the Atlantic.

FOR FURTHER READING

Crews, C. Daniel, *Johann Friedrich Peter and His Times* (Winston-Salem, NC: Moravian Music Foundation, 1990)

Curcio-Nagy, Linda A., *The Great Festivals of Colonial Mexico City: Performing Power and Identity* (Albuquerque: University of New Mexico Press, 2004)

Hall, Douglas, *In Miserable Slavery: Thomas Thistlewood in Jamaica, 1750–86* (London: Macmillan, 1989)

Higgins, Kathleen J., *"Licentious Liberty" in a Brazilian Gold-Mining Region: Slavery, Gender, and Social Control in Eighteenth-Century Sabará, Minas Gerais* (University Park: Pennsylvania State University Press, 1999)

Music and Urban Society in Colonial Latin America, ed. Geoffrey Baker and Tess Knighton (Cambridge: Cambridge University Press, 2011)

The Music of the Moravian Church in America, ed. Nola Reed Knouse (Rochester, NY: University of Rochester Press, 2008)

Russell, Craig H., "The Splendor of Mexican Matins: Sonority and Stucture in Jerusalem's Matins for the Virgin of Guadalupe," *Colloquium Journal* (Yale Institute of Sacred Music) 4 (Fall 2007), www.yale.edu/ism/colloq_journal/vol4/russelll.html

———, *From Serra to Sancho: Music and Pageantry in the California Missions* (New York: Oxford University Press, 2009)

ⓢ **Additional resources available at wwnorton.com/studyspace**

CHAPTER TWELVE

St. Petersburg under Catherine the Great

Eighteenth-century St. Petersburg was a new city, founded by the ruler from whom it took its name as the capital of the huge empire that he transformed into a major European power. Peter the Great, czar of Russia from 1689 to 1725, was not much interested in music. He did so little to bring European music to Russia that in 1729 the editor of the *St. Petersburg Gazette* felt it necessary to define the word "opera" for his readers. But the process of Europeanization that the czar initiated made St. Petersburg later in the century one of Europe's most exciting musical capitals.

Peter brought his empire, hitherto isolated on the edge of Europe, into closer contact with the West. In 1697–98 he made a Grand Tour, visiting Dresden, Amsterdam, London, and Vienna (his conspicuous omission of Italy signaled his lack of interest in music). Five years later he founded St. Petersburg, which he hoped would represent the best of European civilization—and a link between Russia and the West. It rose quickly from the marshes and islands where the Neva River flowed into the Baltic Sea (Fig. 12.1). In an effort to make it a metropolis that rivaled those he admired on his travels, the czar summoned European architects, artists, and engineers. They directed the work of thousands of serfs and soldiers who came from all over Russia.

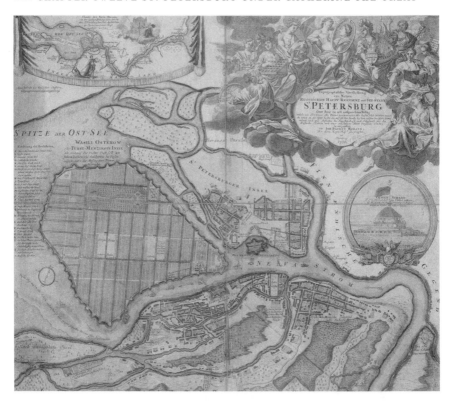

Figure 12.1: *Map of St. Petersburg by Johann Baptist Homann, ca. 1720*

St. Petersburg quickly became a focal point of interaction between European and Russian culture, which bore architectural fruit in the form of palaces and churches that lined the city's rivers, canals, and avenues. Bartolomeo Rastrelli, an Italian who came to Russia as a teenager and achieved a brilliant synthesis of Italian and Russian architectural traditions, designed many of them (Fig. 12.2).

Peter's niece Anna, who ruled Russia from 1730 to 1740, made up for her uncle's lack of support of music. One of her first acts as empress was to invite a traveling troupe of Italian singers and actors, who presented the comedy *Calandrano*, possibly the first Italian opera performed in Russia. She soon assembled a resident opera company in St. Petersburg. The Neapolitan musician who served as its music director, Francesco Araia, initiated a succession of Italian and French composers (Table 12.1) who presided over opera in St. Petersburg, directing performances and composing new works. The list is shorter than that of foreign musicians who worked at the King's Theatre in London (see Table 7.1), but it contains a higher proportion of first-rate composers. Italian opera continued to flourish under Anna's successor Elizabeth, who signaled her fondness for modern, galant music by having Johann Adolf Hasse's *La clemenza di Tito* (The Clemency of Titus) performed at her coronation in 1740. But it was not until the accession of Catherine the Great that St. Petersburg entered a true golden age of opera.

Figure 12.2: *Bartolomeo Rastrelli's Church of the Resurrection at the Smolny Convent, St. Petersburg, 1748–64*

Table 12.1: *Composers of Italian opera and opéra comique serving as music directors in St. Petersburg*

COMPOSER	TENURE
Francesco Araia	1735–1758
Vincenzo Manfredini	1762–1765
Baldassare Galuppi	1765–1768
Tommaso Traetta	1768–1775
Giovanni Paisiello	1776–1783
Giuseppe Sarti	1784–1786
Domenico Cimarosa	1787–1791
Vicente Martín y Soler	1790–1794
Giuseppe Sarti	1793–1801
François Adrien Boieldieu	1803–1810
Daniel Steibelt	1810–1823

CATHERINE THE GREAT AS OPERATIC PATRON

Catherine reigned from 1762 to 1796. She joined the ranks of highly educated, intellectually curious, and artistically adventurous monarchs so characteristic of our period. Born in Germany and fluent in French as well as Russian, she stayed closely in touch with developments in the capitals of western Europe by voracious reading and private correspondence with several leading writers and artists. Although she professed (perhaps in imitation of Peter the Great) a lack of musical knowledge and understanding, her actions spoke louder than her words.

Catherine invited from Paris a troupe that performed the latest opéras comiques as well as spoken comedies. The court and the aristocracy especially liked opéra comique, which brought together Italianate music with a language that Russians were more familiar with than Italian. Opéra comique served as the principal model for opera in Russian, as it had for Singspiel in Germany (see Chapter 9). One of the earliest Russian operas with spoken dialogue was *Anyuta*, based on a comedy by the French playwright Charles-Simon Favart, performed in 1772. Catherine herself, by writing several librettos in Russian, played a role in the early development of Russian opera.

In her patronage of Italian opera, Catherine brought excellent composers into an environment that encouraged them to do extraordinary work. She replaced Araia and Vincenzo Manfredini—no more than competent musicians— with several of Italy's leading composers. Lured by high salaries, they took turns in making the long journey to Russia, where they found an audience intensely aware of the latest artistic developments in Paris, London, Vienna, and Berlin. They also found a uniquely Russian musical tradition: choral singing fostered by the Russian Orthodox Church. "I have never heard such a magnificent choir in Italy," exclaimed Baldassare Galuppi.

Among the cultural developments in western Europe that Catherine read about was the attempt being made during the 1760s in several European capitals (as discussed in Chapter 8) to unite the vocal virtuosity and melodic charm of Italian music with French operatic spectacle, especially as embodied in dance and chorus. Tommaso Traetta's innovative operas in Parma and Vienna, Christoph Gluck's *Orfeo ed Euridice* (first performed a few months after Catherine came to power; see Chapter 8), and Niccolò Jommelli's novelties in Stuttgart must have stimulated much curiosity in St. Petersburg. In engaging Traetta in 1768, Catherine placed her capital at the cutting edge of European opera.

TRAETTA'S *ANTIGONA*

Tommaso Traetta (1727–1779) was probably as impressed as Galuppi by the chorus he had at his disposal. In one of his first productions for St. Petersburg, he revised his earlier setting of Pietro Metastasio's *L'Olimpiade* (The Olympiad) by adding new choruses, sung by 50 members of the imperial chapel. Choristers trained to sing a cappella sacred music in Church Slavonic (the ancient language of the Orthodox liturgy) were now singing Italian words—in the service of a synthesis of Italian vocal display and French spectacle.

In 1772 a librettist and a singer with whom Traetta had previously worked in some of Europe's most creative theatrical centers arrived in St. Petersburg. The librettist, Marco Coltellini, had collaborated with Traetta on *Ifigenia in Tauride* (Iphigenia in Tauris; Vienna, 1763). The singer, Caterina Gabrielli (whose career we followed in Chapter 4), had created several important roles for Traetta in Parma and Vienna. This alignment of theatrical stars—like the similar constellation in Vienna a decade earlier—produced several important operas, including *Antigona* (Antigone), first performed at the Imperial Theater on November 11, 1772.

Based on a tragedy by Sophocles, *Antigona* takes place in the aftermath of a duel between two royal brothers, Eteocles and Polynices. They had agreed to share power; but when Eteocles claimed the throne for himself, Polynices tried to take it by force. The opera opens with a pantomime depicting the duel, which results in the death of both brothers. Creon, the new king, orders that Eteocles be given a hero's funeral but that Polynices, as the aggressor, should be left unburied. Antigone, the dead men's sister, protests, but without success. The ensuing drama follows Antigone as she strengthens her revolve to organize and preside over the funeral of Polynices in secret (Act 1); carries out her plan, confesses her deed, and is sentenced to death by Creon (Act 2); faces her punishment and is about to die when Creon is moved to pity and forgives her (Act 3; the happy ending is a typically eighteenth-century variation on a story that in Sophocles ends with the heroine's suicide).

The opera placed Gabrielli, as Antigone, at the center of the action and exploited all her dramatic and musical abilities. Largely built of big set pieces involving dance and choral music as well as solo song, the opera displays Traetta's powers at their prime.

Singer and composer contributed equally to the first scene in Act 3, in which preparations are made for Antigone to be buried alive, the people of Thebes bewail her approaching death, her sister Ismene begs to be killed along with her, and Antigone declares herself ready and willing to die. The scene opens with a chorus, *Piangi, o Tebe* (Weep, Thebes), in the minor mode and full of intense dissonance (see Anthology 16). Antigone makes her first speech, *O Tebe, o cittadini* (Oh Thebes, oh citizens), in orchestrally accompanied recitative. Ismene, before being forcibly separated from her sister, expresses her desperation in a frantic aria. Antigone, in contrast, approaches death with resignation—she even welcomes it, as it will finally end her suffering—and bids farewell to her compatriots. The tonal instability and irregular phrase structure of her long orchestrally accompanied recitative find resolution in the tender melody of *Non piangete i casi miei* (Do not bewail my fate), an aria that made the most of Gabrielli's ability to sing not only spectacular coloratura but lyrical lines of great simplicity and emotional power. The chorus recapitulates its monumental lament, *Piangi, o Tebe*, while Antigone approaches the cave that is to serve as her tomb.

PAISIELLO'S *IL BARBIERE DI SIVIGLIA*

Traetta left Russia in 1775, soon to be replaced by the considerably younger Giovanni Paisiello (1740–1816), who first appeared in St. Petersburg at a concert at court. Like the concerts at Mannheim when its famous orchestra was on display, this occasion involved card playing and conversation. Yet Paisiello managed to attract attention to himself and his music. Melchior Grimm, a German intellectual who lived in Paris and who kept Catherine informed of cultural developments in the French capital, was visiting St. Petersburg when Paisiello made his appearance. He wrote:

> The empress, who is not passionately fond of music, was struck singularly by the vigor of his style and the novelty of his ideas. The grand duke and grand duchess, and the entire court, were enchanted and people clapped hands in the throne room as if at a public spectacle. After the first piece and after Paisiello kissed the empress's hand she began to play cards but she deputized the grand equerry and other messengers of the kind to make the most agreeable compliments to him, and as she forbade me to approach her table for fear of distracting me from the music, she later deputized me in addition as an ambassador to compliment him on his success, so general and so complete.

Paisiello composed mostly serious operas during his first three years in St. Petersburg. But with a comedy that he wrote for a newly formed opera buffa company in 1779, *I filosofi immaginari* (The Imaginary Philosophers), he achieved a new level of success. Catherine expressed delight in a letter to Grimm:

> The more I see it the more astonished I am at his singular control of tone and sounds. Even a cough becomes harmonious and full of sublime follies. You cannot guess how this magician makes even less sensitive ears, like mine, pay attention to the music. I leave the performance with my head full of music; I can recognize and almost sing his composition. Oh what an extraordinary head is Paisiello's! I have ordered the score transcribed for you, who will find it full of sublime things. It passes understanding.

Remarkable praise, coming from someone who repeatedly denigrated her own musicality. Paisiello's music, Catherine discovered, made her a more sophisticated and perceptive listener; it made her newly aware of the dramatic possibilities of musical theater. She recognized and appreciated a special quality in his comedy that she found lacking in his serious operas.

Paisiello's success with comic opera made him regret the absence in St. Petersburg of a first-rate Italian librettist to work with on future projects. He tried to commission a libretto from the Neapolitan poet Giovanni Battista Lorenzi, specifying in a letter the maximum number of acts (two), the maximum number and the types of singers for which he intended to compose the opera, and insisting that recitative should be kept short because his audience in St. Petersburg did not understand Italian. Lorenzi apparently did not send a libretto. When, about a year and a half later, Paisiello brought his masterpiece *Il barbiere di Siviglia* (The Barber of Seville) to the stage, it was with an anonymous libretto to which he himself may have contributed.

The lack of an Italian librettist in St. Petersburg was not the only unusual condition under which Paisiello transformed Pierre-Augustin Caron de Beaumarchais' celebrated play *Le barbier de Séville* into a scintillating comic opera in 1782. In the libretto printed for the first production, both the composer and the unnamed librettist, addressing the empress, referred to the opera's brevity. Paisiello wrote: "Madame! *Le barbier de Séville* having been enjoyed by Your Imperial Majesty, I thought this same play could not displease you in the form of an Italian opera. I have therefore made an extract of the play, which I have tried to make as short as possible while preserving (insofar as the special character of Italian poetry allows) the contents of the original, without adding anything." Someone identifying himself as "the translator" added: "If in translating [the French play] I shortened it, I did so only to adapt myself to the taste of this imperial court, in the hope that the music would compensate for the beauty of the scenes that I had to omit to make the performance as short as possible."

The libretto follows Beaumarchais' play closely, which accounts for its unconventional structure of four short acts, only the third and fourth of which end with finales. The story takes place in the Spanish city of Seville, where Count Almaviva (tenor) has fallen in love with Rosina (soprano), the ward of Bartolo (bass), a rich old doctor who wants to marry her himself and tries to keep other possible suitors away. Almaviva disguises himself as a poor young man, so that if Rosina agrees to marry him it will not be for his title and wealth. With the help of the clever barber Figaro (bass) and liberal disbursements of cash, Almaviva finds his way to Rosina. Having won her love, he reveals his identity; Bartolo is forced to give up Rosina and bless the marriage.

Paisiello's opera combined brevity and musical elaboration. It reduced the dialogue in recitative and kept the number of arias to a minimum; several arias and ensembles are shorter than normal. This concision allowed Paisiello to be occasionally expansive. Several times he abandoned the opera's rapid dramatic pace to luxuriate in long moments of lyrical beauty, most of which are associated with Rosina—such as her aria *Giusto ciel* (Just heaven) at the end of Act 2 and the aria she sings during her music lesson (with Almaviva disguised as her teacher),

Già riede primavera (Spring is smiling). These numbers are expansive not only in length but also in instrumental color, with pairs of clarinets and bassoons in dialogue with each other and with the strings in *Giusto ciel* and the warm spring breezes in *Già riede primavera* depicted by clarinet and bassoon solos.

The opera's combination of elaboration and concision are on display at the end, when Almaviva has won Rosina's love, but obstacles still stand in their way. Rosina, on learning that a letter she wrote to the man she knows as Lindoro was delivered to Count Almaviva, believes that Lindoro courted her only to procure her for a nobleman. When Almaviva (still pretending to be Lindoro) arrives to take Rosina away, she accuses him of treachery. He finally identifies himself, tossing off his cloak and, to Rosina's astonishment, revealing a magnificent suit. That *coup de théâtre* signals the beginning of the finale.

The finale was one of opera buffa's most important contributions to European musical dramaturgy. Invented in Italy around the middle of the eighteenth century, the finale is an ensemble at the end of an act that depicts a series of events by means of several passages differing in tempo, meter, key, and orchestration, and yet closely linked in a single movement that coheres musically as well as dramatically. By the 1780s finales were often enormously long, but *Il barbiere di Siviglia* ends with a relatively short one (see Anthology 17).

MUSIC AND THE NOBILITY: NICHOLAS AND PRASCOVIA

In Russia as in western Europe, the aristocracy imitated the court. The richest noble families of St. Petersburg built splendid residences in much the same style as the imperial palaces. Some of the noble houses contained theaters for the performance of the same kinds of plays and operas admired at court. The nobility derived much of its wealth from huge numbers of serfs who farmed its land. Some of these serfs also served as theatrical craftsmen, artists, and musicians.

The Sheremetevs, the richest of the Russian noble families, owned 200,000 serfs. Count Nicholas Sheremetev (1751–1809) experienced Italian and French opera during a Grand Tour in the early 1770s. He returned to Russia with several trunks filled with musical scores. To teach his serfs to act, sing, dance, and play in his orchestra, he engaged a German violinist, a French singing teacher, a teacher of French and Italian, several European ballet masters, and a Russian choir director. They supervised performances in private theaters at several Sheremetev residences.

Although Nicholas's repertory of more than 50 operas included some by Russian composers, most of the works he presented were French *opéras comiques* in Russian translation. When Nicholas had André Grétry's *Les mariages samnites* (The Samnite Marriages) performed during a visit by Empress Catherine, the language in which it was sung caused a French diplomat to think it was a Russian

opera with music by a serf, but his account did not otherwise exaggerate the role
that serfs played in the production:

> A Russian grand opera was performed in a beautiful theater; everyone who
> understood the libretto found it interesting and well written. I could judge
> only the music and the ballets; the former astonished me with its harmo-
> nious melody, the latter by the elegant richness of the costumes, the grace
> of the ballerinas, and the quickness of the male dancers. What seemed
> almost inconceivable to me was that the librettist and the composer who
> wrote the opera, the architect who built the theater, the painter who deco-
> rated it, the actors and actresses of the opera, the dancers both male and fe-
> male, and the musicians in the orchestra are all Count Sheremetev's serfs.

The star of Nicholas's troupe was the serf soprano Prascovia Ivanovna
Kovalyova (1768–1803), the daughter of a blacksmith. She made her debut in
1779, at the age of 11. Impressed by her beauty and talent, Nicholas soon gave her
leading roles. During the 1780s and 1790s she was one of Russia's finest singers,
winning special admiration for her portrayal of Eliane in *Les mariages samnites*,
which she sang from 1785 to 1797 (Fig. 12.3).

Figure 12.3: *The serf soprano Prascovia
Ivanovna Kovalyova in the role of Eliane in
André Grétry's* Les mariages samnites

The count, taking advantage of the almost absolute power with which he controlled his serfs, slept with several of his female singers, including Prascovia. But the same system that condoned such exploitation also forbade a master to marry a serf. When Nicholas fell in love with her, the only course open to him was to make her his mistress. In 1797 illness (probably tuberculosis) forced her to leave the stage. With the end of her career, Nicholas lost interest in opera and disbanded his troupe. He gave Prascovia an apartment in his palace in St. Petersburg and finally, in 1801, married her in a secret ceremony. Although he freed her from serfdom before the wedding, his relations with a former serf and a former singer scandalized his friends and family, many of whom abandoned him. Prascovia died a year after the wedding, and a few weeks after giving birth to a son, at the age of 34. Nicholas, one of the richest men in St. Petersburg, to whose operas and concerts the nobility had flocked for years, was left practically alone to grieve.

GIUSEPPE SARTI, DMITRY BORTNIANSKY, AND RUSSIAN CHURCH MUSIC

Although Catherine brought Italian composers to Russia primarily to write operas, some also wrote music for the Russian Orthodox Church. An Italian particularly well prepared for the composition of church music was Giuseppe Sarti (1729–1802), who had served as music director for the Cathedral of Milan before coming to Russia in 1784. In Russia he found a tradition of sacred music restricted to a cappella singing, in this respect different from most of what he knew in Italy. But he skillfully adapted the mixture of learned and galant idioms typical of modern European sacred music to the unaccompanied choral singing of Russian Orthodoxy.

Sarti composed *Nïne silï nebesnïya* (Now the powers of heaven) for the Liturgy of the Presanctified Gifts, a ceremony unique to the period of Lent. What in the terminology of western European music might be called a motet, *Nïne silï nebesnïya* accompanies the Great Entrance—the solemn moment when the sanctified Host (bread miraculously transformed into the body of Christ) is carried to the main altar in preparation for Communion.

Working in a language that must have been completely unfamiliar to him before coming to Russia, and in a liturgy different from that of Catholicism, Sarti managed to bring the text to life. The opening section, with its emphasis on the minor mode, slowly moving harmonies, and intense dissonances, evokes the mystery of transubstantiation. The sopranos' repeated ascent up to A is a stunning depiction of heaven (Ex. 12.1). Sarti declaimed the word "king" (*tsar*) in massive chords, while he conveyed the idea of "glory" (*slavi*) in a sudden outburst of melismatic counterpoint in the major mode.

Example 12.1: *Giuseppe Sarti, Nïne sili nebesnïya, mm. 1–9*

Now the powers of heaven serve invisibly with us

The second part begins with a respite from the high drama of the Great Entrance. It takes the form of a dialogue: the four lowest voices repeatedly declaim "pristupim" (let us draw near), while the sopranos, mostly in parallel thirds, sing "veroyu i lyuboviyu" (in faith and love). The gentle lyricism of this passage sets the stage, in turn, for the brilliant Alleluia with which the motet ends.

The Ukrainian Dmitry Bortniansky (1751–1825) sang in the Imperial Chapel as a boy, studied composition with Galuppi, and spent several years in Italy. In 1779 he returned to St. Petersburg, where he composed opera and church music and in 1796 became the first director of the Imperial Chapel born within the Russian Empire. His large output of a cappella choral music formed the foundation for the nineteenth-century repertory of the Orthodox Church. Both his career and his music exemplify the interaction of Russian and western European (particularly Italian) musical culture that also produced Sarti's liturgical music. When Hector Berlioz visited St. Petersburg in 1847, he heard the Imperial Chapel singing music by Bortniansky; his ecstatic description of the performance (quoted by Walter Frisch in Chapter 5 of *Music in the Nineteenth Century*) suggests something of the effect that *Nïne silï nebesnïya* might have produced in its liturgical context.

THE RUSSIAN HORN BAND

Composers from western Europe or Russians under the influence of European music composed most of the music referred to in this chapter. A uniquely Russian kind of instrumental music also flourished during our period, but it too had its origins in the work of a foreigner. Around 1750 Jan Antonín Mareš (1719–1794), a Bohemian hornist in the employ of a Russian prince, took advantage of two things he found in Russia: a virtually unlimited supply of cheap labor, and the *Rog*, a horn (often made of wood) that had long been used to communicate among hunters in the Russian woods. Mareš constructed a set of *Rog*-like horns, each producing only a single note. These instruments, made of brass or wood, came to be known as Russian horns. Mareš taught some of the prince's serfs to play them, with each player responsible for a single pitch. The prince liked the sound, and soon noblemen all over Russia formed horn bands, ranging in size from 30 to 60 players (Fig. 12.4).

Figure 12.4: *A Russian horn band, with the longest instruments (on the right) supported by a horizontal rail*

A French traveler in St. Petersburg near the end of Catherine's reign recognized the horn band, in its dependence on serfdom, as a distinctively Russian institution. Although he admired the ensemble's sound, he could not help thinking of the extreme inequality of the society in which such music-making was possible. He particularly disliked the idea of men counting vast numbers of rests, waiting for their chance to play a single note and without any chance to play a melody: "I doubt that it would be possible to establish this strange ensemble outside of Russia, because it would be difficult to find fifty men willing to sacrifice their life to the playing of a single note on a horn. . . . For such precision could only be demanded from an automaton, an organ pipe, or a slave." But another French visitor, the painter Elisabeth Vigée Lebrun, felt no such scruples when she heard a horn band in St. Petersburg in 1795. Invited to a nobleman's villa outside the city, she enjoyed the view from a terrace overlooking the Neva and the "delightful instrumental music" that sounded throughout dinner: "I was greatly surprised when Count Stroganov informed me that each of the musicians played but one note; it was impossible for me to conceive how all these individual sounds could form into such a perfect whole, and how any expression could grow out of such a mechanical performance."

JOHN FIELD'S FORWARD-LOOKING PIANO MUSIC

As St. Petersburg's wealth and musical sophistication increased, so did the number of leading instrumental virtuosos willing to make the long trip to Russia, and sometimes even to settle there. Among those who stayed the longest and contributed the most to its musical life was the Irish pianist and composer John Field (1782–1837).

Born in Dublin, Field made such rapid progress on the piano that at the age of ten he played a concerto in public. Shortly thereafter he moved with his family to London. His father apprenticed him to the pianist and composer Muzio Clementi (1752–1832), who was also active in the instrument-selling and music-publishing businesses. Field paid for his lessons by demonstrating pianos in Clementi's showroom, presumably playing music that his master had for sale. Under Clementi's guidance he blossomed as a composer; he was just 16 when he played a concerto of his own composition in 1799.

In 1803 Clementi took Field with him on a business trip that included a visit to St. Petersburg. The young virtuoso charmed the Russian court and nobility. When Clementi returned to England, Field stayed in Russia. For the next 20 years he lived mostly in St. Petersburg and Moscow, teaching and playing in the nobility's musical salons.

Field developed in Russia a pianistic style of unsurpassed grace and elegance—characteristics he distilled in his nocturnes, the compositions for

Example 12.2: *John Field, Nocturne No. 5 in B♭ Major, mm. 1–8*

which he is most famous. He helped to establish this genre by applying the word (hitherto used for several different musical genres, not all of them for piano) to a particular kind of melancholy, lyrical piano piece in slow to moderate tempo, in which the right hand spins out a melody over an arpeggiated accompaniment, as in the Nocturne No. 5 in B♭ Major, published in St. Petersburg in 1817 (Ex. 12.2). The nocturne is a typically Romantic genre that Frédéric Chopin would take up and develop in the middle of the nineteenth century (see Chapter 6 of Walter Frisch's book). In publishing his first three nocturnes in St. Petersburg in 1812, near the end of the period covered by this book, Field helped to open a new epoch in the history of European keyboard music.

The women who ruled Russia after Peter the Great differed from him (and more closely resembled rulers in western Europe) in using music to project an image of wealth and power. Under the empresses Anna, Elizabeth, and Catherine the Great, St. Petersburg vied with London, Berlin, and Vienna in the cultivation of Italian opera. The resulting interaction of Italian and Russian culture was productive. Like its exuberant churches and palaces, the operas written for St. Petersburg were mostly created by foreigners. But Italian composers did not limit themselves to opera; some of them contributed to the rich literature of sacred music for the Orthodox Church.

The empress's patronage whetted the aristocracy's musical appetite. Russian noblemen, many of whom owned hundreds of serfs, trained some of them to be singers, dancers, and instrumentalists—a development that reached its zenith in Count Sheremetev's theaters and the triumph of Prascovia. Russia's vast supply of cheap labor led to the development of one of its most distinctive musical phenomena: a horn band in which each musician played a single pitch. In satisfying the Russian nobility's thirst for the most up-to-date piano music, John Field wrote the nocturnes that constitute one of the foundations of the nineteenth century's keyboard repertory.

FOR FURTHER READING

Figes, Orlando, *Natasha's Dance: A Cultural History of Russia* (New York: Holt, 2002)

Heartz, Daniel, *Music in European Capitals: The Galant Style, 1720–1780* (New York: W. W. Norton, 2003), 929–64

Lincoln, W. Bruce, *Sunlight at Midnight: St. Petersburg and the Rise of Modern Russia* (New York: Basic Books, 2002)

Massie, Robert K., *Catherine the Great: Portrait of a Woman* (New York: Random House, 2011)

Naroditskaya, Inna, *Bewitching Russian Opera: The Tsarina from State to Stage* (New York: Oxford University Press, 2011)

Ricks, Robert, "Russian Horn Bands," *Musical Quarterly* 55 (1969): 364–71

Ritzarev, Marina, *Eighteenth-Century Russian Music* (Aldershot: Ashgate, 2006)

Smith, Douglas, *The Pearl: A Tale of Forbidden Love in Catherine the Great's Russia* (New Haven, CT: Yale University Press, 2008)

Ⓢ **Additional resources available at wwnorton.com/studyspace**

CHAPTER THIRTEEN

Foreigners in Paris

Gluck, Mozart, Salieri, Cherubini

During the years leading up to, during, and following the French Revolution (1789–99), music in Paris benefited greatly from the work of composers born elsewhere. But not all of the talented foreigners who came to Paris succeeded equally in dealing with the complex and rigid institutional framework (discussed in Chapter 6) of French musical life. Some of those who achieved success under one set of political conditions were unable to repeat that success when conditions changed. This chapter examines the experiences in Paris of four foreigners during the last 30 years of the eighteenth century, each of whom contributed significantly yet differently to music in the French capital.

GLUCK AT THE OPÉRA

In 1770 the dauphin (crown prince) Louis—the future King Louis XVI—married Archduchess Marie Antoinette of Austria (daughter of Empress Maria Theresa and sister of Emperor Joseph II). The wedding initiated a period in which musicians associated with the Viennese court played an important role in French musical life. Christoph Gluck (1714–1787), whose early life and contributions

to Viennese music we have already considered in Chapter 8, knew Marie Antoinette personally and may even have given her some lessons. With the operas
he wrote for Paris in the 1770s, under her patronage, he transformed French
musical theater as dramatically as *Orfeo ed Euridice* had reformed Italian opera
a decade earlier.

Around the same time as Marie Antoinette's marriage to the dauphin, Gluck
began working with a French diplomat in Vienna, François Roullet, on *a tragédie
lyrique, Iphigénie en Aulide* (Iphigenia in Aulis). The librettist asked the Opéra
to consider it for performance. Its initial rejection—causing a minor uproar in
Paris as journalists and pamphleteers argued over the opera's merits—was soon
overturned when Marie Antoinette's wishes gave the edge to Gluck's partisans.
The successful staging of *Iphigénie en Aulide* in 1774 led to the composition of
several more operas in which Gluck brought a lifetime of operatic experience
into a fruitful marriage with the rich traditions and ample resources of the
Opéra.

Gluck confronted and embraced those traditions most dramatically in
Armide, based on a libretto by Philippe Quinault that Jean-Baptiste Lully had
set to music almost a century earlier. Lully's opera, one of the mainstays of the
Parisian stage, had been performed into the 1760s (see Fig. 6.2). Gluck's *Armide*
pays homage to Lully and Quinault, but it also demonstrates the distance that sep-
arates the musical style of the 1680s from that of the 1770s, and the strength
and distinctiveness of Gluck's musical and theatrical personality.

One of more than 100 operas and ballets based on the story of Armida
and Rinaldo, as told by Torquato Tasso in his epic poem *Gerusalemme liberata*
(Jerusalem Liberated) of 1581, Gluck's *Armide* takes place during the First
Crusade. Armide, a Moslem sorceress, uses magic and feminine allure to defeat
the Christian knights who hope to conquer the Holy Land. Only one knight, the
handsome Renaud, can resist her power; he robs her of victory by freeing the
Christian prisoners she has taken. Armide, finding Renaud alone, causes him
to fall into a magic sleep. But when she approaches him with the intention of
stabbing him to death, she cannot bring herself to do so. Overcome with love,
she uses her magic powers to make Renaud fall in love with her and to transport
them both to "the end of the universe." There, in an enchanted palace, they live
in a state of erotic bliss—but not for long. Christian knights come in search of
Renaud; they successfully fend off monsters sent by Armide and demons who
take the form of seductive women. Finding Renaud momentarily alone, they
persuade him to leave Armide and rejoin the Christian forces. Armide pleads in
vain for him to stay. Alone, she drives off in a chariot pulled by dragons and calls
on her demons to destroy the palace.

Gluck mobilized all the musical and scenic resources of the Opéra to transform
this story into an opera remarkable for its sense of continuity and forward
momentum. Orchestrally accompanied recitatives, arias, ensembles, choruses,

and dances follow one another in a seemingly unstoppable succession. Gluck's music conveys triumphant joy, painful indecision, passionate love, heartfelt pity, and extreme rage with equal vividness.

An example of both continuity and expressive intensity is Armide's monologue at the end of Act 2, *Enfin, il est en ma puissance* (At last he is in my power). This scene must have been especially familiar to Gluck's audience because Lully's setting of the same words had been the object of a famous debate in the 1750s between Jean-Philippe Rameau (who praised Lully's music) and Jean-Jacques Rousseau (who rejected it). As Armide approaches the sleeping Renaud with dagger in hand, the orchestra depicts her excitement and lethal single-mindedness with energetic music in A minor. A few moments into her recitative, rapid ascending scales correspond to her aggressive gestures: she is about to strike. But soon another motive, *legato* and *piano*, hints that Renaud's sleeping face exerts its own magical power over Armide, which keeps her from killing him (Ex. 13.1a).

Example 13.1: *Christoph Gluck,* Armide, Enfin, il est en ma puissance

(a) *mm. 10–19*

At last he is in my power, this deadly enemy, this proud conqueror. Sleep's charm delivers him to my vengeance. I will pierce his invincible heart.

(b) *mm. 49–57*

How cruel it would be to take his life!

The motive associated with Renaud's beauty dominates the first part of Armide's aria *Ah! quelle cruauté de lui ravir le jour* (How cruel it would be to take his life), in which she decides to enchant him into falling in love with her (Ex. 13.1b). Her melody begins with a beautifully ornamented version of a melodic-harmonic schema—a descent from the fifth scale degree down to the third over I–V–I harmony—that eighteenth-century composers used often. In the Andante that follows, she summons demons to transform themselves into gentle breezes and carry Renaud and her away. The constant syncopations and triplet figures in the accompaniment depict the wind that Armide conjures up. In a magnificent postlude—one of the great act endings in all opera—the orchestra uses these same motives in a sonic evocation of Armide's magic flight.

Throughout the scene, modal shifts reflect Armide's changing—and partly suppressed—feelings toward Renaud. The aria begins in E minor (see Ex. 13.1b), but in the course of a six-measure orchestral introduction it modulates to G major—and that is the key in which this part of the aria ends, creating a strong association in listeners' minds between G major and Armide's love. In the final Andante, a binary movement in E minor, we expect the first half of the structure to end in G major (the relative major) or B minor (the dominant). Instead it ends in D (the dominant of G major), as if G major (associated with love) serves as a kind of implied tonic, hidden behind the veil of E minor.

MOZART IN PARIS'S SALONS AND CONCERT ROOMS

The young Mozart (1756–1791) visited Paris on three separate occasions. Traveling through Europe on their protracted Grand Tour of 1763–66, the Mozart family lived in the French capital from November 1763 to April 1764 and again from May to July 1766. Wolfgang returned with his mother 12 years later, living and working in Paris from March to September 1778.

On their arrival in Paris in 1763, seven-year-old Wolfgang and his twelve-year-old sister Nannerl (also a gifted pianist) quickly immersed themselves in private music-making. The death of La Pouplinière (the rich tax farmer we met in Chapter 6) a year earlier had removed from the scene one of the city's most generous and energetic patrons, but many other musical salons opened their doors to the Mozarts. Music lovers showered the children with presents—gold snuffboxes, a gold toothpick case, a gold watch, a silver writing case, a ring, all eagerly collected and enumerated by their father Leopold—in exchange for their performances.

A painting of Mozart at the keyboard in the residence of the Prince of Conti conveys the character of the salons in which he and Nannerl appeared (Fig. 13.1). While Mozart and two or three other musicians play, about 16 of the prince's elegantly dressed guests divide their attention between music, tea, and conversation. For a good idea of the kind of music that Mozart played on such occasions we can turn to his first published works, the sonatas for keyboard and violin, K. 6–9. Paris was Europe's capital of music printing and publishing. In publishing Wolfgang's sonatas there, Leopold took advantage of the city's preeminence in this important aspect of musical culture, just as Luigi Boccherini was doing around the same time (see Chapter 5).

When Mozart returned to Paris in 1778, he was no longer a child prodigy playing for valuable trinkets but a mature artist in search of commissions and

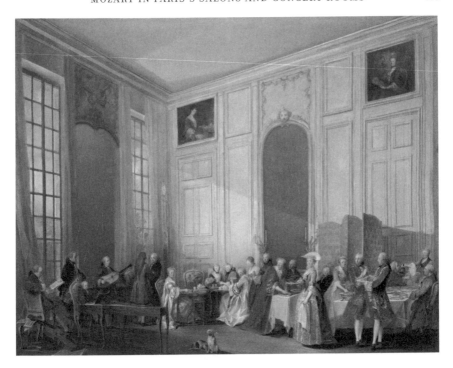

Figure 13.1: *The child Mozart performing at a Parisian salon. Painting by Michel-Barthélémy Ollivier.*

employment. He found commissions but no position. His most useful contact was Jean Le Gros, director of the Concert Spirituel, who asked him to write several works for the venerable concert series.

In composing a symphony for Le Gros (K. 297, known as the *Paris* Symphony), Mozart took care to appeal to French taste. A wretched rehearsal left him worried that the performance would be a failure. But his fear was unfounded. He wrote to his father: "In the middle of the first Allegro there was a passage that I felt sure must please. The audience was quite carried away—and there was a tremendous burst of applause. But as I knew, when I wrote it, what effect it would surely produce, I had introduced the passage again at the close—where there were shouts of 'Da Capo.'"

Mozart probably referred here to the thrilling musical fireworks in the exposition's closing material, where he presented the movement's opening motive in diminution and in imitation between winds and bass, while the violins, playing *tremolo*, sustain an A-major chord (Ex. 13.2). In taking credit for repeating this passage near the end of the movement, he was disingenuous, as sonata form all but required him to do so. He continued:

The Andante also found favor, but particularly the last Allegro, because, having observed that all last as well as first Allegros begin here with all the instruments playing together and generally *unisono*, I began mine with two violins only, *piano* for the first eight bars—followed instantly by a *forte*; the audience, as I expected, said "hush" at the soft beginning, and when they heard the *forte*, began at once to clap their hands. I was so happy that as soon as the symphony was over, I went off to the Palais Royal, where I had a large ice, said the Rosary as I had vowed to do, and went home.

Mozart did not call attention to another important concession to Parisian taste: his decision to write his symphony in three movements (without a minuet) acknowledged the popularity of three-movement symphonies in Paris in the 1770s (whereas most Austrian composers, following the example set by Haydn in symphonies such as those discussed in Chapter 10, favored the four-movement symphony).

Also for the Concert Spirituel, Mozart wrote a symphonie concertante (a concerto for more than one solo instrument) for flute, oboe, bassoon, and horn. It does not survive, but the work known today as the Concerto for Flute and Harp, K. 299, which he wrote for a Parisian nobleman, is really a symphonie concertante; it testifies vividly to the charm and brilliance that this typically French kind of concerto inspired in Mozart. He did not write the greatest of his "French" works, the Symphonie Concertante for Violin and Viola, K. 364, until he returned to Salzburg.

Although Mozart thought about composing an opera for Paris, he did not do so. Like many other visitors to France, he disliked the distinctively French style of singing and vocal composition. He wrote to his father: "What annoys me most of all in this business [of composing for French audiences] is that our French gentlemen have only improved their *goût* [taste] to this extent: that they can now listen to good stuff as well. But to expect them to realize that their own music is

Example 13.2: *Wolfgang Amadeus Mozart, Symphony No. 31 in D Major, K. 297, movement 1, mm. 93–96*

bad or at least to notice the difference—Heaven preserve us! And their singing! Good Lord! Let me never hear a Frenchwoman singing Italian arias. I can forgive her if she screeches out her French trash, but not if she ruins good music! It's simply unbearable."

In addition to his antipathy to French vocal music, two barriers—one institutional, one emotional—discouraged Mozart from writing an opera for Paris. First, the Opéra operated under rules that made it difficult for foreign composers to win commissions. It was only after an energetic publicity campaign by his supporters—and a friend at the highest levels of the court—that Gluck had gained access to the Opéra in 1774. Second, Mozart was in love with a young German singer, Aloysia Weber, whom he hoped to transform into an opera seria star. He dreamed of traveling with her to Italy and of writing Italian operas for her. That dream left no place in his mind or heart for *tragédie lyrique*.

ANTONIO SALIERI AND *LES DANAÏDES*

Antonio Salieri (1750–1825), later to become Mozart's operatic rival in Vienna, was in a better position than Mozart to overcome the obstacles that faced foreign musicians hoping for operatic success in Paris. As Gluck's protégé and a favorite of Emperor Joseph II, he received the help of both in getting his foot in the Parisian operatic door. His first French opera, *Les Danaïdes* (The Danaids), began as a commission for Gluck, who may have started to write the music, with Salieri assisting him in preparing the score. But at some point their roles changed: Salieri became the composer, Gluck his advisor. Taking advantage of Gluck's record of success in Paris, they presented the finished opera as mostly the work of Gluck. Only after it was successfully performed in April 1784 did Gluck claim that Salieri had written the entire opera, thus allowing the younger composer to take full credit for its success. Salieri dedicated the printed score to Marie Antoinette, in gratitude for her support in bringing the opera to the stage.

Based on a particularly gruesome Greek myth, *Les Danaïdes* takes its name from the 50 daughters of King Danaus. As the opera begins, Danaus swears an oath of friendship to the family of Egyptus, his brother and archenemy, whose eldest son, Lyncée, now leads the family. To seal their reconciliation, Lyncée and his 49 brothers are betrothed to the daughters of Danaus; Lyncée himself will wed his beloved Hypermnestre, eldest of the Danaids.

Alone with his daughters, Danaus reveals that the reconciliation is a trick; he orders them to kill their husbands on their wedding night. All except Hypermnestre agree to do so. The audience's knowledge of what lies ahead enhances the emotional tension of the wedding scene, for which Salieri composed much festive choral and dance music. The brilliance of that music contrasts effectively with the tenderness with which Hypermnestre and Lyncée interact in the few moments they have together. She reveals her father's plot, but not in time for Lyncée to save his brothers. The Danaids enter with bloody swords. Lyncée attacks the palace, slaughtering the Danaids and their father. The palace is destroyed, the ruins engulfed in flames.

The opera's final scene shows the Danaids imprisoned in the underworld and Danaus chained to a rock, his entrails devoured by a vulture, while a chorus of Furies promise eternal torment. The music combines the minor mode, syncopations, *sforzandi*, tremolos, diminished seventh chords, and full orchestra (including trombones) to produce an overwhelming evocation of horror.

This scene made a strong impression on William Bennett, an Englishman on the Grand Tour who attended a performance in 1785:

> The music loud and noisy in the French taste, and the singers screamed past all power of simile to represent. The scenery was very good, no people understanding the *jeu de theatre* or tricks of the stage, so well as the French. We had in the dark scenes not above one light, and in the bright ones above twenty large chandeliers, so as to make a wonderful contrast, nor was there the least error or blunder in changing the scenes, except once when a candle pulled up too hastily, was very near to setting fire to a whole grove of trees. The stage being deeper than ours, was filled sometimes with fifty persons, a great advantage to the Chorus's and bustling parts [scenes with much activity on stage]. Our Opera ended with a representation of Hell, in which the fifty Danaides were hauled and pulled about as if the Devils had been going to ravish them. Several of them in the violence of the French action being literally thrown flat upon their backs; and they were all at last buried in such a shower of fire, that I wonder the Playhouse was not burned to the ground.

This wonderful report, so expressive of the astonishment and delight that *tragédie lyrique* could arouse, contains yet another negative assessment of French singing. But we should probably attribute Bennett's discomfort to his unfamiliarity with the distinctive quality of vocal production at the Opéra rather than to any inherent defect in its singers.

LUIGI CHERUBINI AND THE FRENCH REVOLUTION

Luigi Cherubini (1760–1842) stands out among the relatively few foreign musicians who stayed in Paris during the Revolution and thrived in those tumultuous times. Born in Florence, he studied with Giuseppe Sarti, whose music for the Russian Orthodox Church we admired in Chapter 12. He came to Paris in 1786 and adapted quickly and expertly not only to its operatic traditions but also to the ever-changing, sometimes dangerous political situation.

Cherubini's first major patron in France was Marie Antoinette, who supported him as strongly as she had supported Gluck and Salieri. It was almost certainly through her that a team including Cherubini and the celebrated violinist Giovanni Battista Viotti (yet another of the queen's musical protégés) gained permission from King Louis XVI to form a company for the production of Italian comic operas in Paris, flouting the Opéra's old monopoly on the use of recitative in musical theater. The new troupe, with Cherubini as music director, made its debut in January of the fateful year of 1789. Its first home was the Théâtre de Monsieur, so named because it was located in the Tuileries Palace (see Fig. 6.1), the residence of the king's younger brother, the Count of Provence, whose traditional appellation was "Monsieur."

The Revolution broke out in July 1789 when a crowd stormed the Bastille, the state prison less than two miles from the Tuileries, killing its warden and several guards. During the political upheavals that followed, Cherubini's fate was intertwined with that of the French monarchy. He survived; it did not.

After the destruction of the Bastille the king and his family took refuge at Versailles, but in October rioters forced them to come to Paris and they were put under house arrest in the Tuileries. Cherubini's opera company had to vacate the palace, occupying a temporary home until, at the beginning of 1791, it moved to a new theater on the Rue Feydeau. It opened there with *Le nozze di Dorina* (The Marriage of Dorina), a comic opera by Cherubini's teacher Sarti. Six months later the royal family escaped from the Tuileries by night and attempted to flee; captured at Varennes, near the French border, they were brought back to Paris and imprisoned. Rising hostility toward the royal family caused the Théâtre de Monsieur to be renamed after the street on which it was located. The repertory of the Théâtre Feydeau, reflecting the increasing nationalism of the Revolution, shifted from Italian comic opera to opéra comique.

Cherubini produced his first opéra comique, *Lodoiska*, on July 18, 1791, less than a month after the arrest of Louis and Marie Antoinette at Varennes. It was an immediate hit with Parisian audiences, who recognized its effective use of opéra comique's mixture of spoken dialogue and orchestrally accompanied song in a drama that conveyed some of the ideals of its violent age. (Despite the genre's name, in this and many other opéras comiques of the 1790s, heroic and sentimental content superseded comedy.) Like several operas that followed, *Lodoiska* involves the rescue of a virtuous person from prison. It brings together characters from a wide spectrum of social classes, and it focuses the audience's admiration on characters who, regardless of their place in society, display generosity and heroism.

The Revolution gained strength. In September 1791 the king reluctantly accepted a constitution that took away most of his power, making France a constitutional monarchy. Following the wishes of those who wanted to export the Revolution to other parts of Europe, France declared war on its former ally Austria, initiating a period of intermittent conflict that would last until 1814. Lack of success on the battlefield led to riots and political repression. The Théâtre Feydeau was forced to shut down and Viotti fled to England. (We will meet him again in Chapter 16, performing with Haydn during that composer's second visit to London.) Cherubini also withdrew from Paris, but not nearly so far away. During much of 1792 and 1793 he lived quietly with a friend in Rouen, about 60 miles from the capital.

In September 1792 the National Assembly abolished the monarchy and declared France a republic. In January 1793 a new legislative body, the National Convention, condemned Louis to death; Marie Antoinette followed him to the guillotine in October 1793 (Fig. 13.2). Their deaths signaled the beginning of the most violent phase of the Revolution, the Reign of Terror, when Jacobins (radical revolutionaries) under the leadership of Maximilien Robespierre and his Committee of Public Safety put to death at least 1,200 people, mostly suspected of counter-revolutionary activities. In December 1793 the army launched its first attack against a royalist rebellion in the Vendée (a part of western France). The Reign of Terror ended in mid-1794 with the arrest and execution of Robespierre and the adoption of a new constitution. The stage was set for the rise of Napoleon, to be discussed in Chapter 17.

Cherubini, in the meantime, kept his head, figuratively and literally. He returned to Paris in the summer of 1793, in time to witness the Reign of Terror;

Figure 13.2: *Marie Antoinette, 37 years old, on the way to the guillotine. Drawing by Jacques-Louis David.*

he kept a low profile and, when the crisis ended, took advantage of the lack of musical leadership that it had left in its wake. The former beneficiary of Marie Antoinette's patronage established his republican credentials with patriotic works intended to be performed during political rallies: *Hymne à la fraternité*, *Hymne au Panthéon*, *Le salpêtre républicain* (to celebrate the opening of a salt-peter mine, for the production of gunpowder), and *Hymne et marche funèbre* (on the death of General Hoche, who had brutally suppressed the rebellion in the Vendée, killing many thousands).

Cherubini returned to the composition of opéra comique. With *Elisa, ou Le voyage au glaciers du Mont St-Bernard* (Elisa, or The Voyage to the Glaciers of Mount St. Bernard, 1794), he exploited a French fondness for operas with Alpine settings. With *Médée* (Medea, 1797) he put the generic conventions of opéra comique at the service of Greek tragedy. These operas did not only appeal to French audiences; translated into German, they were performed to great applause in much of the German-speaking part of Europe. Cherubini's international success as a composer of opéra comique illustrates the ability of this genre (and of Cherubini himself) to transcend national prejudices, even during a time of revolution and war.

CHERUBINI'S *LES DEUX JOURNÉES*

With *Les deux journées* (The Two Days, 1800), another rescue opera, Cherubini's popularity reached its zenith. The action takes place in Paris in the seventeenth century. Mikéli, the hero, has come to Paris with his family from the Alps, and makes a simple but honest living transporting water in a cart. Count Armand, leader of the French parliament, is being hunted down by the repressive forces of Cardinal Mazarin. He takes refuge in the house of Mikéli, who declares his humanitarian beliefs in *Guide mes pas, ô providence* (Guide my steps, oh Providence). At the end of a century that had associated operatic heroism with royalty and nobility, an aria in which a humble workingman prays earnestly for help in achieving a heroic deed must have struck audiences as novel and moving.

Act 2, which takes place at night, begins with an orchestral unison, *fortissimo*, followed immediately by a diminuendo in which the instruments stop playing in turn until only the double basses sound. Drawn into this near silence, the audience pays close attention as the strings play a *pianissimo* chromatic passage. In the complete silence that follows, a bell tolls in the distance. The ringing of a distant bell in the theater or concert hall appealed to the Romantic imagination: we hear it again in several works discussed by Walter Frisch in *Music in the Nineteenth Century*, including Berlioz's *Symphonie fantastique*, the Wolf's Glen scene in Carl Maria von Weber's *Der Freischütz*, and Giacomo Meyerbeer's *Les Huguenots*.

Later in the act, soldiers looking for Count Armand stop Mikéli, who has hidden Armand in his water barrel. Mikéli sends the soldiers on a wild goose

Example 13.3: *Luigi Cherubini,* Les deux journées, *finale of Act 2, mm. 209–220*

Flute, oboes, clarinets, bassoons, horns, strings

chase, and they run off to the sound of a festive march. Mikéli opens his barrel; Armand comes out and escapes. While this is happening, Cherubini repeats the march in various parts of the orchestra, first accompanying the voices of the departing soldiers as they anticipate their arrest of Armand, then without voices and *pianissimo*, to end the act (Ex. 13.3). The march begins with a pair of two-measure phrases, but then becomes more unbalanced and unpredictable, corresponding to the increasing consternation of the soldiers wandering off into the darkness on their fruitless search.

Queen Marie Antoinette, of whose musical childhood in Vienna we read in Chapter 8, played a role in the lives of all four of the musicians whose contributions to French music we have followed in this chapter. A consideration of them from her point of view dramatizes the differences in their experiences in Paris.

The 56-year-old Christoph Gluck, comfortably ensconced in Vienna, would probably not have entered the contentious world of the Opéra if an Austrian archduchess had not married the future king of France; and without her support such operas as *Armide* might not have achieved as much success as they did. Wolfgang Amadeus Mozart and Marie Antoinette, almost exactly the same age, had played together as children when the Mozart family visited Vienna in 1762, but in Paris Mozart never managed to parlay his personal connections to the queen into artistically satisfying and financially rewarding projects. Building on Gluck's achievements of the 1770s, and working with the vast musical and scenic resources of the Opéra, Mozart might have surpassed even Gluck in the composition of French opera. His failure to write an opera for Paris constitutes one of the great lost opportunities of his career, and is perhaps the most tantalizing "might-have-been" of eighteenth-century music.

With *Les Danaïdes* (the printed score of which he dedicated to Marie Antoinette), Antonio Salieri established himself as Gluck's Viennese successor at the Opéra; he followed up its success with that of *Tarare* (1787). He intended to return to Paris, but the French Revolution, and especially the execution of the queen, produced conditions under which musicians active in Vienna could no longer accept, or even expect, commissions from Paris. An opera that Salieri had planned to present in Paris had to be recast as an Italian opera and performed in Vienna.

We will see in Chapter 16 that during the Revolution, London became a favorite destination for many traveling musicians who preferred to avoid Paris; they included some, like the pianist Jan Ladislav Dussek, who had enjoyed the patronage of Marie Antoinette. But one of the queen's protégés evidently found artistic inspiration in the violence and political instability of the Revolutionary era: Luigi Cherubini survived the Revolution that killed his former patron, contributed crucially to post-Revolutionary opera, and helped shape France's musical life well into the nineteenth century, notably as the powerful director of the Paris Conservatoire from 1822 to 1842.

FOR FURTHER READING

Dean, Winton, "Opera under the French Revolution," *Proceedings of the Royal Musical Association* (1967–1968): 76–96

Deane, Basil, *Cherubini* (London: Oxford University Press, 1965)

Doyle, William, *Oxford History of the French Revolution*, 2nd ed. (Oxford: Oxford University Press, 2002)

Heartz, Daniel, *Music in European Capitals: The Galant Style, 1720–1780* (New York: W. W. Norton, 2003), 801–81

Johnson, James H., *Listening in Paris: A Cultural History* (Berkeley: University of California Press, 1995)

The Letters of Mozart and His Family, 3rd ed., translated and annotated by Emily Anderson (New York: W. W. Norton, 1985)

Music and the French Revolution, ed. Malcolm Boyd (Cambridge: Cambridge University Press, 1992)

Rice, John A., *Antonio Salieri and Viennese Opera* (Chicago: University of Chicago Press, 1998), 307–29

Ⓢ **Additional resources available at wwnorton.com/studyspace**

CHAPTER FOURTEEN

Mozart's Vienna

On March 16, 1781, the 25-year-old Mozart arrived in Vienna in the entourage of his employer, the Archbishop of Salzburg, who was visiting the Habsburg capital. The musical conditions he found resembled in many respects those (described in Chapter 8) with which he was familiar from his boyhood visits to Vienna. The Habsburg court continued to dominate musical life. The Burgtheater and the theater at the Kärntnertor, under the supervision of court officials and of the emperor himself, remained Vienna's principal theaters and, as such, centers of musical activity. Vienna continued to attract young, ambitious musicians to compose, perform, and settle there. When Mozart broke free of his job, his father, and his birthplace to establish himself in Vienna, he chose that city for many of the same reasons that had drawn Christoph Gluck, Johann Baptist Vanhal, and Antonio Salieri, and that would persuade Beethoven to settle there in 1792.

But Vienna was also changing rapidly in 1781, and some of the changes resulted from the actions and policies of Emperor Joseph II. Empress Maria Theresa's eldest son, Joseph had shared from 1765 responsibility for ruling the vast, multinational, multilingual Habsburg monarchy. But it was not until the empress's death in 1780 that he ruled alone, which left him only nine years before his own death in 1790.

"I assure you this is a splendid place—and for my craft the best place in the world," Mozart wrote to his father, shortly after arriving in Vienna. Intoxicated by the richness of the city's musical life—numerous opportunities to give concerts, to perform in the private salons of wealthy music lovers, to compose, and to teach—Mozart almost immediately resented the restrictions the archbishop placed on his activities. His repeated testing of those restrictions led, within a few weeks, to his being fired: literally kicked out of the archbishop's residence. With that kick Mozart became a freelance musician whose financial and artistic fate was, for the rest of his life, inextricably tied to Vienna.

JOSEPH AS ENLIGHTENED MONARCH

No eighteenth-century ruler better exemplified the concept of enlightened absolutism than Emperor Joseph II (1741–1790). His ideals were those of the Enlightenment: he often used the equivalent German word, *Aufklärung*, in announcing and explaining his policies. As a ruler, he took it as his duty to increase the education, prosperity, and happiness of his subjects, and he assumed (very much in the spirit of his age) that all these things were interdependent. But he also assumed that his subjects needed a benevolent and powerful ruler to make decisions for them, and that his subjects should obey the ruler without question.

These beliefs and assumptions might make sense in an imaginary world in which rulers are infallible and their subjects uniformly intelligent, malleable, and virtuous. But in the real world of eighteenth-century Europe they were a recipe for conflict and failure. Joseph began the 1780s as full of energy, ambition, and self-confidence as Mozart was at the time, absolutely sure of his obligation and ability to strengthen the monarchy and improve the lives of his subjects. Whereas Maria Theresa had pushed her reforms forward slowly, negotiating and cajoling, Joseph ruled by fiat. He issued a steady stream of laws, rules, and proclamations with the goals of increasing the efficiency of tax collection, the use of the German language in government and education, and the freedom of the press; reforming the legal system; emancipating serfs; and in many other ways transforming economic, political, and religious life throughout the monarchy.

Many of Joseph's reforms made good sense and deserved to be called enlightened, or even revolutionary. But naturally they stirred up resentment in the many people whom they affected negatively. This resentment, increased by the lack of sensitivity and tact with which Joseph imposed his reforms, led some parts of the monarchy into full-scale rebellion. He died at the age of 49 a broken man, mentally as well as physically, leaving the Habsburg monarchy on the verge of disintegration.

RELIGIOUS REFORMS AND CHURCH MUSIC

Some of the most pervasive of Joseph's reforms involved attempts to limit the power, wealth, and influence of the Catholic Church, which predominated in most of the monarchy. He repealed some of the laws restricting the rights of

Protestants and Jews. He ordered that hundreds of monasteries be closed so that their wealth could be put to more constructive use: for the building of parish churches and schools and for the salaries of teachers. Joseph's paternalistic eagerness to supervise the lives of his subjects down to the smallest detail led him to prescribe their religious ceremonies, which were to be as simple as possible, both to reduce expense and to discourage what he considered superstitious ritual; he restricted the number of processions, statues, and candles.

During the early 1780s Joseph issued a series of decrees that limited the occasions when the most elaborate church music could be performed. His regulations never completely forbade such performances, but the spirit of his regulations, and his anticlerical stance in general, discouraged the performance of elaborate church music. As early as 1782 a report from Vienna could state (with some exaggeration): "orchestrally accompanied music has now been entirely eliminated from the churches, except for very important feastdays."

We saw in Chapter 8 something of the richness of Viennese sacred music during the reign of Maria Theresa. In the 1770s Mozart composed much magnificent church music for Salzburg; we might have expected that his decade in Vienna would have yielded an equally rich harvest of church music, but it did not. Mozart suddenly turned away from church music after 1783, doing what he had never been able to do earlier in Salzburg: he focused all his creative energy on secular music. The success he achieved in instrumental music and opera during the 1780s owes something, indirectly, to Joseph's religious reforms. The decline of Viennese church music left him free to concentrate on other genres.

JOSEPH AS OPERA DIRECTOR: SINGSPIEL

Joseph's supervision of the court theaters exemplifies his strengths and weaknesses as a ruler. An experienced musician (Fig. 14.1) who performed almost daily with his own private chamber music group when he was in Vienna, he combined in his theatrical management real musical knowledge and sophistication with a tendency to micromanage and to act suddenly, drastically, and undiplomatically.

Already in 1776, well before Joseph became sole ruler, Viennese opera felt the effects of his reformist zeal. Dissolving the contract with the impresario struggling to manage the court theaters, he brought them under his direct authority. He dismissed the opera buffa and ballet troupes, together with the orchestra of the Kärntnertor Theater. All that remained were a troupe for the performance of spoken dramas in German and the Burgtheater orchestra, to play overtures and incidental music.

As was often the case with his reforms, Joseph seems to have disregarded the practical implications of his theatrical reorganization. Many of his most powerful subjects—those who might have helped him implement his more important

Figure 14.1: *Joseph II, preparing to accompany two of his sisters in a duet by Salieri. More commonly he made music with a private group of instrumentalists consisting only of men. Painting by Joseph Hauzinger.*

reforms in the political, economic, and religious arenas—loved opera and ballet. His reorganization caused financial difficulties for many: more than 100 people (singers, dancers, instrumentalists, and administrators) lost their jobs. No ruler could afford to make so many enemies among those with close connections with the court. It is not surprising that Joseph's reorganization, like so many of his reforms, had to be modified and to some extent reversed.

The first of these modifications was the reestablishment in the Burgtheater of an opera troupe organized and subsidized by the court. In 1778 Joseph added to the troupe of German actors enough singers to make possible the performance of operas in German. The German singers made their debut in February 1778 with an opera by Ignaz Umlauf (1746–1796), *Die Bergknappen* (The Miners).

This work is typical of the operas written for Joseph's troupe in borrowing from several theatrical traditions. Viennese librettists and composers were inspired by the Singspiele of northern Germany (of which we saw an example, Johann Adam Hiller's *Die Jagd*, in Chapter 9); opéra comique, so popular in Vienna in the 1750s and 1760s; and Italian opera, both comic and serious. *Die Bergknappen* has simple, folk-like songs such as one finds in Hiller's Singspiele. But the big trio *Erinnere dich stets meiner Schwüre* (Always remember my oath), with several changes of tempo, resembles the finale of an opera buffa; and the heroine's accompanied recitative is clearly inspired by opera seria, as is the virtuoso coloratura aria *Wenn mir der Himmel lacht* (If heaven smiles on me). The opera's final number is an ensemble of a kind common in opéra comique, in which each of the principal characters sings one verse (the hero and heroine sing one verse together) and the rest join in a repeated refrain.

MOZART'S *DIE ENTFÜHRUNG AUS DEM SERAIL*

Although *Die Bergknappen* was no longer in the repertory when Mozart arrived in Vienna, Joseph's Singspiel troupe was still active and still performing works that followed the pattern established by Umlauf's opera. Mozart, eager to show off his extraordinary talents in any genre, and not particular about what kind of music he composed, coveted above all Joseph's recognition. He wrote to his father: "My chief object here is to introduce myself to the emperor in some becoming way, for I am absolutely determined that he shall get to know me." It was natural that he should be drawn to the genre and the troupe that Joseph had established in Vienna. Mozart's *Die Entführung aus dem Serail* (The Abduction from the Seraglio), begun a few months after his arrival in Vienna, represents his first great success in the Habsburg capital and the culmination of the short-lived tradition of Singspiel in the Burgtheater.

Mozart combined in *Die Entführung* the same generic elements and national styles that Umlauf combined in *Die Bergknappen*. But Mozart had much more experience as a dramatic composer than Umlauf and had composed works in many of the genres from which he was expected to draw as a composer of Singspiel. Clearly aware of what worked in the theater and what did not, he collaborated with his librettist Gottlieb Stephanie in recasting a libretto of the kind that Hiller might have set to music in Leipzig in the 1760s, in this case a lighthearted romance concerning the rescue of a Spanish lady from an Ottoman harem, or seraglio. Mozart and Stephanie added many new musical numbers, arias and ensembles, some of which replaced spoken dialogue. The changes increased Mozart's opportunities for musical characterization and depiction of relations between characters.

Mozart wrote happily to his father letters that express the enthusiasm, energy, and theatrical insight with which he composed *Die Entführung* (SR 140; 5/19), endowing his score with a richness of musical ideas and techniques that Umlauf and his Viennese colleagues could not match, including a taste of the Turkish janissary music that had offended the ears of Frederick the Great's sister, Princess Wilhelmina, half a century earlier (see Chapter 11). It was probably to this abundance that the emperor, sarcastic by nature, alluded when he said: "Too beautiful for our ears, and far too many notes, my dear Mozart." Joseph probably agreed with Mozart's response, "Just as many, Your Majesty, as are needed," if for no other reason than that *Die Entführung* was a great popular success. The Viennese greeted the premiere, on July 16, 1782, with loud applause, and Mozart's opera received more performances than any other during the short time that remained for the Singspiel troupe in the Burgtheater.

Joseph's promotion of German opera did not cause Viennese opera lovers to lose their fondness for Italian opera. *Die Entführung* brought enthusiastic crowds into the Burgtheater whenever it was performed, but the German troupe could not survive on one work or on the work of one composer. This is probably why Mozart did not write another German opera for the Burgtheater. In late 1782, as he continued to enjoy the success of *Die Entführung*, he had already turned his attention to Italian opera.

NEW PATTERNS OF PATRONAGE

Music "is the only thing about which the nobility shows taste," according to an account of Viennese musical life published in 1784. The Viennese aristocracy, its wealth largely generated by the labor of thousands of serfs, was able and willing to spend large amounts of money on music. But the methods by which noblemen bestowed their patronage changed during the second half of the eighteenth century. A midcentury patron might employ musicians on a full-time basis and require that they work for him alone, as when Haydn agreed, on joining the household of Prince Paul Esterházy in 1761, that his compositions would be reserved "for the exclusive use of His Highness" (see Chapter 10). Such strict, long-term agreements became less common later in the century, replaced by arrangements whereby a patron would engage a musician for a single concert or series of concerts, or for the composition of a single work or series of works. The transition from the one kind of patronage to the other was not always easy. Mozart's confrontation with the archbishop of Salzburg in 1781 that led to his settling in Vienna was fundamentally a conflict between the older style of patronage and the newer: between steady employment and its many restrictions and the life of a freelance musician—riskier, but potentially more stimulating and rewarding.

Prince Dmitry Golitsin, the Russian ambassador in Vienna from 1762 to 1792, was a generous bestower of the new kind of patronage. For many years he gave weekly concerts in his Viennese residence at which the leading musicians of the city were invited to perform. During Lent 1784 Mozart appeared almost every Thursday at Golitsin's concert. He must have welcomed the opportunity to earn cash and gain access to the high nobility without having to go through the difficult and time-consuming process of organizing his own concerts, and without having to give up his freedom to make music where and when he pleased.

Mozart had a more influential patron in Baron Gottfried van Swieten (1733–1803). A diplomat early in his career, he got to know the music of Handel and Johann Sebastian Bach in Berlin. On his return to Vienna he became director of the court library and one of the chief architects of Emperor Joseph's reforms in education, religion, and censorship. He invited musicians to the court library for weekly music-making. Mozart joined Swieten's circle soon after settling in Vienna, and it was not long before he too became fascinated by the learned polyphony at the center of attention at these musical gatherings. (His contrapuntal studies bore fruit in works such as the String Quartet in A Major, K. 464, to be discussed below.) Swieten continued to enrich Viennese musical life as Haydn's patron and collaborator in the 1790s, as we will see in Chapter 17.

PUBLIC CONCERTS

Although the Viennese court did not maintain a monopoly in the organization of public concerts within the city walls, as it did in the public performance of operas, the Burgtheater nevertheless remained the focus of concert life. Individual concerts and series of concerts were organized in other places, but these rarely developed into long-lasting institutions like the Bach-Abel Concerts in London (see Chapter 7).

Vienna lacked aggressive and imaginative concert impresarios such as Johann Peter Salomon, who (as we will see in Chapter 16) brought Haydn to London and organized his concerts there. London's much larger population allowed public concerts to continue through most of the winter and spring, competing for audiences with operas and spoken plays. In Vienna public concerts were mostly limited to Advent and Lent, when the performance of opera was generally forbidden. The court made its theaters available to individual virtuosos, who organized their own concerts, engaging musicians and selling tickets.

When Mozart arrived in Vienna, the public concert was one of the aspects of musical life that most excited him. The concert seasons became periods of hectic activity, as he moved quickly from public concerts in the court theaters to subscription concerts in other halls and appearances in the private salons of wealthy patrons like Prince Golitsin. Leopold Mozart visited his son in Vienna during Lent 1785; in a letter to his daughter he described vividly the exhausting activity of the concert season:

> We never get to bed before one o'clock and I never get up before nine. . . .
> Every day there are concerts; and the whole time is given up to teaching,
> music, composing and so forth. Where am I to go? If only the concerts
> were over! It is impossible to describe the trouble and the commotion.
> Since my arrival your brother's fortepiano has been taken at least a dozen
> times to the theater or to some other house.

Leopold described one of Wolfgang's subscription concerts in the Mehlgrube, a hall often used for musical events. The concert contained the typical mixture of symphonies, arias, and concertos; typical too was Mozart's involvement in every aspect of the concert, from renting the hall to overseeing the music copying:

> Each person pays a souverain d'or or three ducats for the six Lenten concerts. Your brother . . . pays only a souverain d'or each time for the hall. The concert was magnificent and the orchestra played splendidly. In addition to the symphonies a female singer of the Italian theater sang two arias. Then we had a new and very fine concerto by Wolfgang [K. 466 in D Minor; see below], which the copyist was still copying when we arrived, and the rondo of which your brother did not even have time to play through [in rehearsal], as he had to supervise the copying.

MOZART'S PIANO CONCERTOS

Mozart was a prolific composer of symphonies before he came to Vienna, but he wrote relatively few keyboard concertos; in Vienna the reverse was true. Although public concerts in Vienna typically contained at least one symphony, they were primarily vehicles for soloistic display, vocal as well as instrumental. These concerts thus stimulated Mozart's ambitions and talents as a pianist and as a composer of music for piano and orchestra. On the 17 piano concertos that he wrote during his Viennese decade (1781–91) he lavished some of his richest inventiveness and most exquisite craftsmanship.

Because opera was not given in Vienna during Lent, opera-loving Viennese looked to concerts for the forbidden pleasures of the operatic stage. They wanted and expected music performed in concerts to be theatrical in effect. Here again we can sense why Mozart favored the piano concerto over the symphony after his arrival in Vienna: the concerto, with its interaction of soloist and orchestra, was more susceptible to the incorporation of operatic drama. One of the most patently operatic aspects of concertos was the opportunity they gave the soloist to improvise. Mozart often wrote plain melodies in the solo part, with the expectation of ornamenting the line in performance. Near the end of some movements he placed a fermata, telling the orchestra to pause while he (like a singer near the end of an aria) improvised a cadenza. Mozart's piano concertos do not tell stories; yet they vividly convey the passion and violence, the gaiety and laughter, and the sheer theatricality of the Viennese stage.

KEYS AND THEIR ASSOCIATIONS

Many eighteenth-century musicians and theorists attributed a particular character and expressive potential to each key. Although Mozart wrote very little on this subject, he would certainly have agreed that his choice of key was one of the first and most important decisions that he made in planning a large-scale orchestral work, with implications for its texture, instrumentation, dynamics, melodic style, and, consequently, for its expressive content and dramatic character. Mozart wrote piano concertos in many different keys, as if eager to explore the full potential of the concerto as a dramatic genre.

Composers often associated E♭ with seriousness and nobility, perhaps partly because the violin's open G string encouraged composers to write rich, sonorous E♭ major chords, with the violin's lowest note providing a low and resonant third degree; eighteenth-century woodwind instruments, moreover, tend to produce a comparatively muted sound when playing in this key. Mozart chose to write *Die Zauberflöte* (The Magic Flute, 1791) in E♭—that is, it begins and ends in this key. The Piano Concerto in E♭ Major, K. 482, with its sumptuous writing for clarinets, evokes the calm nobility of Sarastro's realm.

The Concertos in C Major, K. 467 and 503, both project the brightness and grandeur that he associated with that key. Brilliant works, evocative of royal celebration and triumph, they belong to the expressive world of Mozart's opera *La clemenza di Tito* (The Clemency of Titus), also in C and written for the coronation of Emperor Leopold II in 1791. Trumpets and drums, traditionally associated with music in C and D and missing from most of the concertos in other keys, add to the majestic, festive effect of the C-major concertos.

The Concerto in D Minor, K. 466, in stark contrast, evokes the tragic stage. Mozart could hardly have made a more adventurous choice for a piano concerto than D minor, strongly associated in operas and ballets with vengeance and violence, the supernatural, the underworld, and the Furies. Both Gluck's Don Juan (in his ballet of 1761) and Mozart's Don Giovanni (in his opera of 1787) are dragged down to hell to the sound of D minor; when the Queen of the Night (in *Die Zauberflöte*) invokes the vengeance of hell, she does so in this key.

Violence and anger pervade the first movement of the Concerto in D Minor, written by Mozart for his Lenten concerts of 1785 and admired by Leopold Mozart when his son performed it in the Mehlgrube. The quiet opening, with menacing syncopations in the violins, low in their register, and sinister rumblings in the bass, inspires awe. But the music's full fury is held back until the full orchestra enters, *forte*, with trumpets and drums, the strings playing fiery arpeggiation and tremolos. The soloist enters as Orpheus might confront the Furies in the underworld, playing a tender melody completely different from the orchestra's stormy introduction. We must imagine the intensity of the drama at

Example 14.1: *Wolfgang Amadeus Mozart, Piano Concerto in D Minor, K. 466, movement 1, mm. 77–88*

this moment as Mozart, performing the concerto for the first time, seemingly improvised this passage, reaching an expressive climax as he stretched to play his piano's highest note, F above high C (Ex. 14.1).

Mozart and his contemporaries often used G major, a key in which the lowest string of the violin could serve as a tonic drone and in which flutes and oboes could be played with greater ease than in some other keys, as a pastoral key. Johann Baptist Vanhal wrote his *Missa pastoralis* in G (see Chapter 8); Mozart associated the key with the peasants in *Le nozze di Figaro* (The Marriage of Figaro, 1786; see below) and *Don Giovanni* and with the rustic Papageno and Papagena in *Die Zauberflöte*. In the Piano Concerto in G Major, K. 453, the pastoral connotations of the key led him to accompany his cheerful opening melody with a bagpipe-like drone and to intersperse the melody with birdlike twittering in the woodwinds (Ex. 14.2).

Example 14.2: *Wolfgang Amadeus Mozart, Piano Concerto in G Major, K. 453, movement 1, mm. 1–5*

The finale of the Concerto in G Major consists of variations on a theme that Papageno the bird catcher might have sung (Ex. 14.3). Mozart, shortly after completing the concerto, explicitly associated the melody with a bird. He bought

Example 14.3: *Wolfgang Amadeus Mozart, Piano Concerto in G Major, K. 453, movement 3, mm. 1–4*

a pet starling, which learned to sing the theme's first phrase, albeit with some inaccuracies. Mozart transcribed the starling's version in a notebook and commented: "That was nice!" (Ex. 14.4).

Example 14.4: *Wolfgang Amadeus Mozart, Piano Concerto in G Major, K. 453, movement 3, mm. 1–4, as sung by Mozart's starling and transcribed by the composer in May 1784*

All of Mozart's piano concertos have three movements, with the central slow movement in a key other than the tonic, allowing the composer to move away from the concerto's prevailing color and mood before returning to it in the finale. In the Concerto in G Major the relaxed, rustic tone of the first and third movements gives way in the Andante to something darker and more complex (see Anthology 18). This binary movement is in C major, but without the trumpets and drums it lacks the festive character of so much of Mozart's orchestral music in that key. The opening melody, with a sarabande-like emphasis on the second beat, is left incomplete, contributing to the movement's enigmatic, unstable atmosphere. The second part of the binary structure wanders to extremely distant keys before a modulation of stunning audacity and expressivity leads back to the tonic.

MUSIC IN THE HOME

Michael Kelly, the Irish tenor of whose arrival in Naples as a student in the 1770s we read in Chapter 3, and who sang Italian opera in Vienna from 1783 to 1787, was greatly impressed by Viennese musicality: "All ranks of society were doatingly fond of music," he wrote in his memoirs, "and most of them perfectly understood the science." Music played an important role in the daily life of many of the city's residents. In the taverns one could drink to the sound of Haydn minuets; in the ballrooms during carnival an orchestra played dance music by Mozart and his contemporaries from nine in the evening to five in the morning. And in private apartments and palaces many people spent their leisure in a wide variety of music-making.

Vienna's small but growing upper middle class participated enthusiastically in its culture of domestic music. Instead of paying professional musicians to play for them, most Viennese music lovers made music for themselves and their private guests. Haydn's friend and patron Marianne von Genzinger, for example, organized musical soirées in her home. A fine musician whose husband, a doctor, had been ennobled by Empress Maria Theresa, Marianne and her friends played pleasant, light music on such occasions, sipped coffee, tea, or chocolate, and engaged in casual conversation. Women played as important a role in music-making as men in these contexts, especially as pianists and singers. Late-eighteenth-century illustrations of private music-making often show women at the keyboard, and composers dedicated much of their published piano music to women.

One of the liveliest and most stimulating of Vienna's musical salons took place on Saturday nights at the residence of Marianna Martines (1744–1813). As a girl Martines studied keyboard and composition with Haydn. During the 1760s and 1770s she composed tirelessly: masses and other sacred music, keyboard concertos and sonatas, and Italian arias and cantatas. She wrote less after 1780, as she focused on teaching voice and on her weekly musical salon. Mozart frequently attended Martines's parties and enjoyed playing piano duets with her. Through her soirées as well as her compositions she contributed significantly to the richness of Viennese musical life.

Closely connected with the spread of music-making in the home was the development of the Viennese music publishing industry. Before the 1780s little music was published in Vienna, compared with the vast quantities produced by the flourishing music businesses of Paris and London. Most music circulated in manuscript. As the number of amateur musicians increased, in Vienna as in the rest of Europe, publishers were quick to see the profitable possibilities of the musical market. The Italians Carlo and Francesco Artaria, among the first to do so, were joined by the Bohmian composer and pianist Leopold Kozeluch and the Austrian composer Franz Anton Hoffmeister. Few if any Viennese composers made a living from their published music alone, but the growth of music publishing (which continued and accelerated in the nineteenth century, as Walter Frisch shows in his book in this series), offered them an important way to supplement their income and made their music available to more performers than ever before.

THE STRING QUARTET

Disappointed by the performance of one of Mozart's piano quartets (for piano, violin, viola, and cello) by unskilled amateur musicians at a private concert, a critic writing in 1788 recommended that such a work be performed "by four talented musicians, who have probably studied it, in a quiet room where not even the suspension of each note escapes the ear, in the presence of two or three attentive people." This kind of performance suited a string quartet (for two violins, viola, and cello) just as well. But although women were often involved in chamber music that included keyboard, the string quartet seems to have been closely associated with men—as composers, performers, and listeners.

Kelly described a party that took place in Vienna in 1784, in which some of the finest male musicians in the city entertained themselves and a few male friends with string quartets (Kelly also attended Martines' mixed-gender musical salons, and it is clear from his account that this occasion was quite different):

> The players were tolerable; not one of them excelled on the instrument he played, but there was a little science among them, which I dare say will be acknowledged when I name them:

> The First Violin . . . HAYDN.
>   "   Second Violin . . . BARON DITTERSDORF.
>   "   Violoncello . . . VANHALL.
>   "   Tenor [Viola] . . . MOZART.

> The poets [Giambattista] Casti and Paesiello [the composer Giovanni Paisiello] formed part of the audience. I was there, and a greater treat, or a more remarkable one, cannot be imagined. . . . After the musical feast was over, we sat down to an excellent supper, and became joyous and lively in the extreme.

The Viennese string quartet was not a genre for all men, of course, but for musical professionals and connoisseurs. Haydn, Mozart, Vanhal, Carl Ditters von Dittersdorf, and their contemporaries wrote quartets with the assumption that they would be executed by skillful, knowledgeable musicians who played for their own amusement and who might have practiced their parts carefully. (Mozart was a child prodigy on the violin as well as the piano, but in later years he stopped playing string instruments in public.) Descriptions of quartet playing rarely mention an audience of more than a few, and these were often themselves fine musicians, like Kelly, who listened attentively and appreciatively.

HAYDN'S OPUS 33 QUARTETS

The six quartets by Haydn that Artaria published in 1782 with the opus number 33 set a standard of intricacy and wit for all Viennese composers of string quartets during the 1780s. Throughout the set Haydn replaced the word "minuet" with "scherzo" (Italian for "joke"). Although the scherzi, considered as a group, do not differ much from movements that Haydn referred to as minuets (many of which are as fast and energetic as these scherzi), the word in itself is important: with it, Haydn alluded to the sophisticated playfulness that pervades the set.

We find good examples of Haydn's musical wit in the way two of the quartets begin: with material that clearly identifies itself as belonging somewhere else. The Quartet in B Minor starts with two phrases from the second melodic area, in the relative major, D. We have to wait until measure 10 for the first V–i cadence in B minor, which encourages us to hear the first nine measures, in retrospect, as a kind of introduction. The Quartet in G Major, the first work in the original set, begins with a V⁷–I cadence and a melodic ascent of a fourth (from D up to G; Ex. 14.5a), from which Haydn generated much of the movement that follows, including the first theme (see mm. 7–10) and the final measures (where the players first toss the motive from one to another, then present it in

Example 14.5: *Joseph Haydn, String Quartet in G Major, Op. 33, No. 5, movement 1*

(a) *mm. 1–10*

(b) *mm. 297–305*

exactly the same homophonic context as at the beginning, and finally play it in octaves; Ex. 14.5b). Whereas the Quartet in G begins with an ending, the Quartet in E♭ (later nicknamed "The Joke") ends with a beginning. In many other respects as well, its final rondo (see Anthology 19) epitomizes the wit of Opus 33.

MOZART'S "HAYDN" QUARTETS

Four years after the publication of Haydn's Opus 33, Artaria issued another set of six quartets, by Mozart. It was no accident that he dedicated these works to Haydn, whose Opus 33 supplied him with an important source of ideas for his own set. In his dedication, addressed "to my dear friend Haydn," Mozart wrote of the labor these works had cost him; Haydn could, and did, appreciate the craft, the attention to detail, and the originality that distinguish Mozart's quartets. Haydn expressed his opinion to Leopold Mozart during the performance of three of the "Haydn" Quartets in Mozart's apartment during Lent 1785. Here was another intimate, all-male setting, with as few as five people in the room. Probably the musicians took turns listening while the others played. Haydn said to Mozart's father: "Before God and as an honest man I tell you that your son is the greatest composer known to me either in person or by name. He has taste and, what is more, the most profound knowledge of composition."

Although Haydn could have found things to admire in all six of the quartets dedicated to him, the Quartet in A Major, K. 464, might have particularly pleased him because it shows Mozart confronting a challenge that Haydn loved: the derivation of a wide variety of musical material from a few basic ideas. The quartet, like all six "Haydn" Quartets, is in four movements. The first and fourth, both marked Allegro, are in sonata form. The second movement, an intricately contrapuntal minuet and trio (see Anthology 20), is followed by a long Andante consisting of a theme, six variations, and a coda.

The opening themes of all four movements make prominent use of the melodic descent from the fifth scale degree to the third that Gluck elaborated so beautifully in the aria *Ah! quelle cruauté de lui ravir le jour* in *Armide* (see Ex. 13.1b). In the first movement, an eight-measure period elaborating the $\hat{5}$–$\hat{4}$–$\hat{3}$ descent, *piano*, is followed by a gruff unison passage, *forte*, in which a two-measure idea is repeated one step higher (Ex. 14.6a). The minuet begins with a reincarnation of these elements, but in reverse order, with a unison passage first and the $\hat{5}$–$\hat{4}$–$\hat{3}$ descent (condensed to four measures and decorated with appoggiaturas) second. The theme subjected to variation in the third movement, with the rhythmic characteristics of a gavotte (two upbeats preceding the first downbeat), takes up the second movement's $\hat{5}$–$\hat{4}$ and $\hat{4}$–$\hat{3}$ appoggiaturas (Ex. 14.6b). The fourth movement compresses the $\hat{5}$–$\hat{4}$–$\hat{3}$ descent into a single four-note chromatic motive, but then (in an allusion to the first

Example 14.6: *Wolfgang Amadeus Mozart, String Quartet in A Major, K. 464 (numbers above the notes refer to scale degrees)*

(a) *movement 1, mm. 1–16*

(b) *movement 3, mm. 1–4*

(c) *movement 4, mm. 1–8*

movement) uses that motive as part of a larger, eight-measure realization of the 5̂–4̂–3̂ descent (Ex. 14.6c).

The same motivic economy that links the movements of this quartet unifies the individual movements. In the Andante, for example, the thirty-second notes that the first violin plays in variation 1 are transferred to the second violin in variation 2; later, in variation 6, the remarkable drumlike music introduced by the cello is taken over in turn by the viola, second violin, and first violin in the coda, at the end of which the cello finally reclaims its idea. The finale takes motivic economy to an extreme, with ideas from the exposition's opening melodic area playing an essential role in the bridge, the second melodic area, and the closing material.

OPERA BUFFA

In 1783 Emperor Joseph gave up his project to make Vienna a center in the performance of Singspiel, and assembled a troupe for the performance of Italian comic opera. Already in Vienna were two first-rate composers, Mozart and Antonio Salieri (whom we last saw in Paris in Chapter 13), both experienced in Italian opera. Joseph liked Salieri, whom he had known personally for 17 years, but he had the musical sophistication to appreciate the newcomer Mozart and the generosity to support him with commissions and, from 1788, a salary from the court. Two talented librettists, Giambattista Casti and Lorenzo Da Ponte, inspired Joseph's composers.

True to his character, Joseph maintained control over the whole complex enterprise. Kelly remembered him fondly: "As the theatre was in the palace, the Emperor often honoured the rehearsals with his presence, and discoursed familiarly with the performers. He spoke Italian like a Tuscan, and was affable and condescending. He came almost every night to the opera. . . . He was passionately fond of music, and a most excellent and accurate judge of it." Without Joseph's direction, Viennese opera in the 1780s would have developed differently; we have Joseph as well as Mozart and Da Ponte to thank for the Italian operas that still today firmly maintain a place in the repertory.

That Joseph's Italian troupe specialized in comic opera, not serious, is itself a product of the emperor's tastes. The best Italian composers of the 1780s—including Giovanni Paisiello, Domenico Cimarosa, and Giuseppe Sarti—put as much energy and creativity into opera seria as opera buffa; most cities that cultivated Italian opera, both in Italy and the rest of Europe, performed serious as well as comic opera. But Joseph strongly preferred comic opera.

In his fondness for opera buffa Joseph resembled Empress Catherine the Great, who, as we saw in Chapter 12, made St. Petersburg a thriving center of Italian comic opera in the early 1780s. Indeed, Joseph was very much aware of operatic developments in the Russian capital, and especially the success that Paisiello achieved with such operas as *Il barbiere di Siviglia* (The Barber of Seville). About two months before the debut of his own opera buffa troupe, Joseph thanked his ambassador in St. Petersburg for sending him a copy of *Il barbiere di Siviglia*: "I hope to have it performed after Easter by a new troupe of Italian comic singers that I have had engaged and that should be good. You will also do me the pleasure of buying all the works in this genre (i.e., not serious) composed by Paisiello whenever they appear." Joseph evidently hoped to rival Catherine as a promoter of Paisiello's comic art. He succeeded. *Il barbiere di Siviglia*, as popular in Vienna as in St. Petersburg, paved the way for the acclaim that greeted Paisiello on his arrival in Vienna in 1784 and for the success of the opera he wrote for Joseph's company, *Il re Teodoro in Venezia* (King Theodore in Venice).

MOZART'S *LE NOZZE DI FIGARO* AND *COSÌ FAN TUTTE*

But the most important repercussion of the success of Paisiello's *Il barbiere di Siviglia* in Vienna was in inspiring Mozart to write a sequel. During the first two years in which Joseph's Italian troupe was active, 1783–84, Mozart worked on several operatic projects, but none of them came to fruition. Only in 1785 did he and Da Ponte begin working on an operatic treatment of Beaumarchais' *Le mariage de Figaro* (The Marriage of Figaro), the second play in what would eventually become a trilogy that begins with *Le barbier de Seville*. In *Le nozze di Figaro*, Mozart's second response to Emperor Joseph's operatic policies, he showed that he had mastered opera buffa as brilliantly as he had mastered Singspiel in *Die Entführung aus dem Serail*.

First performed in the Burgtheater on May 1, 1786 (by a cast including our old friend, the Irish tenor Michael Kelly), *Figaro* inspired strongly contrasting feelings among Viennese operagoers. The *Wiener Zeitung*, a newspaper that contained hardly any serious musical criticism, printed an exceptionally detailed report:

> Herr Mozart's music was generally admired by connoisseurs already at the first performance, if I except only those whose self-love and conceit will not allow them to find merit in anything not written by themselves. The *public*, however . . . did not really know on the first day where it stood. It heard many a *bravo* from unbiassed connoisseurs, but obstreperous louts in the uppermost storey exerted their hired lungs with all their might to deafen singers and audiences alike with their *St!* and *Pst!* And consequently opinions were divided at the end of the piece. Apart from that, it is true that the first performance was none of the best, owing to the difficulties of the composition. But now, after several performances, one would be subscribing either to the cabal or to tastelessness if one were to maintain that Herr Mozart's music is anything but a masterpiece of art. It contains so many beauties, and such a wealth of ideas, as can be drawn only from the source of innate genius.

The reference to the difficulty of Mozart's music is typical of early responses, not only to *Figaro* but to his new works in general. He presented performers as well as audiences with music unusually challenging in its wealth of ideas and intricacy of craftsmanship. The admiration with which a large part of its early audiences welcomed *Figaro* is a tribute to Vienna's musical and theatrical sophistication.

The success of *Figaro* led to the commissioning of two more operas from Mozart and Da Ponte—perhaps the greatest composer–librettist team in operatic history. *Don Giovanni*, first performed in Prague in October 1787, will be discussed in Chapter 15. *Così fan tutte*, the last work written for Joseph's Italian company, reached the stage just a few weeks before the emperor's death in 1790.

Così fan tutte (All Women Act Like That) has the subtitle *La scuola degli amanti* (The School for Lovers). The lovers are two idealistic young military officers, Ferrando and Guglielmo, who believe their fiancées, Dorabella and Fiordiligi, incapable of infidelity. Alfonso, an older man of great experience, is unconvinced, so the young men challenge him to a bet. He agrees, putting into motion an elaborate scheme by which the young men pretend that they have to join their regiment, but then disguise themselves and try to seduce each other's fiancées. They eventually succeed, thus losing the bet and demonstrating the truth of the opera's title.

Così fan tutte is remarkable for the delicate equilibrium that Da Ponte and Mozart achieved between comic and serious and between sincerity and deceit. They rarely encouraged the audience to laugh out loud, except in a few sustained comic situations such as the first-act finale. But moments of complete seriousness—seriousness not undermined by parody—are also rare. The very first sound of the opera, a C-major chord with the violins playing double-stopped E and high C, and orchestrated with trumpets and drums, has the majestic, serious quality that Mozart often associated with this key (Ex. 14.7a). Yet this majestic opening is prelude to the scurrying Presto, in which a dialogue for oboe, flute, and bassoon just as vividly evokes lighthearted playfulness (Ex. 14.7b).

Example 14.7: *Wolfgang Amadeus Mozart,* Così fan tutte, *overture*

(a) *mm. 1–4*

(b) *mm. 29–37*

The trio *Una bella serenata* (A beautiful serenade), again in C major, begins
with a grand Allegro in the serious style, as Ferrando, full of confidence and
joy, declares how he will spend his winnings: he will present a serenade (probably meaning, in this context, an outdoor concert) to his beloved (Ex. 14.8a);
Guglielmo responds that he will give a lavish dinner party. But Alfonso un-
dercuts the celebratory tone with a mocking question ("Will I be among the
guests?"), accompanied by laughing strings (Ex. 14.8b). Alfonso again introduces a comic element in the tender, sad quintet *Di scrivermi ogni giorno* (To write to
me every day). He finds the lovers' heartbreaking farewell (the women expressing sincere sorrow, their lovers faking it, but with music just as ravishing) highly amusing; he murmurs to the audience, with a disjunct melody clearly comic in
character, that he will burst if he does not laugh. One of the dramatic high points
of *Così fan tutte*, the duet *Fra gli amplessi in pochi istanti* (In a few moments I will
reach the embrace), depicts the moment when Fiordiligi, the more serious and
steadfast of the two women, finally allows herself to be seduced by the stranger
who is actually Ferrando in disguise (see Anthology 21). Unlike Zerlina, who
gives in quite easily to Don Giovanni in the seduction duet *Là ci darem la mano*

Example 14.8: *Wolfgang Amadeus Mozart, Così fan tutte, trio:* Una bella serenata

(a) *mm. 3–6*

A Beautiful serenade . . .

(b) *mm. 23–28*

Will I be among the guests?

(see Chapter 15), the noble Fiordiligi struggles valiantly against Ferrando's pleading. Her capitulation is consequently much more passionate and dramatic.

———

Così fan tutte represents Viennese opera buffa at its best: the product of a complex combination of genres and the collaboration of some of Europe's best librettists, singers, and composers, all under the supervision of an experienced musician, Emperor Joseph II himself. Joseph's reign as sole ruler of the Habsburg monarchy coincided quite closely with the period Mozart spent in Vienna. Mozart arrived in 1781, a few months after Maria Theresa's death; he died in 1791, less than two years after Joseph. The emperor's cultural policies, the concentration of musical talent in Vienna, the city's insatiable appetite for fine music, and the presence of an extraordinary musical genius united to make the decade of 1781–91 one of the most productive in the history of music.

FOR FURTHER READING

Beales, Derek, *Joseph II: Against the World, 1780–1790* (Cambridge: Cambridge University Press, 2009)

Grave, Floyd K., and Margaret G. Grave, *The String Quartets of Joseph Haydn* (Oxford: Oxford University Press, 2006)

Heartz, Daniel, *Mozart, Haydn, and Early Beethoven, 1780–1802* (New York: W. W. Norton, 2009)

———, *Mozart's Operas.* Edited, and with contributing essays, by Thomas Bauman (Berkeley: University of California Press, 1990)

Hunter, Mary, *The Culture of Opera Buffa in Mozart's Vienna: A Poetics of Entertainment* (Princeton, NJ: Princeton University Press, 1999)

———, *Mozart's Operas: A Companion* (New Haven, CT: Yale University Press, 2008)

Landon, H. C. Robbins, *Mozart: The Golden Years, 1781–1791* (New York: Schirmer, 1989)

Link, Dorothea, *The National Court Theatre in Mozart's Vienna: Sources and Documents, 1783–1792* (Oxford: Oxford University Press, 1998)

Morrow, Mary Sue, *Concert Life in Haydn's Vienna: Aspects of a Developing Musical and Social Institution* (Stuyvesant, NY: Pendragon, 1989)

Wolff, Christoph, *Mozart at the Gateway to His Fortune: Serving the Emperor, 1788–1791* (New York: W. W. Norton, 2012)

ⓢ Additional resources available at wwnorton.com/studyspace

CHAPTER FIFTEEN

Prague

Prague, capital of the kingdom of Bohemia, enjoyed a reputation in the eighteenth century as a city that fostered music with exceptional energy and success. It shared with Vienna the role of providing Mozart, during the last ten years of his life, with major commissions and enthusiastic audiences.

Prague lies about 150 miles northwest of Vienna, on both sides of the Vltava (Moldau in German) River. A bend in the river embraces the flat district on the east bank, the Staré Mesto (Old City). On the west bank, on a bluff rising above the Vltava, stands Prague Castle, a giant complex that includes the Gothic cathedral of St. Vitus. Hemmed in between the river and castle is the Malá Strana (Small Side), dominated by the dome of St. Nicholas's Church. For centuries the only way across the river was by boat or by the Charles Bridge, an elegant span decorated with sculptures (Fig. 15.1). Those standing on the bridge today have a view of domes, fortifications, palaces, and parks much like what Mozart might have enjoyed during his four visits to Prague.

IN THE SHADOW OF WHITE MOUNTAIN

Many eighteenth-century Europeans looked back to the wars of the previous century (and to the War of the Spanish Succession that finally ended in 1713) as having led to the conditions under which they now enjoyed relative peace

Figure 15.1: *A view of Prague with the Charles Bridge, Malá Strana, the castle, and the Cathedral of St. Vitus*

and prosperity. Bohemia, in contrast, attributed its present circumstances to a single event: the Battle of White Mountain (Bílá Hora) in 1620.

Since 1526 Bohemia had been part of the monarchy (as defined in Chapter 8), inherited by one Habsburg from another and ruled from Vienna. Like much of northern and central Europe, Bohemia was caught up in war during the first half of the seventeenth century, as Emperor Ferdinand II, bearing the flag of the Counter-Reformation, imposed Catholicism on his largely Protestant Bohemian subjects. Ferdinand defeated the Bohemian rebels at White Mountain, near Prague, and gained absolute control over the kingdom. He handed religious matters over to the Jesuits, who imposed a rigorous program of Catholic indoctrination on the populace. He confiscated the old Bohemian nobility's land and transferred it to a newly created Catholic aristocracy with close ties to the imperial court in Vienna. The Battle of White Mountain was the single great event that shaped Bohemian society for the next two centuries.

Prague, as the capital of Bohemia, exerted little political power after 1620. A satellite of Vienna, Prague offered an opportunity for the victors at White Mountain to display their power. To the beautiful medieval city the Habsburg emperors and the new Bohemian nobility added lavish palaces. The Jesuits built churches and schools. The splendid Church of St. Nicholas in the Malá Strana rose between 1711 and 1753 as a celebration of the triumph of the Counter-Reformation.

Music also owed much of its character to White Mountain. Musical education in eighteenth-century Bohemia was largely the work of the Jesuits, who had noted the importance of music in the Lutheran liturgy and the role that music played in Lutheran efforts to win Catholic converts. Fighting fire with fire, the Jesuits made music a central element in their campaign to wipe out Protestantism in Bohemia.

MUSIC IN BOHEMIAN SCHOOLS

"I had frequently been told," wrote Charles Burney, "that the Bohemians were the most musical people of Germany, or, perhaps, of all Europe; and an eminent German composer, now in London, had declared to me, that if they enjoyed the same advantages as the Italians, they would excel them." Before he visited Bohemia, such reports might have led Burney to assume that Bohemians were innately musical. But his travels led him to realize that Bohemia's elementary schools were the foundation of its musical achievements: "I found out at length, that, not only in every large town, but in all villages, where there is a reading and writing school, children of both sexes are taught music."

Some village schools approached the cacophony that Burney encountered in the conservatories of Naples (see Chapter 3). Of Cáslav, for example, Burney wrote: "I went into the school, which was full of little children of both sexes, from six to ten or eleven years old, who were reading, writing, playing on violins, hautbois [oboes], bassoons, and other instruments. The organist had in a small room of his house four clavichords, with little boys practicing on them all: his son of nine years old, was a very good performer." Little did he know that this boy, Jan Ladislav Dussek, would become one of Europe's greatest pianists (see Chapter 16).

The prominent place of music in the Bohemian schools went hand in hand with the practice, common in the kingdom, of choosing domestic servants partly on the basis of their musical abilities, which allowed noble households to use their valets, footmen, and secretaries in private wind ensembles and orchestras. A society that employed large numbers of competent musicians as part-time players required and rewarded the mass production of instrumentalists that existed in Bohemia. But that same society produced conditions unacceptable to some of the most serious and talented musicians, who wanted to devote all their time and energy to music. Many of these went elsewhere to seek their fortune; we have met Christoph Gluck in Paris and Vienna, Johann Baptist Vanhal in Vienna, Josef Mysliveček in Naples, Johann Stamitz in Mannheim, and Jan Antonin Mareš in St. Petersburg; in Chapter 16 we will re-encounter Dussek (at the height of his career) in London.

The musical talent developed by Bohemia's schools found employment all over Europe, but it also contributed to the vitality of music in Prague. Many of the musicians who eventually left Bohemia first worked in its capital, serving as singers, instrumentalists, and music directors in the city's churches, palaces, and theaters. Among the musicians who stayed in Prague was František Brixi (1732–1771), who quickly rose to the top of his profession, as organist at St. Nicholas's Church and then at the Cathedral of St. Vitus. Enormously prolific, he wrote more than 500 sacred works—including 100 masses—during his short life. In the realm of secular music, two of the leading figures were the pianist, music teacher, and composer František Dušek and his wife Josepha, a singer. At Bertramka, their villa in the suburbs, the Dušeks presided over one of Prague's liveliest musical salons.

ITALIAN OPERA

The new Catholic aristocracy of Bohemia, imitating the court at Vienna, turned to Italian opera as a means of projecting its power, wealth, and taste. Within a few months of the spectacular production of Johann Joseph Fux's *Costanza e fortezza* (Constancy and Strength) in celebration of the coronation of Charles VI as king of Bohemia in 1723 (see Fig. 2.4), Count Franz Sporck engaged an Italian impresario to present operas in his palace. Sporck's theater became, in effect, Prague's first public opera house. Although it lasted only about a decade, it played a crucial role in establishing a vibrant tradition of Italian opera in Prague. It probably gave Gluck his first taste of Italian opera, inspiring him to devote his life to musical theater.

In the decades that followed, several opera troupes performed in a variety of venues, bringing to increasingly sophisticated music lovers a steady diet of first-rate Italian opera. But it was not until the early 1780s that Prague had a theater that matched in size and magnificence the quality of the operatic productions to which it had grown accustomed.

In 1783 Count Franz Nostitz, governor of Bohemia, opened the National Theater in the Staré Mesto. As if to compensate for its political subservience to Vienna, Prague made its theater bigger and finer than Vienna's Burgtheater, which was awkwardly wedged into a corner of the imperial residence and grotesquely overshadowed by the Imperial Riding School (see Fig. 8.2). The National Theater in Prague, imitating the theater that Frederick the Great built in Berlin in the early 1740s (see Fig. 9.3), stood proudly alone, a monument to Bohemia's wealth and good taste (Fig. 15.2). It still stands, though unfortunately much altered from its original state.

To present opera in the new theater, Nostitz engaged an Italian impresario named Pasquale Bondini, of whom a German visitor to Prague wrote: "This impresario offers good salaries, and pays promptly. . . . He spares no expense in acquiring the best and newest scores, in paying good men and women singers so that they are happy to work with him. . . . The costumes and settings are excellent." The orchestra that accompanied Bondini's singers was small but fine, according to Franz Xaver Niemetschek, a resident of Prague who wrote an early biography of Mozart: "It does not count famous concerto soloists or virtuosi

Figure 15.2: *An early-nineteenth-century view of the Estates Theater, formerly known as the National Theater and the Nostitz Theater*

among its members, but all its members are skilled and thorough, many are first-rate artists, fired by a sense of honor, who through renunciation of personal priority and a long period of continuous playing together, produce a remarkably unified whole that seems to come forth as from a single soul." Bondini's troupe presented Italian operas largely imported from Italy and Vienna. The several Viennese operas performed in Prague in 1786 included Mozart's *Le nozze di Figaro* (The Marriage of Figaro), premiered in Vienna a few months earlier.

MOZART IN PRAGUE

By the mid-1780s Prague knew some of Mozart's music well. His Singspiel *Die Entführung aus dem Serail* had been performed there with great success in 1783, in a production that marked the beginning of the city's love affair with the composer, according to Niemetschek: "It was as if what had been heard and known before were not music! Everyone was overcome with enchantment; everyone was astonished at the new harmonies, the hitherto unheard wind parts. Now the Bohemians began to seek out his works, and in this same year, Mozart's symphonies and piano music were to be heard at all the best concerts."

Mozart had close personal friends and admirers among the city's leading musicians and musical patrons. Count Johann Thun was an old friend of the Mozart family as well as a connoisseur of Italian opera. František and Josepha Dušek had known the Mozart family since they visited Salzburg in 1777.

These personal connections, the high quality of Bondini's troupe and of the orchestra of the National Theater, the musical and operatic sophistication of the Bohemian audience, and its fondness for Mozart's music, together made Prague an ideal place for a production of *Figaro*, a work that, as we saw in Chapter 14, challenged Viennese musicians and audiences alike. So successful were the performances of Mozart's opera during the fall of 1786 that he was invited to come to Prague. There he enjoyed the kind of celebrity he had rarely experienced since his days as a child prodigy.

On the evening of his arrival, January 11, 1787, Mozart attended a ball at which some of the music consisted of arrangements of arias and ensembles from his latest opera. He wrote to a friend that he did not dance: "But I looked on with the greatest pleasure, while all these people flew about in sheer delight to the music of my *Figaro* arranged for contredances and German dances. For here they talk about nothing but *Figaro*. Nothing is played, sung, or whistled but *Figaro*. No opera is drawing like *Figaro*. Nothing, nothing but *Figaro*. Certainly a great honor for me!" A few days later Mozart directed a performance of *Figaro* from the keyboard; the audience welcomed him with enthusiastic applause. Two other high points of Mozart's first visit to Prague were a concert for his own benefit that he gave in the National Theater and the conclusion of a contract in which he agreed to write an opera for Prague.

Niemetschek wrote of the concert:

> Never was the theater so crowded as on this occasion; never such intense and unanimous delight as was aroused by his divine performance [at the piano]. Indeed we could not decide what we should admire more: his extraordinary composition or his extraordinary playing. Both together produced on our souls a total effect that resembled sweet enchantment! But after Mozart, at the end of the concert, improvised alone at the piano for more than half an hour, and aroused our pleasure to the highest degree, this spell was broken by a storm of loud applause. And in fact this improvisation went beyond any keyboard playing that could be imagined, because it combined the highest level of compositional art with the most perfect virtuosity of performance. It is certain that, just as this concert represented a unique event for Prague, so Mozart counted this day as one of the finest in his life.

THE *PRAGUE* SYMPHONY

Mozart's benefit concert included at least two symphonies, one of which was in D major—probably the Symphony in D, K. 504, that he had finished in Vienna at the beginning of December 1786, and that later became known as the *Prague* Symphony. Whether he wrote this symphony with the intention of presenting it in Prague we do not know. But it is tempting to hear in it a tribute to the sophistication of Prague's music lovers and to the abilities of the National Theater's orchestra.

The symphony is in three movements: two fast movements frame a central slow one. Even in the 1780s the minuet was not an essential part of the symphony; indeed some theorists, such as Heinrich Christoph Koch, still regarded the fast-slow-fast format as the norm (SR 126: 807–8; 5/5: 73–74). All three movements are in sonata form. The majestic slow introduction announces the symphony's seriousness and grand scope (see Anthology 22). Its emphasis on the key of D minor anticipates the expressive world of *Don Giovanni*, in which that key plays a crucial role. In the Allegro that follows, Mozart achieved a perfect equilibrium of galant and learned. The slow movement uses a combination of pedal points, $\frac{6}{8}$ meter, and the key of G major to evoke the pastoral realm. The finale recalls the first movement not only in the complexity and brilliance of its counterpoint, but in its frequent use of an upbeat motive consisting of three eighth notes, related to the three-note upbeat motive that dominates the second melodic area of the first movement.

DON GIOVANNI

Mozart returned to Vienna with the money that he made from the concert and the contract for an opera with which he hoped to match the success of *Figaro*. That opera was *Don Giovanni*, performed in the National Theater less than a year later. Its origins offer us a case study in how operas came into existence in the eighteenth century.

ORIGINS AND REHEARSALS

Mozart, like most professional composers of his time, rarely set to work on an opera without knowing when, where, and by whom it would be performed, and how much he would be paid. Because copyright as we know it hardly existed, the only fees that an opera composer could realistically hope to earn were those associated with the original production and stipulated by contract. Once the score was in the hands of copyists it was essentially in the public domain, and operas could be performed widely without the composer receiving any payment. In the case of *Don Giovanni*, the commission seems to have promised two kinds of payment: a flat fee of 100 ducats and the proceeds of the fourth performance.

Operatic commissions usually allowed the commissioner to choose the libretto. Bondini left this decision to his successor, Domenico Guardasoni, who took over the company in 1787. Mozart's popularity gave him influence over Guardasoni—in regard to the choice of both libretto and librettist. Many years later Lorenzo Da Ponte, librettist of the Italian opera troupe in Vienna from 1783 to 1791, reported that Guardasoni offered Mozart a libretto by Giovanni Bertati on the story of Don Juan, first performed just a few months earlier in Venice; Mozart accepted the idea of a Don Juan opera but insisted that Da Ponte be commissioned to write a new libretto.

Bertati's libretto was one of several tellings of the story of Don Juan performed in the 1780s. But the history of Don Juan dramas goes back much farther. A legendary Spanish nobleman of prodigious sexual appetite and irresistible attractiveness to women, Don Juan had been the subject of plays since the first half of the seventeenth century. In carnival 1787—just as Mozart was enjoying his first triumph in Prague—Bertati presented his version of the Don Juan legend in a two-part libretto. The first part, entitled *Il capriccio drammatico* (Theatrical Caprice), depicted a traveling troupe of Italian opera singers who argue about what opera to perform next. Their manager proposes a Don Juan opera, and after much debate the singers agree. The second part consists of the actual performance of *Don Giovanni o sia Il convitato di pietra* (Don Giovanni, or The Stone Guest). Mozart, realizing that Bertati's one-act treatment needed expansion, turned naturally for this task to Da Ponte, with whom he had successfully worked on *Figaro*. Da Ponte not only expanded but almost entirely rewrote the second part of Bertati's libretto.

Mozart had probably finished most of the score by the time he returned to Prague in early October 1787. Da Ponte soon joined him, to fulfill the duties—normally assigned to librettists—of what today we call a stage director. *Don Giovanni* was originally planned for a gala performance on October 14, but because it was not yet ready, the premiere had to be delayed. Mozart, writing to a friend, blamed the delay on others: "In the first place, the stage personnel here are not as smart as those in Vienna, when it comes to mastering an opera of this kind in a very short time. Secondly, I found on my arrival that so few preparations and arrangements had been made that it would have been absolutely impossible to produce it on the 14th, that is, yesterday." But Mozart deserves some of the blame, as his arrival in Prague less than two weeks before the scheduled premiere did not allow nearly enough time to rehearse a big, complex opera, even for the most skillful and experienced singers. The premiere was postponed until October 24, but the illness of a singer caused another delay. *Don Giovanni* eventually reached the stage on October 29. Even then the overture had to be played more or less at sight, because Mozart had not managed to get it down on paper until the night before.

Anecdotes related to the rehearsals suggest that, in addition to learning their music, their dialogue in recitative, and their movements on stage, the singers developed a framework within which they improvised some of their interaction. Luigi Bassi, the first Giovanni, compared later performances of the supper scene (near the end of the opera) to that of the original production: "That is all nothing. It lacks the liveliness, the freedom, that the great master wanted in this scene. In Guardasoni's company we never sang the scene the same from one performance to the next. We did not keep the beat exactly, and instead used our wit, always new things, and paying attention only to the orchestra; everything *parlando* [speech-like] and almost improvised—that is how Mozart wanted it."

The singer who portrayed Zerlina (a peasant girl whom Giovanni tries first to seduce and then to rape) had to do more than just sing beautifully, according to a story written down in the 1820s: "At the first rehearsal of this opera in the theater, Signora Bondini, as Zerlina, when she is seized by Don Giovanni at the end of Act 1, was unable to scream properly and at the right moment, even after several repetitions. Mozart left the orchestra, went on stage, and directed that the scene be repeated yet again. At the moment in question he seized the actress so abruptly and forcefully that she screamed in terror. 'That's the way,' he said to her approvingly, 'that's how to scream.'"

COMEDY AND HORROR

In *Don Giovanni*, as in all his Italian operas, serious and comic, Mozart adopted a basic musical and dramatic framework in which arias, ensembles, and choruses punctuate dialogue in simple recitative. The comic operas differ from the serious ones in their wider variety of styles in the arias (reflecting, as in Gaetano Latilla's *La finta cameriera* and Niccolò Piccinni's *La buona figliuola*, a wider variety of character types and social classes) and in using more ensembles. Among the glories of Mozart's comic operas, including *Don Giovanni*, are the finales: the act-ending ensembles of which we have seen (in Chapter 12) a fine example in Giovanni Paisiello's *Il barbiere di Siviglia*.

At one end of the stylistic spectrum in *Don Giovanni* are the heroic speeches of the aristocratic Ottavio and his fiancée Anna. As the opera approaches its conclusion, Anna shares with Ottavio her feelings of love, sorrow, and hope in an orchestrally accompanied recitative and an aria, *Non mi dir bell'idol mio* (Do not say, my darling), with music evoking the nobility of opera seria—both the long, gracefully sinuous lines of the opening Larghetto and the fiery coloratura of the concluding Allegretto moderato. At the other stylistic extreme is the vividly pictorial comic aria in which Leporello, Giovanni's servant, summarizes the contents of a list of the women seduced by his master (see Anthology 23). Somewhere between the two extremes is the suavely beguiling duet *Là ci darem la mano* (There we will give each other our hands; Opera Sampler), in which Giovanni practices his arts of seduction on the unworldly Zerlina. She gives in quickly, and the duet ends with music in which Giovanni and Zerlina, singing mostly in parallel tenths, look forward to having sex.

The finales with which both acts end are but the longest and most complex of the opera's many ensembles, which include some of its most broadly comic moments. These usually involve Leporello: for example the supper scene, accompanied by a wind ensemble playing excerpts from familiar operas, in which the servant furtively samples his master's dinner, and the sextet *Sola, sola in buio loco* (Alone in this dark place), in which Leporello, disguised as Giovanni, tries to escape Elvira's endearments and the anger of the other characters. The *introduzione* (the finale-like ensemble at the beginning of the opera; Opera Sampler) begins comically: Leporello, outside Anna's residence, complains, with a mainly disjunct melody and an accompaniment that often doubles the voice, of having to stand guard while his master makes yet another conquest. But it suddenly descends into tragedy when Anna's father, having challenged Giovanni to a duel, is stabbed to death.

A death on stage! For those familiar with nineteenth-century opera, it is difficult to imagine a time when such an event would have shocked an operatic audience. But death is rare in opera of our period, even so-called opera seria. When Da Ponte, reminiscing about his collaboration with Mozart on *Don Giovanni*, referred to the composer's wish to make the opera "exclusively serious," he probably had such moments in mind: the first in a series of violent events that pervade it—despite its comic episodes—from beginning to end. Mozart called attention to this violence with his music, and it differentiates this opera from all his others.

Nowhere is Mozart's interest in dramatizing violence more apparent than in the finale of Act 2, when the statue of the man Giovanni killed—the "Stone Guest" of the opera's subtitle—comes to life and drags him down to the underworld. But even here comedy is not absent. Mozart used the resources of the finale—its potential for depicting a wide range of characters and dramatic situations within a single coherent musical structure—to juxtapose Leporello's comic reaction to the statue's approach (he looks for a place to hide, using the same key and much the same melodic style that he used in the opera's opening scene) and the statue's first words. This Andante in D minor, orchestrated with trombones, is one of the most chilling moments in all of opera (Ex. 15.1). By quoting the music of this scene at the beginning of the overture, where its ominous D-minor chords stand out, Mozart told his audience that the horror of Giovanni's fate lies at the heart of the opera. And in getting the original Zerlina to scream—really scream—during the finale of Act 1, he emphasized the same aspect of the drama: the violence of the attempted rape anticipates the violence with which Giovanni himself is abducted at the end of the opera.

Example 15.1: *Wolfgang Amadeus Mozart,* Don Giovanni, *finale of Act 2, mm. 426–443*

[Leporello] *I don't want to see your friend; I'll quietly go and hide. [Il Commendatore]*
Don Giovanni, you invited me to dinner, and I have come.

Eighteenth-century conventions demanded that the unrepentant Giovanni
be punished for his crimes, but they also led audiences to expect a happy ending.
Could an opera end with an event as terrifying as Giovanni's death? At the end
of *The Beggar's Opera* (see Chapter 7) the fictive author of the play comes on stage
to spare Macheath's life, "for an opera must end happily." Da Ponte and Mozart
found a different, less subversive, way to a happy ending, while still having

Giovanni suitably punished. They added to the story a final scene in which all the characters except Giovanni and the statue return to the stage and cheerfully draw a moral from the sinner's fate.

A CORONATION OPERA FOR THE "GERMAN TITUS"

When Joseph II died in February 1790, his brother and successor Leopold inherited the monarchy in crisis. Joseph had not managed most aspects of his reign as successfully as he had managed his theaters. Through despotically imposed reforms and arrogant and autocratic behavior, he had alienated himself from many of his subjects, even from those, such as the peasants and the urban working class, whom his reforms had generally benefited. An unpopular war with Turkey was going badly for the Austrians. War taxes and forced conscription increased discontent. The nobility in Bohemia and Hungary, alarmed by his attempts to better the peasants' lot, threatened to rebel; already the Austrian Netherlands were in open revolt. With the outbreak in 1789 of the French Revolution, a dynasty closely allied to the Habsburgs by marriage, and the tradition of absolute monarchy in general, faced a dangerous challenge.

Leopold dealt with the internal threats with a skillfully applied strategy of divide and conquer. Using a mixture of negotiation, concession, and (in the case of the Austrian Netherlands) armed force, he brought the monarchy under control. One of the ways in which Leopold defused Bohemia's anger was to agree to be crowned king of Bohemia. Through the coronation oath he acknowledged the ancient rights that the Bohemian nobility enjoyed in exchange for granting him the crown. The coronation, in other words, was a kind of contract that reassured the nobility that Leopold would rule with respect for its traditional rights and privileges. The festivities surrounding the coronation on September 6, 1791, thus celebrated the reconciliation between the Bohemian nobility and their new ruler.

Music played an important role in the festivities. Coronation day involved two great ceremonial events. The coronation itself took place in the morning in the cathedral high above the river; the coronation opera took place in the evening in the National Theater in the Staré Mesto. Antonio Salieri, imperial court music director, conducted music for the coronation; Mozart composed and directed the opera. Trumpets and drums sounded in the cathedral as the archbishop of Prague placed the crown of St. Wenceslaus, Bohemia's patron saint, on Leopold's head. Trumpets and drums sounded again that evening, when, in the presence of the emperor and his family, courtiers, and members of the Bohemian nobility, Mozart directed the premiere of *La clemenza di Tito* (The Clemency of Titus).

The opera had come into existence quickly. About six weeks earlier the governor of Bohemia concluded an agreement with Guardasoni in which the impresario promised to present a new opera, to be composed by "a famous composer." After Salieri refused the commission, Guardasoni offered it to Mozart. In August 1791, only a little more than three months before his death, Mozart came to Prague for the last time to finish and rehearse *Tito* and to conduct its first performance in the same theater that had witnessed the triumphs of *Figaro* and *Don Giovanni*.

The libretto by the late Viennese court poet Pietro Metastasio (see Chapters 4 and 8) was one of his most popular dramas, having been set to music some 40 times since it first reached the stage in 1734. It takes as its hero the Roman emperor Titus, who ruled from 79 to 81 c.e. Metastasio built the dramatic action out of an aborted rebellion that took place during Titus's reign. But beyond that, *Tito*, like many operas purporting to be based on historical events and characters, is mostly fiction.

Eighteenth-century audiences were used to seeing their rulers allegorically portrayed in opera. No one watching Carl Heinrich Graun's *Montezuma* in Berlin in 1755 (see Chapter 9) could have avoided identifying the Aztec ruler with Frederick the Great. A book published in 1793 drew a parallel between the lives and characters of Titus and the Habsburg emperor Leopold, whom it called the "German Titus." That parallel leaves little doubt that the first audiences of Mozart's opera made the same connection. Having done so, the audience could recognize, in the violent and frightening rebellion with which Act 1 of *Tito* ends, the revolutionary movements and restive special-interest groups—including the Bohemian aristocracy—that confronted Leopold.

Caterino Mazzolà, the Viennese court theater's house poet in 1791, worked with Mozart to bring Metastasio's libretto up to date. He shortened it by cutting some of the dialogue in blank verse, omitting several arias, and recasting its three acts into two. He transformed some of the remaining dialogue into ensembles and increased the chorus's prominence. He thus played a crucial role in the creation of many of the opera's most powerful numbers, such as the politically charged ensemble at the end of Act 1.

In Metastasio's libretto the rebellion takes place offstage; it is described only briefly by a minor character. Mazzolà gave Mozart an opportunity to depict revolutionary violence in music. As a fire set by the conspirators spreads, a combination of minor mode, fast tempo, syncopations, rapid shifts in dynamics, and augmented-sixth harmony conveys the confusion and fear that the rebellion arouses. Suddenly, in the distance, the people of Rome cry out on a diminished seventh chord. This vivid evocation of political turmoil ends quietly, with the soloists and a distant crowd expressing their shock and grief at the news of Titus's death (Fig 15.3).

Figure 15.3: *The end of Act 1 of Mozart's* La clemenza di Tito, *as depicted on the cover of a piano–vocal score published in Leipzig in 1795*

In Act 2 we learn that Titus survived the assassination attempt and suppressed the rebellion. He forgives the rebels and the opera ends with a chorus of praise in which the key of C major and the sound of trumpets and drums bring listeners back to the festive realm of the overture. For the opera's first audience, this music represented a return also to the sounds of the coronation earlier the same day. At the end of Act 1, Mozart conjured up a musical image of revolution in all its horror and tragedy; at the end of Act 2 he depicted with equal power the grandeur of enlightened absolutism.

In a land that specialized in the education of musicians, Prague had access to a steady supply of musical talent and audiences that recognized, appreciated, and rewarded musical excellence. It was close enough to the larger city of Vienna to make travel from one city to the other relatively easy. Many musicians trained in Prague and the surrounding countryside settled in Vienna. But Prague also attracted and inspired a composer living in the Habsburg capital. It warmly appreciated Mozart, and its best orchestra played his complex and difficult music with precision and enthusiasm. The operas that he wrote for Prague, *Don Giovanni* and *La clemenza di Tito*, were fruits of the symbiotic relations between a city and a musician.

FOR FURTHER READING

Durante, Sergio, "The Chronology of Mozart's 'La clemenza di Tito' Reconsidered," *Music and Letters* 80 (1999): 560–94

Freeman, Daniel, *The Opera Theater of Count Franz Anton von Sporck in Prague (1724–1735)* (Stuyvesant, NY: Pendragon, 1992)

Heartz, Daniel, *Mozart, Haydn, and Early Beethoven, 1781–1802* (New York: W. W. Norton, 2009), 164–97

Kelly, Thomas Forrest, *First Nights at the Opera* (New Haven, CT: Yale University Press, 2004), 65–126

Landon, H. C. Robbins, *1791: Mozart's Last Year* (London: Thames and Hudson, 1988)

Rice, John A., *W. A. Mozart: La clemenza di Tito* (Cambridge: Cambridge University Press, 1991)

Rushton, Julian, *W. A. Mozart: Don Giovanni* (Cambridge: Cambridge University Press, 1981)

Sisman, Elaine, "Genre, Gesture, and Meaning in Mozart's 'Prague Symphony,'" in *Mozart Studies 2*, ed. Cliff Eisen (Oxford: Oxford University Press, 1997), 27–84

◎ Additional resources available at wwnorton.com/studyspace

CHAPTER SIXTEEN

London in the 1790s

The French Revolution transformed France's cultural landscape, including its music. But Europe as a whole also felt effects of the Revolution. As we saw in Chapter 15, Mozart's *La clemenza di Tito*, performed in Prague in 1791, could have communicated a counter-revolutionary message to its first audience. Another city that heard the Revolution's musical reverberations was London. Throughout the century London had drawn talented and ambitious musicians from the Continent; but during the Revolution, musicians previously active in Paris, or who might have settled there, came to London instead. In 1793 one of the daily papers marveled at the large number of such musical refugees: "Nothing less than the demolition of one Monarchy, and the general derangement of all the rest, could have poured into England and settled such a mass of talents as we have now to boast. Music as well as misery has fled for shelter to England."

RIVAL CONCERT SERIES

The death in 1782 of Johann Christian Bach, who had helped to organize concerts at the Hanover Square Rooms since they opened in 1774, led to the end of the popular Bach-Abel Concerts. But they were quickly replaced by other series, several of which also took place at Hanover Square: the Hanover Square Grand

Concert (1783–84), the Professional Concert (1785–93), and Salomon's Concert (1791–94). The last was the brainchild of the violinist and impresario Johann Peter Salomon, yet another German immigrant, who brought the public concert to an unprecedented level of artistic excellence.

All three of these series presented 12 or 13 concerts (one each week) during a season that began around the middle of the winter and continued until late spring. In trying to win subscribers, their organizers engaged celebrated composers, instrumentalists, and singers to appear regularly, and exclusively, on their series. But the series did not differ much in the format of their programs, which consisted of two parts separated by an intermission. Both parts began with symphonies, often called overtures, a term reflecting the symphony's ancestry in the operatic sinfonia (see Chapter 5). The second part ended with an orchestral work variously called a finale, a full piece, or a symphony. Concerts typically included Italian arias sung by two or three singers, male and female, who often joined in the performance of a duet or trio near the end of the program. Two or three concertos for different instruments, one of which often served as the conclusion of the concert's first half, constituted the third essential ingredient of concerts in London. Audiences loved novelty, and programs frequently called attention to the newness of music that was to be performed.

An announcement in the *Public Advertiser* of the first concert in the Professional Concert's 1790 series, on February 15, contained the evening's program:

ACT I

Overture	HAYDN
Quartetto	PLEYEL

For two Violins, Tenor [viola], and Violoncello, by Messrs. CRAMER, BORGHI, BLAKE, and CERVETTO

Song	Miss CANTELO
Sonata Piano Forte	Mr. DAME
Song	Signora STORACE
Concerto Violin	Mr. CRAMER

ACT II

New Grand Overture	M.S. HAYDN
Song	Miss CANTELO
Concerto Hautboy [oboe]	Mr. PARKE
Song	Signora STORACE
New Overture	M.S. GIROWETZ

This program was exceptional only in that no male singer participated. The songs performed by the evening's vocal soloists, Miss Cantelo (first name unknown) and Nancy Storace, were almost certainly Italian arias. Storace, born in England to an English mother and an Italian father, had sung opera in Italy and Vienna, where she created the role of Susanna in Mozart's *Le nozze di Figaro*. The program emphasized the novelty of the "overtures"—again, probably concert symphonies—that framed the second half by the abbreviation "M.S." (manuscript), implying they had not yet been printed. Only the symphony by the young Bohemian composer Adalbert Gyrowetz could have been really new, as Gyrowetz had recently arrived in London and might have composed it especially for this occasion. But the compositional star of the evening—the only composer named more than once—had not yet written any symphonies for London. In February 1790 he was far from England; during his long life he had never ventured more than about 100 miles from his birthplace near Vienna.

HAYDN'S FIRST VISIT TO ENGLAND

Salomon's efforts during the 1780s to give his concerts an edge over the competition included repeatedly inviting Joseph Haydn—the popularity of whose symphonies in London can be surmised from their prominence on the concert program quoted above—to write symphonies for London and to direct their performance in person. Haydn, busy fulfilling his duties for Prince Nicolaus Esterházy (see Chapter 10) and writing music for other patrons who did not require him to travel, declined Salomon's invitations. But in September 1790 Nicolaus died. His son Anton largely abandoned Eszterháza, Nicolaus's magnificent but isolated palace, and disbanded his father's opera troupe. He kept Haydn on salary but gave him little to do.

Salomon, in Germany hiring musicians for his next concerts, realized that if he was ever to engage Haydn, this was the time. In November or early December he hurried to Vienna and, on being admitted to Haydn's residence, announced: "I am Salomon from London and have come to fetch you. Tomorrow we shall conclude an agreement." In this agreement Haydn promised to write six symphonies and to direct their performance from the keyboard. Some of Haydn's friends doubted that the composer, now 58, could survive the long trip across Europe and find success in a city much bigger than Vienna. Mozart said to him: "You have no training for the great world, and you speak too few languages." Haydn responded: "My language is understood all over the world!"

On December 15 Haydn and Salomon left Vienna together. Following in the footsteps of so many great musicians from the Continent, Haydn arrived in

London at the beginning of January 1791. Thus began the first of two long visits, each of which included two concert seasons.

Haydn wrote to a friend that it took him two days to recover from his journey by coach and boat. "Now, however, I am fresh and well again, and occupied in looking at this endlessly huge city of London, whose various beauties and marvels quite astonished me." He must have been equally surprised at the richness of London's musical life, of which he could have gotten some idea from an announcement in the *Public Advertiser* on January 7, 1791: "Never could this country boast of such a constellation of musical excellence as now illuminates our fashionable hemisphere. No one metropolis can exhibit such a union of masters as London now possesses." There follows a list of the weekly events planned for the upcoming season:

SUNDAY	The Nobleman's Subscription is held every Sunday at a different house.
MONDAY	The Professional Concert—at the Hanover-Square Rooms—with Mrs. Billington.
TUESDAY	The Opera.
WEDNESDAY	The Ancient Music at the rooms in Tottenham Street, under the patronage of Their Majesties.
	The Anacreontic Society also, occasionally, on Wednesday.
THURSDAY	The Pantheon. A pasticcio of music and dancing, in case that the Opera Coalition shall take place; if not, a concert with Mad. Mara and Sig. Pacchierotti.
	Academy of Ancient Music, every other Thursday, at Freemason's Hall.
FRIDAY	A concert under the auspices of Haydn at the Rooms, Hanover Square, with Sig. David.
SATURDAY	The Opera.

With the significant exception of Haydn, all the musicians mentioned on this list were singers: the sopranos Elizabeth Billington and Gertrud Mara, the *musico* Gasparo Pacchierotti, and the tenor Giacomo David were all among Europe's leading performers of Italian opera. Their names again underline the importance of vocal music (and Italian opera arias in particular) in concerts in London, as in the rest of Europe.

The list also reminds us of the crucial role that Italian opera had played in London's musical life since the early eighteenth century (see Chapter 7). Indeed,

Haydn came to England with the expectation of writing not only symphonies but also an opera seria, which was to be entitled *L'anima del filosofo, ossia Orfeo ed Euridice* (The Philospher's Soul, or Orpheus and Eurydice). He came close to completing it and putting it into production, but it fell victim to a rivalry between two theaters competing for the exclusive right to present Italian opera, and was never performed. Fortunately, Haydn had been paid for it in advance; he took it back to Vienna and eventually had parts of it published.

A TRIUMPHANT DEBUT

Salomon soon announced his intention to present 12 concerts on Friday nights, with Haydn directing the performance of a new work for each concert; subscriptions were to cost five guineas. After several delays, Haydn's first series of concerts began on March 11, 1791. He made his debut on a program that began and ended with symphonies by the Bohemians Antonio Rosetti and Leopold Kozeluch, and included arias sung by a soprano and tenor (both prominent opera singers), concertos for oboe and violin, and a symphonie concertante for piano and harp by yet another Bohemian musician, Jan Ladislav Dussek. But the pièce de résistance was Haydn's "New Grand Overture," played at the beginning of the second half of the program.

No fewer than three of the soloists—the pianist Dussek, the harpist Anne-Marie Krumpholz, and the violinist Madame Gautherot—had spent the period immediately before the French Revolution in Paris, exemplifying how London benefited during the Revolution from musical talent developed in France. Also French was the symphonie concertante, a concerto for two or more instruments of which French composers and audiences were particularly fond; Mozart had encountered it in Paris in 1778, as we saw in Chapter 13.

Haydn's "New Grand Overture" was probably his Symphony No. 92 in G Major, composed in 1789: not new, but apparently unknown in London. (Haydn was to present it again in July 1791 in Oxford, on the occasion of his receiving an honorary degree from the university; that performance earned for it the nickname *Oxford* Symphony.) Haydn directed its performance from the keyboard, in the middle of an orchestra whose arrangement was described by an eyewitness:

> The pianoforte was in the centre, at each extreme end the double basses, then on each side two violoncellos, then two tenors or violas and two violins, and in the hollow of the piano a desk on a high platform for Salomon [as concertmaster] and his ripieno [perhaps the first violin section]. At the back, verging down to a point at each end, all these instruments were doubled, giving the requisite number for a full orchestra. Still further back, raised high up, were drums, and on either side the trumpets,

trombones, bassoons, oboes, clarinets, flutes, &c., in numbers according to the requirements of the symphonies and other music to be played on the different evenings.

The *Morning Chronicle* echoed the audience's ecstatic reaction to Haydn's concert: "Never, perhaps, was there a richer musical treat." Not surprisingly, it devoted most of its report to Haydn's symphony:

> It is not wonderful that to souls capable of being touched by music, HAYDN should be an object of homage, and even of idolatry; for like our own SHAKSPEARE, he moves and governs the passions at his will.
>
> His *new Grand Overture* was pronounced by every scientific ear to be a most wonderful composition; but the first movement in particular rises in grandeur of subject, and in the rich variety of *air* and passion, beyond any even of his own productions. The *Overture* has four movements. . . . They are all beautiful, but the first is pre-eminent in every charm, and the band performed it with admirable correctness. . . .
>
> We were happy to see the concert so well attended the first night; for we cannot suppress our very anxious hopes, that the first musical genius of the age may be induced, by our liberal welcome, to take up his residence in England.

Although Haydn's first season in London was marred by the failure to bring *L'anima del filosofo* to the stage, as a symphonist he triumphed. His success came despite his not fulfilling the agreement with Salomon, in which he had promised to write six symphonies. Having been engaged so soon before the beginning of the concert season, and with much of his early weeks in London taken up with the composition of his opera, he had little time to write symphonies. Of those he presented in 1791, only two, Nos. 95 in C Minor and 96 in D Major, are among the 12 that he would eventually compose for London. Salomon allowed him to fulfill his promise with a mixture of new symphonies and works (like the *Oxford* Symphony) new enough not to be familiar in England.

HAYDN'S SECOND SEASON

Haydn's success during the winter and spring of 1791 caused Salomon to ask him to stay in England and to headline the 1792 season. In July 1791 Haydn wrote Prince Anton Esterházy, seeking permission to extend his leave to the following summer. Anton's coldly polite answer, which managed to misspell Haydn's name, was an unpleasant reminder that despite his fame he was still a nobleman's servant:

To the Kapellmeister Hayden:

It is with much pleasure that I learn from your letter of July 20 how much your talents are prized in London and I genuinely rejoice thereat; but at the same time I cannot conceal from you that your present, already extended absence has turned out to be not only very vexatious for me but also very expensive since I was compelled to have recourse to outsiders for the festivities held at Eszterháza this month.

You will not think ill of me therefore that I cannot grant you the requested extension for a further year of your leave of absence; but instead expect to hear from you by the next post the exact time when you will arrive back here again.

Haydn ignored the summons: a personal rebellion that, in its own small way, echoed the Revolution unfolding in France. His experiences in London had taught him his true value. He knew that Anton earned prestige from having him as his music director. He calculated that the prince would not dismiss him, even if he extended his leave without permission. He was right.

The long period between the end of the 1791 concert season and the beginning of the 1792 season gave Haydn time to visit Oxford, to relax at the country estate of a banker who had befriended him, and to write music for his forthcoming concerts. That music included the Symphonie Concertante in B♭ Major (for violin, oboe, cello, and bassoon) and four symphonies, the most celebrated of which (No. 94 in G Major) came to be known as the *Surprise* Symphony because of the *fortissimo* chord, reinforced with a drumbeat, in the otherwise placid slow movement. Another symphony, No. 97 in C Major, is just as finely crafted but less sensational in it effects. Composed within a few months of Mozart's death on December 5, 1791, it exemplifies the brilliance, grandeur, and charm of Haydn's "London" Symphonies and at the same time presents what he might have intended as a gentle, private memorial to his friend.

THE SYMPHONY NO. 97

The Symphony No. 97, like all of Haydn's later symphonies, is in four movements: a Vivace in sonata form, preceded by a slow introduction marked Adagio; a set of variations on a theme, Adagio ma non troppo (see Anthology 24); a minuet marked Allegretto; and a finale that moves freely and unpredictably within the parameters of rondo form. In choosing the key of C major, Haydn also chose a particular orchestral color, dominated by trumpets and timpani, that he associated with this key. The timpani influenced the character of the Vivace's opening theme, with its fanfare-like alternation of the timpani's two notes, C and G (Ex. 16.1).

The slow introduction begins, like Haydn's String Quartet in G Major from the Opus 33 set (see Ex. 14.5), with an ending. But while the cadence at the beginning

Example 16.1: *Joseph Haydn, Symphony No. 97 in C Major, movement 1, mm. 14–25*

of the quartet is a terse, four-note motive harmonized V⁷–I, the symphony begins with a sweetly lyrical cadential phrase (Ex. 16.2a). It draws attention to itself by its unusual location, making it more likely that listeners will recognize it when it returns at the end of the introduction (Ex. 16.2b). The context here is again strange: we expect a slow introduction to end with a half cadence, not a full cadence like this one. By now the cadential phrase has begun to take on special significance, reinforced in the Vivace when it appears yet again in the exposition's closing material (Ex. 16.2c) and one final time in the closing material of the recapitulation. This phrase resembles, in melody and harmony, one of Mozart's most memorable cadences: the moment in *Così fan tutte* when Fiordiligi succumbs to Ferrando's seduction (see Anthology 21, mm. 97–101). Haydn attended a rehearsal of *Così fan tutte* as Mozart's guest in December 1789; the musicologist Daniel Heartz has suggested that he gave this phrase such prominence in a symphony that he wrote shortly after he learned of Mozart's death "because it had great meaning for him after Mozart used it so beautifully in what may be the last work by the younger composer that Haydn heard under its creator's direction."

The attention aroused by the repetition and manipulation of this phrase in the first movement allows listeners to follow other stimulating relationships within and between other movements, and to admire Haydn's inexhaustible inventiveness. The coda in the first movement is one of three codas (the others are in the second and fourth movements), all of which approach the elaborateness with which Beethoven would later treat this compositional element. The second theme in the Vivace, which sounds like a country dance, with the bassoons playing off-beat chords, anticipates in character the trio section of the third movement. There, instead of using repeat signs, Haydn wrote out the repeats, and reorchestrated parts of the trio, including a passage in which the horns play off-beat chords. The very last phrase he scored for solo violin especially for the man who brought him to London and who served as concertmaster during the

Example 16.2: *Joseph Haydn, Symphony No. 97 in C Major, movement 1*

(a) *mm. 1–4*

(b) *mm. 10–16*

(c) *mm. 98–104*

performance of this symphony. He wrote above the violin part: "Salomon solo ma piano" (Salomon alone, but softly).

These passages reminded listeners of other passages in the symphony, but Haydn probably hoped an effect in the minuet would remind them of one of their favorite moments in another symphony first performed in 1792: the timpani-reinforced *fortissimo* in the slow movement of the *Surprise* Symphony. Where listeners expect the minuet to end, it extends itself with a three-note motive passed from violins to oboe to flute to bassoon, until the timpanist suddenly interrupts, *forte*, repeatedly pounding a single drum, as if to tell the winds to stop chatting.

In June 1792 Haydn left London, exhausted but much better off financially than when he arrived 18 months earlier. After London, the smaller city of Vienna probably seemed a little sleepy. Mozart's death had left it a less exciting place for a musician of Haydn's sophistication. Not surprisingly, he jumped at the opportunity to return to London in January 1794.

HAYDN'S SECOND VISIT

Haydn's second visit to England (1794–95) followed closely the schedule of the first. On his arrival he immediately began preparations for the third Salomon–Haydn series, from February to May 1794, in which he shared the spotlight with the violinist Giovanni Battista Viotti (another refugee from Paris, whom we met in Chapter 13 as Luigi Cherubini's partner at the Théâtre Feydeau). Haydn passed the summer and fall sightseeing, socializing, resting, and composing. For his final concert series, beginning in February 1795, Viotti took over Salomon's role as music director and concertmaster, and the concerts took place not at Hanover Square but in a concert hall next to the new King's Theatre in the Haymarket. The series reached its culmination in the concert that Haydn gave for his own financial benefit on May 4, 1795, which included the first performance of his last symphony, No. 104 in D Major. During the second London visit Haydn presented six new symphonies (Nos. 99–104). But he was just as busy composing music for the piano, and in this respect the second visit differed from the first.

CLEMENTI, DUSSEK, AND THE LONDON PIANOFORTE SCHOOL

In the second half of the eighteenth century, several instrument makers from Germany, Switzerland, and the Netherlands made London one of Europe's most productive centers of piano design and construction. Although many of the instruments built in London were square pianos (especially appropriate for music-making in the home), the city also produced a distinctive kind of grand piano. John Broadwood and other piano makers perfected an action, now known as "English action," different from that in Viennese pianos. (A piano's action is the mechanism that transfers the energy in the player's finger to the hammer that strikes the string.) Also different from Viennese instruments are the thick soundboards and the heavy hammers of English pianos, and their triple stringing (a single hammer hits three strings, instead of the two strings

Figure 16.1: *A grand piano by John Broadwood, 1792. Compare with the much earlier grand in Fig. 5.2.*

common in Viennese pianos), all of which give English grands a bigger sound than Viennese ones (Fig. 16.1).

English pianos encouraged composers and performers to explore the new possibilities these instruments opened up. Musicians, in turn, inspired builders to expand the size and power of their instruments still further. The mutually beneficial interaction of musicians and instrument makers led to the formation of what has been called the "London Pianoforte School." The term does not refer to an institution but to a group of pianists and pianist-composers in London during the 1780s and 1790s, with close ties to one another and to Broadwood and other builders.

If anyone can be called the founder or leader of the London Pianoforte School, it was Muzio Clementi (1752–1832). As a talented teenager in Rome, Clementi attracted the attention of a wealthy English nobleman on the Grand Tour, who took him back to England and paid for his musical education. He established himself as a professional musician in London in the mid-1770s. In 1781 he toured France and Germany, giving many performances and engaging in a famous pianistic "duel" with Mozart in Vienna. (Clementi admired his rival's "spirit and grace," but Mozart dismissed the Italian virtuoso as "a mere mechanicus.") He stayed in England for most of the rest of his life, active as a performer, teacher, music publisher, piano salesman, and composer (principally of technically demanding piano sonatas and concertos). Among his students were several who won fame as keyboard virtuosos, including John Field, whom we met in Chapter 12.

In 1789 a brilliant young pianist who had just spent several years in Paris joined Clementi and his pianistic students and colleagues in London. Jan Ladislav Dussek (1760–1812; Fig. 16.2), a soloist in Haydn's very first London concert, was one of many Bohemians who left their native land and enriched the musical life of Europe's capitals. He attended the University of Prague, but by the age of 19 he began travels that would occupy most of his adult life. They took him in 1786 to Paris, where he won the patronage of Queen Marie Antoinette. He might have stayed there had the Revolution not broken out three years later. His close ties to

Figure 16.2: *Jan Ladislav Dussek, at a piano similar to the one in Fig. 16.1. Painting by Henre-Pierre Danloux, 1795.*

the court made France uncomfortable for him. Shortly before the Revolution he moved to London. He lived there for 11 years (1789–99), contributing to musical life in many of the same ways, artistic and commercial, as Clementi.

Dussek made his London debut at the Hanover Square Rooms in February 1789; he quickly developed into the kind of celebrity that thrived in London. The composer Johann Tomaschek believed him to have been the first pianist to place the instrument sideways on stage, "so that the ladies could admire his handsome profile." Tomaschek, who heard him in Prague in 1804, wrote of his playing:

> After the few opening bars of his first solo, the public uttered one general *Ah!* There was, in fact, something magical about the way in which Dussek, with all his charming grace of manner, through his wonderful touch, extracted from the instrument delicious and at the same time emphatic tones. His fingers were like a company of ten singers endowed with equal executive powers and able to produce with the utmost perfection whatever their director could require.

Dussek composed a wide variety of works involving piano: concertos, sonatas for piano and for piano and violin, and trios for piano, violin, and cello. Like many of his contemporaries, he liked program music, exciting applause with a *Military Concerto* and celebrating a British victory with a piano sonata, *The Naval Battle and Total Defeat of the Grand Dutch Fleet by Admiral Duncan* (1797). *The Farewell*, a sonata that he dedicated to Clementi and published in 1800, shortly after leaving London, was presumably meant as a parting gesture to the city and its music lovers. Dussek took full advantage of the big, vibrant instruments at his disposal in London and encouraged builders to expand their range and power even further. He developed close relations with Broadwood, who delivered to him one of his first pianos with a five-and-a-half-octave keyboard in 1791; three years later he was one of the first pianists to play Broadwood's six-octave piano in public. He also introduced structural innovations in his compositions, such as the slow introduction with which the Concerto in C Major, Op. 29 (published in 1795) begins and the return of material from that slow introduction in both the second and third movements.

When Queen Marie Antoinette died on the guillotine on October 16, 1793, Dussek reacted quickly. Before the end of the year he published *The Sufferings of the Queen of France: A Musical Composition Expressing the Feelings of the Unfortunate Marie Antoinette during her Imprisonment, Trial, &c.* The score consists of ten movements: *The queen's imprisonment* (Largo, C minor), *She reflects on her former greatness* (Maestosamente, E♭ major), *They separate her from her children* (Agitato assai, C minor), *They pronounce the sentence of death* (Allegro con furia, E♭ minor), *Her resignation to her fate* (Adagio innocente, E♭ major), *The situation and reflections the night before her execution* (Andante agitato, A♭ major), *March*

(Lento, D minor), *The savage tumult of the rabble* (Presto furioso, B♭ major), *The queen's invocation to the Almighty just before her death* (Molto adagio, Devotamente, E major), and *The Apotheosis* (Allegro maestoso, C major).

Some of the movements deal with a single circumstance or emotion; others present contrast or change. The depiction of the queen's "former greatness" (major mode, dotted rhythms, *fortissimo*) gives way to a soft passage in the minor mode marked "doloroso" (grieving). The following movement uses a fast tempo and constant syncopations to depict the queen's despair at being separated from her children; then the tempo slows to Andante to depict "the farewell of her children"; pairs of quarter notes in different registers, with the second note always on a strong beat, probably represent the word "adieu." The penultimate item begins as a tender slow movement (Ex. 16.3a), but the queen's prayer is suddenly cut off with a glissando representing the guillotine's falling blade (Ex. 16.3b), anticipating the gruesome climax of the *March to the Scaffold* in Hector Berlioz's *Symphonie fantastique* of 1830.

That Dussek ended his musical drama with a triumphant *Apotheosis* (in which Marie Antoinette, her suffering over, enjoys her heavenly reward) makes it not just a royalist political statement but an affirmation of the eighteenth century's prevailing optimism. Even at the height of the Revolution, composers and music lovers maintained their fondness for happy endings in instrumental music no less than in opera.

HAYDN'S LONDON PIANO MUSIC

During his first visit to England, Haydn established contacts with members of the London Pianoforte School, particularly Dussek; but he wrote little piano music. He was no keyboard virtuoso; perhaps the combination of digital virtuosity and compositional prowess of Dussek and Clementi intimidated him. He may have felt uncomfortable with the novel sound and touch of English pianos. But by 1794 he was thoroughly at home with English instruments and had nothing to prove to London's critics—or its professional pianists—about his musicianship. Music publishers may have persuaded him that trios for piano, violin, and cello would be welcomed by amateur pianists who might not attempt the solo sonatas that virtuosos wrote largely for themselves and their professional colleagues. During his second visit Haydn allowed his pianistic muse free rein.

Haydn wrote 12 piano trios during 1794–95, publishing them in London in four sets of three. He dedicated them to women, whom he deliberately chose in order to celebrate and strengthen three relationships important to him. With dedications to the widow of Prince Anton Esterházy and to the wife of the current Prince Nicolaus II, he communicated to Nicolaus his desire for continued employment. The dedication to Rebecca Schroeter was a gesture of love to

Example 16.3: *Jan Ladislav Dussek*, The Sufferings of the Queen of France

(a) *No. 9*, The queen's invocation to the Almighty just before her death, *mm. 1–4*

(b) *No. 9, mm. 20–22 and No. 10*, The Apotheosis, *mm. 1–7*

the woman with whom he enjoyed an intimate friendship during his years in London; the dedication to Therese Jansen Bartolozzi was a declaration of admiration and respect from one professional musician to another.

Therese Jansen (ca. 1770–1843) was a leading female member of the London Pianoforte School and, like several other members of the group, German by birth. The daughter of a dancing master, she moved to England as a child and studied piano with Clementi. She married the art dealer Gaetano Bartolozzi in 1795, with Haydn serving as a witness. To judge from the music Haydn wrote for her, she was a brilliant pianist, but like many female instrumentalists she mostly played in private. In the early 1790s both Clementi and Dussek acknowledged and enhanced her status by dedicating publications to her. Haydn, dedicating to her a set of piano trios, not only added to her luster but publicly claimed a place for himself within the London Pianoforte School.

Haydn made similar gestures in private, composing for Jansen at least two sonatas for unaccompanied piano during his second visit to London. He wrote on the autograph of the Sonata in E♭ Major, Hob. XVI: 52: "Sonata composed for the celebrated Signora Teresa de Janson . . . by me, Giuseppe Haydn, 1794." It was not published until 1798. The Sonata No. 50 in C Major was published in London around 1800 as *A Grand Sonata for the Piano Forte composed expressly for and dedicated to Mrs. Bartolozzi by Haydn*. That Haydn did not publish these sonatas immediately after he wrote them suggests a continued reluctance to have his music publicly compared to that of the London Pianoforte School in the genre for which it reserved some of its most brilliant displays of compositional innovation and technical skill.

Jansen's virtuosity, the powerful pianos she and Haydn had access to in London, and the stimulating example of Clementi and Dussek inspired Haydn to a level of ingenuity and originality that makes the Sonata in E♭ Major one of his finest works. Two spacious sonata-form movements in E♭ (see Anthology 25) frame a central slow movement in **ABA′** form, for which Haydn chose the remote key of E major. But he laid the groundwork for this choice in the first movement's development section, where a theme heard earlier in that movement in B♭ and C returns in E. He tied the first and second movements together in another way: by ending the Adagio with a short coda that recapitulates the striking harmonic progression with which the first movement begins (Ex. 16.4). While this slow movement conveys much the same meditative character as Dussek's E-major portrait of Marie Antoinette in prayer, a playful spirit suffuses the finale, beginning with a theme whose droning accompaniment gives it the character of a rustic dance. But Haydn balanced the lightness of the thematic material with a working-out as thorough and as fascinating as in the first movement.

───────────

The outbreak of the French Revolution, the deaths of Emperor Joseph II and Mozart, and Haydn's first trip to London all took place within two and a half years (1789–91). This eventful period separated Mozart's Viennese decade from the years, discussed

Example 16.4: *Joseph Haydn, Piano Sonata No. 52 in E♭ Major, movement 2, mm. 49–54*

in this chapter, in which London benefited from the presence of many talented musicians who might, without the Revolution, have contributed to music in Paris.

Musicians who came to England profited from a characteristic feature of musical life in Europe's largest and richest city: a culture of celebrity that placed particular value on the attractiveness of a musician's looks and personality. Londoners wanted not only to hear the works of the best composers but also to see them conducting their music from the keyboard and to interact with them at receptions and dinners.

Joseph Haydn was the greatest of the composers who came to England in the 1790s. His visits had nothing to do with the Revolution, directly at least, but he certainly gained—creatively as well as financially—from the richness of London's musical life and its culture of celebrity. With his help London produced more first-rate music during the first half of the decade than any other city. Its efficient publishing industry quickly disseminated that music to sophisticated music lovers all over Europe, including Vienna. There, as we will see in Chapter 17, London's musical achievements had a significant impact.

FOR FURTHER READING

Brown, A. Peter, *The First Golden Age of the Viennese Symphony: Haydn, Mozart, Beethoven, and Schubert* (Bloomington: Indiana University Press, 2002), 243–300

Heartz, Daniel, *Mozart, Haydn, and Early Beethoven, 1781–1802* (New York: W. W. Norton, 2009) 421–551

Landon, H. C. Robbins, *Haydn: Chronicle and Works*, Vol. 3, *Haydn in England* (Bloomington: Indiana University Press, 1976)

McVeigh, Simon, *Concert Life in London from Mozart to Haydn* (Cambridge: Cambridge University Press, 1993)

Milligan, Thomas B., *The Concerto and London's Musical Culture in the Late Eighteenth Century* (Ann Arbor, MI: UMI Research Press, 1983)

Plantinga, Leon, *Clementi: His Life and Music* (Oxford: Oxford University Press, 1977)

Price, Curtis, Judith Milhous, and Robert D. Hume, *Italian Opera in Late Eighteenth-Century London,* 2 vols. (Oxford: Oxford University Press, 1995–2001)

Ringer, Alexander, "Beethoven and the London Pianoforte School," *Musical Quarterly* 56 (1970): 742–58

Ⓢ Additional resources available at wwnorton.com/studyspace

CHAPTER SEVENTEEN

Vienna in the Napoleonic Era

The wars that shook Europe during and after the French Revolution made France and Austria implacable enemies. Queen Marie Antoinette was the sister of the Austrian Emperors Joseph II and Leopold II and the aunt of Emperor Francis (who ruled from 1792 to 1830); her imprisonment and execution aroused Austrian fear and hostility. So did the threat that France, in exporting revolution to other parts of Europe, presented to the Habsburg Empire. From the French Republic's point of view, Austria's allegiance to the monarchic form of government presented an equally dangerous threat.

The wars produced a great French leader whose heroic exploits mesmerized Europe, even those parts of Europe that hated and feared him. The prestige that Napoleon Bonaparte (1769–1821) gained from his military victories allowed him to build up political power. Initially promising to preserve the Republic (as First Consul in 1799), he later crowned himself emperor (1804). His image so dominated Europe that it makes sense to call the 20-year period in which he rose to power and ruled France (1795–1815) the Napoleonic Era.

Music continued to flourish in Vienna throughout the wars, and sometimes composers found inspiration in the momentous events taking place around them. Haydn's *Missa in tempore belli* (Mass in Time of War, 1796) ends with a

Figure 17.1: *The title page of Beethoven's* Wellington's Victory *in the first edition of the keyboard reduction (Vienna: Steiner)*

martial Agnus Dei, in which trumpets and drums provide an ominous background to the prayer "Give us peace." Beethoven, writing the *Eroica* Symphony (1804) to celebrate Napoleon, and then ripping up the title page when he learned that the general had crowned himself emperor, was in the sway of great political events. A decade later he celebrated the defeat of France at the Battle of Vittoria in *Wellington's Victory*, a musical depiction of the battle, complete with national anthems and percussion-simulated gunfire (Fig. 17.1).

This might lead us to suppose that the musical cultures of Paris and Vienna, so closely linked during much of the eighteenth century, diverged during and after the Revolution. In some respects they did. We saw in Chapter 13 that Antonio Salieri, who wrote three operas for Paris in the 1780s and whose experiences there strongly influenced his compositional style, found it impossible to return to Paris after 1789. While Parisian aristocrats, leading patrons of the ancien régime, disappeared from musical life, the Viennese nobility projected its wealth and power with a self-conscious promotion of "greatness" in music, at the expense of music that it perceived as merely entertaining or pleasing; it was largely Viennese noblemen who created the artistic climate in which Beethoven reached artistic maturity and Haydn created his last masterpieces. Yet during the brief lulls between military campaigns, French music lovers awarded a medal to Haydn and Viennese operagoers rediscovered the delights of opéra comique. Perhaps the single most important French influence on Viennese music was Napoleon himself, and the image of heroism, energy, and decisiveness that he projected so charismatically.

BEETHOVEN IN VIENNA: THE 1790S

Bonn, the small city where Ludwig van Beethoven (1770–1827) was born, was almost as far from Vienna as it was possible to be in the German-speaking part of Europe. But as the residence of Maximilian, archbishop of Cologne and the brother of Emperors Joseph and Leopold, Bonn had close dynastic connections to Vienna. When young Beethoven, the son of a tenor employed by Maximilian, emerged as a prodigy, it was natural that the archbishop and other patrons in Bonn should think of sending him to Vienna to develop his talents to their fullest.

In 1792, less than a year after Mozart's death, Beethoven traveled to Vienna to study with Haydn. He took with him a letter from Count Ferdinand Waldstein, who helped organize his journey, expressing hope that the brilliant young pianist would one day equal Mozart: "You are going to Vienna in fulfillment of your long frustrated wishes. The Genius of Mozart is mourning and weeping the death of her pupil. She found a refuge but no occupation with the inexhaustible Haydn; through him she wishes once more to form a union with another. With the help of assiduous labor you shall receive *Mozart's spirit from Haydn's hands*."

With recommendations from such music lovers, Beethoven quickly found patrons among Viennese aristocrats, delighted to play a role in the narrative that Waldstein sketched out so attractively. Beethoven himself played his part, devoting special attention throughout his life to genres in which Mozart and Haydn had been particularly successful. In a series of piano sonatas he directed all his virtuosity into an exploration of the coloristic and harmonic possibilities offered by the quickly evolving instrument. With the string quartets of Opus 18 he established a reputation as a composer of chamber music with the potential to equal the achievements of his great predecessors. And in the symphony too he cultivated a style that caused listeners to make comparisons with Haydn and Mozart, and to think of him as the youngest in a trio of great masters. A critic writing in 1803 (who thus could have known only his first two symphonies) praised him for combining in his symphonies "Mozart's universality and wild, extravagant audacity with Haydn's humorous caprice."

THE EARLY PIANO SONATAS

As a piano virtuoso Beethoven focused much of his compositional energy on the sonata, dedicating one of his earliest major publications, the three piano sonatas of Opus 2, to Haydn. In the piano sonata his models were not only the works of Haydn and Mozart, but also the sonatas published in the 1790s by such pianist-composers as Muzio Clementi and Jan Ladislav Dussek, who were energetically taking advantage of the instrument's rapid development in London (see Chapter 16). Beethoven knew the works of the London Pianoforte School, and by the mid-1790s he probably knew English pianos as well. The Austrian pianist and composer Johann Nepomuk Hummel (1778–1837), who visited London in 1791, evidently brought a piano back to Vienna with him. Before his concert in the Burgtheater in 1794, the *Wiener Zeitung* made a special point of announcing that he would perform on his own "English grand pianoforte."

Although the three-movement, fast-slow-fast format pioneered in the keyboard sonatas of Carl Philipp Emanuel Bach (see Chapter 9) predominated in the sonatas of Haydn and Mozart, Beethoven began his career preferring to write sonatas in four movements, following the fast-slow-minuet (or scherzo)-fast pattern that Haydn and Mozart associated with the symphony and string quartet. The fourth and final movement of the Sonata in A Major, Op. 2, No. 2 (1795; see Anthology 26) reveals the young Beethoven at his most melodious and ingratiating; and it serves as a fine example of the sonata-rondo: a rondo incorporating elements of sonata form.

This music reminds us of Beethoven's capacity to delight and charm his audience; but it also is true that in the genre of the piano sonata he achieved some remarkably early breakthroughs to the impetuous, heroic style that became characteristic of his work as a whole only later. In the Sonata No. 8, Op. 13 (*Grande Sonate Pathétique*, 1798), for example, he explored the tumultuous C-minor realm to which he much later returned in the Fifth Symphony's first movement.

Beethoven published the *Pathétique* Sonata individually, rather than as part of a set, thus promoting it as a work of special interest and value. Dedicated to his patron Prince Carl von Lichnowsky, it broke no new ground in large-scale organization, and indeed in its three-movement layout—fast-slow-fast—Beethoven returned to the practice of Haydn and Mozart after his earlier four-movement experiments. In beginning the first movement with a slow introduction (Ex. 17.1), he may have been responding to Clementi, whose Sonata in G Minor, Op. 34, No. 2 (1795) begins with a ten-measure slow introduction that anticipates melodically and rhythmically the opening theme of the Allegro con fuoco (Ex. 17.2). Beethoven's introduction is also ten measures long, but richer and more adventurous harmonically, texturally, and rhythmically. At the same time, the sudden changes of dynamics, the many sighing appoggiaturas, and the improvisatory runs hark back to such works as C. P. E. Bach's Fantasia in C Minor (see Anthology 11).

Example 17.1: *Ludwig van Beethoven,* Grande Sonate Pathétique, *Op. 13, movement 1, mm. 1–5*

Example 17.2: *Muzio Clementi, Sonata in G Minor, Op. 34, No. 2, movement 1, mm. 1–13*

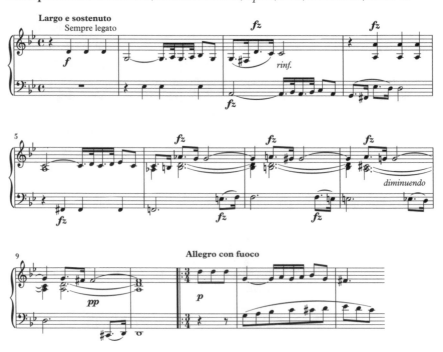

Like Clementi, Beethoven integrated his slow introduction into the sonata-form movement that follows; its portentous dotted rhythms return at the beginning of the development and near the end of the coda. He enhanced the music's darkness by setting the second melodic area in E♭ minor; the expected E♭ major (the relative major) does not arrive until the beginning of the cadential area. He compounded this departure from convention in the recapitulation, where the second melodic area (which we expect to be entirely in tonic C minor or major) begins instead in F minor.

The slow movement of the *Pathétique* Sonata is a rondo in A♭ major with a sweetly euphonious theme. If this Adagio constitutes in many ways the polar opposite of the first movement, the finale reconciles the opposites. It is another sonata-rondo, thus combining the sonata form of the first movement and the rondo of the second. An episode in A♭ major at the center of the movement juxtaposes the key of the second movement with that of the first. The coda combines the stormy C-minor tonality and syncopations of the first movement with a short, quiet passage in A♭ just before the end: a final, fleeting recollection of the Adagio.

GOTTFRIED VAN SWIETEN AND HAYDN'S *THE SEASONS*

We met Baron Gottfried van Swieten, one of the most discerning and influential patrons in Vienna at the end of the eighteenth century, as a patron of Mozart in the 1780s, when his music-making was mostly private (Chapter 14). In the 1790s Swieten took on a more public role as one of the city's musical trendsetters, earning this encomium from a musical almanac: "Practically a patriarch in music, his taste is only for the great and the elevated. . . . Every year he gives some very large and magnificent concerts, in which only pieces by old masters are given. He especially loves the Handelian style, and mostly gives large choral works by him." Swieten was one of the founding members of a society of noblemen who organized concerts—including the first performances of Haydn's oratorios *Die Schöpfung* (The Creation, 1798) and *Die Jahreszeiten* (The Seasons, 1801). He extended his patronage to younger composers as well: Beethoven dedicated to him the Symphony No. 1 when it was published in 1800.

Without the baron at his side, the aged Haydn would probably not have written *The Creation* and *The Seasons*. Swieten encouraged Haydn to undertake the projects, supplied him with texts, and even offered musical ideas. In deriving the texts of both oratorios from English poems, Swieten acknowledged the English cultivation of oratorio as a primary source of inspiration for Haydn's late oratorios. We do not know if Haydn attended performances of Handel's oratorios in Westminster Abbey during his visits to London in the 1790s, but he certainly knew about them. His early biographer Giuseppe Carpani asserted that it was not until his first visit to London that he seriously studied Handel's oratorios. Without that study, Carpani believed, "Haydn would not have written that astonishing masterpiece *The Creation*, in which one hears Handel's grandiloquence transfused through Haydn's mind, and wonderfully linked to his richness of orchestration." On his return to Vienna he found in Swieten the means to achieve that synthesis.

Swieten arranged the text of *The Seasons*, which depicts a year in the country as experienced by simple peasants, from the poem of the same title by the Scottish poet James Thomson. Only once does the brilliance of the court and aristocracy impinge on these rustic scenes, when a party of hunters on horseback rides noisily through the countryside. Fall is the traditional season for hunting, and it plays a big role in the third part of Haydn's oratorio. The peasant Lukas's account of the killing of hares, in a recitative accompanied by scurrying strings, is interrupted by the sound of horns announcing that another, nobler hunt is about to begin.

The chorus that follows, *Hört das laute Getön* (Listen to the loud noise; see Anthology 27), is a depiction of exactly the kind of hunt that François-André Philidor celebrated in an earlier vocal work based on a British literary source: *Tom Jones*, the opéra comique discussed in Chapter 6. In the aria *D'un cerf dix cors* (A ten-point deer), enlivened with the fanfares of hunting horns, Philidor's Squire Weston extols the pleasure and excitement of the stag hunt, in which men on horseback ride through the countryside, following their dogs as they track, surround, and bring down a deer. Haydn, when he wrote his choral depiction of the hunt 35 years later, turned for inspiration to horn signals quite similar to those used by the Frenchman (see Fig. 6.3).

THE TRIUMPH OF CHERUBINI'S *LES DEUX JOURNÉES*

The Treaty of Lunéville, signed in 1801, the same year as Haydn's *The Seasons*, temporarily ended the fighting between France and Austria. Within a few months of the treaty, post-Revolutionary opéra comique, which had been largely absent from Vienna, flooded the theaters of the Habsburg capital. During the next five years more than 60 opéras comiques were performed in Vienna in German translation. And many of the operas written for Vienna during this period, including the first version of Beethoven's *Fidelio* (1805)—a rousing tale about a heroic woman who frees her unjustly imprisoned husband from his dungeon cell—were settings of German translations of opéra comique librettos.

Les deux journées (The Two Days, 1800), the rescue opera by Luigi Cherubini discussed in Chapter 13, reached Vienna by way of an unprecedented double premiere. The Theater an der Wien (a suburban theater that specialized in the performance of opera in German) presented it on August 13, 1802, anticipating by one day the premiere in the Kärntnertor Theater (one of the two court theaters) of the same opera in a completely different translation. The Viennese adored Cherubini's opera, especially in the version staged in the court theaters, where by the end of the decade it had been performed 140 times.

The Habsburg court traditionally celebrated New Year's Day with a public dinner—a banquet with music as well as food. Following an ancient ritual, the imperial family dined in the presence of a noble audience, who watched and listened to the music. For the public dinner on January 1, 1804, Hummel wrote his Trumpet Concerto in E Major, which acknowledged the festive spirit of the occasion by alluding to several musical works familiar at the Viennese court.

Hummel's concluding rondo begins conventionally, with a galloping melody in the tonic followed by a contrasting episode. The main theme returns, as expected, after this episode; then comes a second episode in the minor mode. The trumpet's repeated triplet B (the dominant of E) seems to promise a return to the tonic and the rondo theme, but contrary to the requirements of rondo form, we never hear the main theme again. Another melody in E replaces it, dominating much of the rest of the movement: the march from *Les deux journées* that accompanies the soldiers who, having been tricked by the heroic water-carrier Mikéli, hurry off, allowing Armand to escape (see Ex. 13.3).

In Cherubini's opera the march insinuates itself into the finale and then dominates it. Likewise the march enters Hummel's instrumental finale and replaces the theme with which the movement began. In the opera the march is always heard in E major. Hummel borrowed the key as well as the tune. His decision to write his concerto in E major (a very unusual key for a concerto) must have been made in conjunction with a plan to quote Cherubini's melody at the very end of the concerto.

Just as Hummel built on the popularity of *Les deux journées*, so Beethoven turned to Cherubini's librettist, Jean-Nicolas Bouilly, as the source for his rescue opera *Fidelio*. (The original French title was *Léonore, ou L'amour conjugal* [Leonora, or Conjugal Love].) And, as we will see below, Beethoven would allude to one of Cherubini's most recognizable arias in his own symphonic paean to heroism.

CHURCH MUSIC AS COUNTER-REVOLUTIONARY SYMBOL

Catholicism suffered under the French Revolution. Anticlerical radicals, hoping to establish a cult of enlightened Reason, nationalized church property and restricted the accouterments of Catholic worship, such as processions and the ringing of bells. Austrians reacted by trying to strengthen Catholicism in their domains. Emperor Leopold reversed the restrictions on church music that his predecessor Joseph had introduced during the 1780s (see Chapter 14), thus helping to inaugurate a period in which Austrian church music thrived. Haydn's last six masses and church music by Beethoven, Hummel, and other composers active in Vienna projected a stirring image of the religious solidarity under which Austrian armies fought against the ungodly French.

Empress Marie Therese (1772–1807), second wife of Emperor Francis, was a leading musical patron in Vienna at the beginning of the nineteenth century. She often participated as a singer in private concerts at court. She commissioned works from many leading composers, sometimes giving them detailed instructions. In her cultivation of church music, she promoted an unusual kind of mass that included not only the five parts of the Ordinary but also a gradual, offertory, and Te Deum. In 1803 she ordered from Michael Haydn (1737–1806), Joseph's younger brother and one of her favorite composers of church music, a mass for the emperor's birthday: "The mass should have small solos . . . of these, the *Et incarnatus est* [in the Credo] should be in four voices, and accompanied only by cello and double bass. The *Benedictus* will be a duet for soprano and bass, with a chorus at the end. The offertory a four-part canon. The whole thing should have two fugues."

The *Missa Sancti Francisci* (St. Francis Mass) that resulted from Haydn's careful adherence to his patron's specifications rivals in quality the masses that his brother composed in the preceding decade. Haydn probably intended the important solo soprano part for the empress to sing; it does not go beyond the relatively narrow compass of parts she sang in other works.

As in many settings of the Mass, the three-part structure of the Kyrie text is reflected in a three-part musical structure. Haydn set the words "Kyrie eleison" (Lord, have mercy) as a majestic slow introduction in D minor, the sounds of the chorus emerging mysteriously from the orchestra. He gave the empress an opportunity to display her virtuosity at "Christe eleison" (Christ, have mercy), a big aria-like solo for soprano with choral interpolations (Ex. 17.3a). This passage, also in D minor, ends on a half cadence, which sets up a fugue in D major that brings the Kyrie to a splendid conclusion (Ex. 17.3b). The fugue's subject was heard earlier, in F major, in one of the choral interludes in the soprano solo. Haydn's use of the

Example 17.3: *Michael Haydn,* Missa Sancti Francisci, *Kyrie*

(a) *mm. 47–59*

Christ, have mercy

(b) mm. 129–138

Lord, have mercy

same tune in the second and third parts of the Kyrie, along with the same tempo and meter, gives these otherwise very different passages a satisfying sense of unity. In this Kyrie the theatrical style and the ecclesiastical style, the galant and the learned, once again found common ground, as effectively as they did in music composed at around the same time: the slow movement of Beethoven's *Eroica* Symphony.

BEETHOVEN'S HEROIC STYLE

Since the nineteenth century Beethoven's biographers have used the word "heroic" in reference to his life and work during the decade that began around 1800. After several years in which he achieved recognition and financial success as a pianist and as a composer of instrumental music and built up an impressive network of mostly noble patrons, around the turn of the century (at the age of 30) he began to lose his hearing. Beethoven withdrew from society and his despair grew to the point where he thought about killing himself. The crisis reached its climax in 1802 with the writing of what has come to be called the Heiligenstadt Testament—a remarkable document in which he revealed the depth of his sadness and isolation but also stated his resolve to prevail, for the sake of his art, over all obstacles.

There is certainly something heroic in the tone and content of the Heiligenstadt Testament. Beethoven's self-consciousness—he addressed parts of the letter to humanity at large and preserved it among his papers for the rest of his life—suggests that he regarded himself, in 1802 and the years that followed, as a musical hero: a man who was overcoming partial deafness to produce music of extraordinary power, expressivity, and originality.

THE *SINFONIA EROICA*

One of the first and greatest fruits of Beethoven's newfound strength in the face of adversity was a symphony that he originally planned to dedicate to or to name after Napoleon, whom he admired as the only leader capable of preserving the achievements of the French Revolution. He later abandoned those plans, as his friend Ferdinand Ries recalled:

> In this symphony Beethoven had Buonaparte in his mind, but as he was when he was First Consul. Beethoven esteemed him greatly at the time and likened him to the greatest Roman consuls. I as well as several of his more intimate friends saw a copy of the score lying upon his table with the word "Buonaparte" at the extreme top of the title page. . . . I was the first to bring him the intelligence that Buonaparte had proclaimed himself emperor, whereupon he flew into a rage and cried out: "Is he then, too, nothing more than an ordinary human being? Now he, too, will trample on all the rights of man and indulge only his ambition. He will exalt himself above all others, become a tyrant!" Beethoven went to the table, took hold of the title page by the top, tore it in two and threw it on the floor.

Even in his disillusionment about Napoleon, Beethoven continued to identify the Third Symphony with heroism. The full title, when it was published in 1806, was *Sinfonia eroica, composta per festeggiare il sovvenire di un gran Uomo* (Heroic Symphony, Composed to Celebrate the Memory of a Great Man). Many writers have suggested possible identifications of the "great man." Napoleon, even though he was no longer the hero that he had been during the last years of the French Republic? Beethoven's former patron Archduke Maximilian, who died in 1801? Prometheus, the mythological hero who brought fire to humanity? Beethoven himself? The musicologist Lewis Lockwood is probably right: "The 'hero' of the *Eroica* is not a single figure but a composite of heroes of different types and different situations."

The symphony's very first moments may depict the hero in prayer. Two measures of E♭ major harmony introduce a theme played by the cellos, which suggest by their baritonal register the presence of a male protagonist or narrator (Ex. 17.4). This opening may have reminded Viennese listeners of an aria they must have known by heart. In *Guide mes pas, ô providence* (Guide my steps, oh Providence), Mikéli's humanitarian credo in Cherubini's *Les deux journées*, the vocal part is preceded by two measures of repeated E♭-major chords, *forte* (Ex. 17.5). By introducing his cello melody in a context that resembles the beginning of *Guide mes pas*, Beethoven may have hoped his audience would associate the symphony's heroism with Mikéli, whose words, in turn, invite us to hear the symphony's opening measures as a supplication by the composer himself:

> Guide mes pas, ô providence   *Guide my steps, oh Providence;*
> D'mon plan seconde le succès.   *favor my plan's success.*

A prayer was perhaps appropriate for a composer embarking on a work as vast and original as Beethoven's *Eroica*: a symphony unprecedented in size and complexity, posing new challenges for performers and audience alike. The symphony is in the four movements standardized by Haydn, but with a scherzo replacing the minuet. The first movement alone, in sonata form, exceeds in length all but a few eighteenth-century symphonies. In composing a long and complex funeral march within a symphony that he originally planned for Napoleon, Beethoven may have appropriated the musical rhetoric of French Revolutionary music (see Anthology 28). Republican festivals, political rallies, and funerals gave composers such as François-Joseph Gossec (see Chapter 6) and Cherubini opportunities to demonstrate their commitment to the revolutionary cause by

Example 17.4: *Ludwig van Beethoven,* Sinfonia eroica, *movement 1, mm. 1–6*

Example 17.5: *Luigi Cherubini*, Les deux journées, aria: Guide mes pas,
ô Providence, *mm. 1–10*

composing grandiose, patriotic works, often requiring vast numbers of performers. The *Hymne et marche funèbre* (Hymn and Funeral March) that Cherubini
wrote in memory of General Hoche, who had crushed the monarchist uprising in
the Vendée, is among several similar works that might have inspired Beethoven.
The scherzo is a celebration of energy and speed. The horn fanfares in the trio
probably allude, like those in Philidor's aria *D'un cerf dix cors* and Haydn's chorus *Hört das laute Getön*, to the masculine joy and excitement of the hunt. The
finale is a set of variations on a theme from Beethoven's own ballet score *Die
Geschöpfe des Prometheus* (The Creatures of Prometheus, 1802). But starting from
scratch, as it were, Beethoven began by presenting just the theme's bass line
(Ex. 17.6a), which, in retrospect, we can hear as an adumbration of the first
movement's opening theme (Ex. 17.6b).

BEETHOVEN'S NOBLE PATRONS

Beethoven's brother Carl, who served as the composer's agent, explained how
Beethoven's instrumental works were commissioned, made available in manuscript, and finally published. "These pieces were mostly commissioned by

Example 17.6: *Ludwig van Beethoven,* Sinfonia eroica

(a) *Movement 4, mm. 12–15*

(b) *Movement 1, mm. 3–6*

music lovers, and with the following agreement: he who wants a piece pays a specified sum for its exclusive possession for a half or a whole year, or even longer, and binds himself not to give the manuscript to *anybody*; after this period the author is free to do as he wishes with the piece." Carl did not mention one important part of the transactions: Beethoven was expected to dedicate a published work to the person who commissioned it. Thus in 1799 he received 400 Gulden from Prince Joseph Lobkowitz for the Opus 18 string quartets, of which the prince probably enjoyed exclusive ownership until they were published in 1801 in an edition dedicated to him.

Prince Lobkowitz was one of Beethoven's most steadfast and generous patrons. A wealthy member of the Bohemian nobility, he spent money on music so lavishly that he eventually brought his family to financial ruin. Not only was he involved in the origins of Beethoven's first set of quartets, but he also organized, in 1804, the first performance of the *Eroica* Symphony in his palace in Vienna.

In early 1809 Lobkowitz joined two of Beethoven's other patrons in agreeing to give the composer an annual stipend of 4,000 Gulden for the rest of his life, or until he received an appointment that brought him the same income. In exchange, Beethoven agreed only to live in Vienna or another city in the Austrian Empire, and to obtain the consent of his patrons before traveling elsewhere. With this agreement, as close as Beethoven could get to a MacArthur Foundation "genius" grant, he received a comfortable income while remaining free to do as he liked in everything connected with his work as a musician. The stark differences between these stipulations and those to which Haydn agreed when he signed a contract with Prince Esterházy in 1761 (see Chapter 10) reflect the increasingly elevated and independent status enjoyed by professional composers in the nineteenth century.

Soon after Beethoven started to receive payments under the contract, he composed and dedicated to Lobkowitz the String Quartet in E♭ Major, Op. 74 (later nicknamed *Harp*). All the string quartets he had written earlier in his career had been conceived and published as sets of six or three. In writing a single quartet and dedicating it to a patron partly responsible for the annuity he had just begun to enjoy, Beethoven may have been expressing his gratitude.

Another nobleman for whom Beethoven wrote quartets (and it should be noted that Beethoven followed Mozart and Haydn in dedicating his quartets exclusively to men) was Count Andrey Kyrillovich Razumovsky, the Russian ambassador to the court of Vienna (successor to Mozart's patron Prince Golitsin). A rich and profligate patron of the arts, Razumovsky was particularly fond of string quartets, and he played an important role in the evolution of both the genre and the ensemble that played it. He participated (as a violinist) in performances of quartets, thus perpetuating the eighteenth-century tradition of informal, amateur performance, but he also sponsored one of the first permanent, professional string quartets.

Although Razumovsky commissioned the three quartets by Beethoven that bear his name before he took over the sponsorship of the professional ensemble, the commission and the sponsorship are closely related. The quartets that Beethoven wrote for Razumovsky, revolutionary in their complexity and difficulty, demand intensive rehearsal by expert players—unlike the amateur musicians for whom Haydn and Mozart wrote many of their quartets (see Chapter 14). Razumovsky's decision to engage such players testifies to the seriousness with which he took the genre; this seriousness is reflected in the quartets that Beethoven composed for him.

THE QUARTET IN C MAJOR, OP. 59, NO. 3

Written mostly in 1806, the three quartets of Opus 59 mark a new epoch in the development of the genre. Beethoven brought to the "Razumovsky" Quartets the inventiveness and energy, the new challenges for both players and listeners, with which he had redefined the symphony in the *Eroica*. These superbly crafted pieces together constitute a composite work—a trilogy—in which Beethoven raised the string quartet to the same level of artistic prestige as the symphony.

One of the elements that tie these quartets together is their use of Russian melodies, in tribute to the dedicatee. Beethoven called attention to two of the melodies with the inscription "Thème russe": the opening melody of the finale of Op. 59, No. 1, and the middle section ("Maggiore") of the Scherzo of Op. 59, No. 2. What might be a third Russian tune—at least it has an intensely Russian flavor—is the principal theme of the slow movement of Op. 59, No. 3.

This third quartet, in C major, consists of the expected four movements, with two fast movements in the tonic framing a slower one in the relative minor and a dancelike one in **ABA** form. More innovative was Beethoven's idea—which he was to develop further in the Fifth Symphony—of connecting the third and fourth movements with a transition passage. The spacious opening movement in sonata form is preceded by a tonally mysterious slow introduction that brings to mind Haydn's depiction of primordial chaos at the beginning of his oratorio *The Creation*. In the second movement the Russian-sounding main theme in A minor alternates with a major-mode melody, presented first in the relatively closely related keys of C and A, then in the much more remote key of Eb.

Instead of the energetic scherzo with which Beethoven normally satisfied his audience's expectation for the dancelike movement in triple meter, here he wrote a real minuet, which he inscribed "grazioso" (graceful). In the midst of all the exciting novelty of this quartet, he cast a nostalgic look back to the eighteenth century and perhaps to his own youth in Bonn, where, as an orchestral violist, he might have played similar dances for balls at court. The adjective *grazioso* takes us back to the rondo of the early Piano Sonata Op. 2, No. 2 (see Anthology 26). The eighteenth century treasured grace as a musical value: think of François Couperin's *Les graces naturelles*. The transition (not really a coda, despite Beethoven's label) sets the stage for the finale: a hybrid movement combining fugue and sonata form that brings to a thrilling close not only this quartet but the Opus 59 trilogy as a whole (see Anthology 29).

The composer Johann Friedrich Reichardt (1752–1814) was in Vienna during 1808 and 1809, when Razumovsky's ensemble was active. He recorded his impressions in a series of published letters that allow us a glimpse at how a musically sophisticated listener might have responded to early performances of the "Rasumovsky" Quartets. At a private concert consisting of three quartets—one by Haydn, one by Mozart, and one by Beethoven—Reichardt likened Haydn's quartet to "a charmingly imagined summerhouse" and Mozart's to a palace. "Beethoven settled down in this palace very early, and thus in order for him too to express his own nature in its own forms, he was left no choice but to build a bold and defiant tower on top of which no one could easily place anything without breaking his neck" (SR 147: 1036; 5/26: 302).

THE *PASTORAL* SYMPHONY AS CELEBRATION OF THE ENLIGHTENMENT

Beethoven came to Vienna as a piano virtuoso—a performer—and no matter how highly the Viennese aristocracy valued his sonatas, quartets, and other chamber music, for much of his life he continued to feel the attraction of presenting his music—including his own piano playing—in public concerts. But encroaching deafness made organizing concerts and performing in them as conductor and pianist increasingly difficult.

One of Beethoven's most famous concerts, in December 1808, was announced as follows in the *Wiener Zeitung*:

> On Thursday, December 22, Ludwig van Beethoven will have the honor to give a musical *Akademie* in the . . . Theater an der Wien. All the pieces are of his composition, entirely new, and not yet heard in public.
>
> First part. 1) A Symphony entitled "A Recollection of Country Life," in F major . . . 2) Aria. 3) Hymn with Latin text, composed in the church style with chorus and solos. 4) Piano Concerto played by himself.
>
> Second part. 1) Grand Symphony in C minor . . . [Fifth Symphony]. 2) Sanctus, with Latin text composed in the church style with chorus and solos. 3) Fantasy for piano alone. 4) Fantasy for piano that ends with the gradual entrance of the entire orchestra and the introduction of choruses as a finale [Choral Fantasy].

In some respects—in the mixture of instrumental and vocal music, the prominence of symphonies, and the opportunity that it gave the soloist to improvise—this concert was typical of its time. Recall the important role that symphonies played in the benefit concert that Mozart gave in Prague in 1787, during which he improvised at the piano for more than 30 minutes (see Chapter 15). In placing symphonies at the beginning of both parts of the concert and a concerto at the end of the first part, Beethoven's concert resembled Haydn's concerts in London, as described in Chapter 16. But this was also an extraordinary event, differing from ordinary concerts in length (four hours), in consisting of music by just one composer, in the large number of important works performed for the first time (including the Fifth and Sixth Symphonies and the Choral Fantasy), in the large amount of sacred music (most if not all of it excerpts from the recently composed Mass in C), and in coming close to collapse due to insufficient rehearsals and miscommunication between Beethoven and the orchestra. Prince Lobkowitz invited Reichardt to join him in his box. "There we sat, in the most bitter cold," wrote the guest, "from half past six until half past ten, and confirmed for ourselves the maxim that one may easily have too much of a good thing, still more of a powerful one" (SR 147: 1036; 5/26: 302).

All of Beethoven's nine symphonies except one consist of the four movements that had become standard since Haydn, more than any other single composer, had codified the form. Into the exceptional *Pastoral* Symphony, first performed at the beginning of the monster concert of December 1808, Beethoven inserted an extra movement—the storm—that interrupts the third movement and leads directly to the finale. The incongruity of the storm in a work otherwise devoted to the depiction of rustic peace and joy is analogous to the incongruity of a fifth movement within a symphonic cycle. For the first edition of the symphony Beethoven supplied explanations of each movement's meaning. The first movement depicts "awakening of cheerful feelings on the arrival in the country"; the second, a "scene by the brook"; the third, "merry gathering of countryfolk"; the fourth, a "thunderstorm"; and the finale, titled *Herdsman's Hymn*, "happy, grateful feelings after the storm."

In the first movement, in sonata form, a gradual building up of musical forces conveys a sense of anticipation and of gradually unfolding impressions. Tonal stasis and repetition of small melodic fragments cast a hypnotic spell as they express the peacefulness and well-being of rural life. Trills imitate birdcalls. No trace of the minor mode clouds this sunny picture; no learned counterpoint reminds the listener of urban artifice.

The picture of the brook in the second movement features an unusual orchestral effect. Two solo cellos play throughout, contributing to the gentle murmuring that represents the brook. The movement's conclusion is delayed twice by the sound of birdcalls; Beethoven identified them carefully in his score as a nightingale, a quail, and a cuckoo.

Where Beethoven's earlier works led his audience to expect a scherzo, here he wrote a series of peasant dances in both triple and duple meter. After a tremolo, *pianissimo*, in the double basses and cellos (distant thunder) stops the dancing, a sonic picture of the peasants scurrying for cover replaces the balanced phrases of the dance music. Almost immediately, with a fury and a dramatic power that few composers could evoke as effectively as Beethoven, the storm breaks. Its impact is intensified by its being the symphony's first music in the minor mode (insofar as this tonally unstable music can be said to be in any mode).

The storm fades, and the final movement begins with the symphony's most explicitly pastoral element; not by accident is this the only movement in which Beethoven, with the title *Herdsman's Hymn*, made reference to the pastoral. It is based on the same cowherd's horn call (Ex. 17.7) that Haydn had quoted in the symphony *Le matin* more than 40 years earlier (see Ex. 10.2) and that Johann Baptist Vanhal had used in his *Missa pastoralis* (see Ex. 8.2). A painting of Heiligenstadt, one of the country villages near Vienna where Beethoven retired during the summer and where he wrote the famous testament of 1802, shows a cowherd playing a trumpetlike instrument as his cows cross a lazy brook (Fig. 17.2). The instrument is probably a small alphorn (a wooden trumpet-shaped instrument also known as the *tuba pastoralis*), used by herdsmen to call their animals. The painting

Example 17.7: *Ludwig van Beethoven,* Pastoral Symphony, *movement 5, mm. 1–5*

Figure 17.2: *A cowherd playing a horn in Heiligenstadt, near Vienna. Watercolor by Laurenz Janscha.*

presents a visual depiction of the country life that Beethoven depicted so vividly in his symphony.

Beethoven could have ended his symphony with the violence of the storm (just as Berlioz was later to end his *Symphonie fantastique* with the horror of the Witches' Sabbath), but he was too much a product of the eighteenth century to do that. In the mid-1780s the Viennese composer Carl Ditters von Dittersdorf (1739–1799) had presented a series of symphonies based on Greek myths, including one (*Phaeton*) that ends with a scene of massive destruction. Dittersdorf, in a pamphlet distributed at a performance of the symphonies, explained: "because this scene, without some consolation, would leave in listeners' souls only sad and disturbing impressions, he [the composer] has moderated its effect by means of the *Doucement* [the slow passage that follows], which paints the pleasurable sensations that we feel when, after a great storm, the sky begins to clear." Likewise Dussek's depiction of the sufferings of Queen Marie Antoinette ends not with the fall of the guillotine's blade but with a joyful *Apotheosis* in C major. Beethoven still thought along the same lines. He could not resist the temptation to leave listeners with a sense of well-being and optimism. Just as characteristic of the eighteenth century was Beethoven's need to reestablish tonal stability after the carefully calculated chaos of the storm. The hymn of thanksgiving celebrates not only Enlightenment ideology but also the key of F major and the power of eighteenth-century tonal architecture.

This chapter has offered a glimpse of Viennese music during the two decades in which Napoleon captured the imagination of Europe. The era ended with Napoleon's final defeat at Waterloo and the Congress of Vienna (1814–15), which Walter Frisch discusses in the next volume in this series. In the years around the Congress, Beethoven wrote few major works. He emerged from that fallow period, in 1818, to compose in a style quite different from that of his heroic period.

Chronological accounts of Beethoven's life and works often treat him as a singular figure, somewhat aloof from his musical contemporaries. The approach in this chapter has differed. We have seen Beethoven in a Viennese context, among patrons (all of them skillful amateur musicians) and professional musicians—Cherubini, Hummel, the Haydn brothers—who knew each other's works and interacted with those works in composing their own. The goal has been to enhance our understanding of music by Beethoven and his contemporaries by depicting them as products of and contributors to Viennese culture during a tumultuous age.

An analogous goal has guided the writing of this book as a whole. As tempting as it may be to see the music of the Encyclopedic Century as a series of artistic triumphs by a handful of great composers, it may be more satisfying and more intellectually stimulating to see it as the product of many musicians of greater or lesser talent—performers and composers, female and male, amateur and professional, instrumentalists and singers—who not only competed with but learned from one another within societies that both restricted and inspired them. Working together with patrons, impresarios, publishers, rulers, and audiences, eighteenth-century musicians contributed to an artistic culture of astonishing complexity and richness, and produced works that continue to delight and to enlighten those who study, perform, and hear them.

FOR FURTHER READING

Burnham, Scott, *Beethoven Hero* (Princeton, NJ: Princeton University Press, 1995)

DeNora, Tia, *Beethoven and the Construction of Genius: Musical Politics in Vienna, 1792–1803* (Berkeley: University of California Press, 1995)

Heartz, Daniel, *Mozart, Haydn, and Early Beethoven, 1781–1802* (New York: W. W. Norton, 2009), 675–789

Jones, David Wyn, *Beethoven: Pastoral Symphony* (Cambridge: Cambridge University Press, 1995)

Landon, H. C. Robbins, *Haydn: Chronicle and Works*. Vol. 4, *Haydn: The Years of "The Creation," 1796–1800;* Vol. 5, *Haydn: The Late Years, 1801–1809* (Bloomington: Indiana University Press, 1977)

Lockwood, Lewis, *Beethoven: The Music and the Life* (New York: W. W. Norton, 2003)

Sipe, Thomas, *Beethoven: Eroica Symphony* (Cambridge: Cambridge University Press, 1998)

Will, Richard, *The Characteristic Symphony in the Age of Haydn and Beethoven* (Cambridge: Cambridge University Press, 2002)

ⓢ **Additional resources available at wwnorton.com/studyspace**

GLOSSARY

a cappella (Italian, "in chapel style") Choral singing without instrumental accompaniment.

Academie Royale de Musique The court-sponsored institution, founded by King Louis XIV, that enjoyed a monopoly over the production of *tragédie lyrique* in Paris.

academy A term frequently used in the eighteenth century in referring to a concert.

accidental Sign that calls for altering the pitch of a note: a ♯ raises the pitch a half step, a ♭ lowers it a half step, and a ♮ cancels a previous accidental.

accompanied recitative Recitative with orchestral accompaniment.

Agnus Dei (Latin, "Lamb of God") Fifth of the five major musical items in the Mass Ordinary.

Alberti bass Broken chord accompaniment used in the second half of the eighteenth century, named after Domenico Alberti, who used this figuration often in his keyboard music.

Appoggiatura Dissonant (literally, "leaning") note usually occupying a strong beat and lying above or below a chord note, to which it resolves by step.

aria Lyrical number for solo voice in an opera, oratorio, or other work for voices and orchestra.

arpeggio Chord in which the individual pitches are sounded one after another instead of simultaneously.

augmented-sixth chord Any of several chords containing the interval of the augmented sixth, a dissonance typically resolved by the higher voice moving up a half step and the lower voice moving down a half step, resulting in the interval of an octave.

ballad opera An eighteenth-century English comic play with songs in which new words are set to borrowed tunes.

barline Vertical line used in a musical score to indicate a division between measures.

basso continuo A system of notation and performance practice involving an instrumental bass line that carries both melodic and harmonic meaning. The line's melodic content is typically presented in performance by one or more bass instruments, such as a cello, double bass, or bassoon, while one or more chordal instruments, such as a keyboard instrument, lute, or harp, realize the bass line's harmonic implications with appropriate chords and improvised melodic lines.

beat　Unit of regular pulsation in musical time.

binary form　Musical form comprising two complementary sections. The first part usually ends in the dominant or the relative major key; the second part returns to the tonic. In binary-form movements in instrumental music, both parts are normally repeated.

brass instrument　Wind instrument with a cup-shaped mouthpiece and a tube that flares into a bell.

cadence　Melodic or harmonic succession that closes a musical phrase, section, or composition.

cadenza　A highly embellished passage for a soloist, improvisatory in character (and sometimes actually improvised). The composer signals its location to the performers by means of a fermata, typically near the end of an aria or concerto movement.

canon　A composition or a passage in which contrapuntal voices enter successively, each with the same melody.

cantabile　Songful, lyrical, in a songlike style.

carnival　Typically extending from Christmas to Shrove Tuesday (Mardi Gras), the carnival season was the most important opera season in eighteenth-century Europe.

castrato (plural, *castrati*)　See *musico*.

cembalo　Today this Italian word means "harpsichord," but in the eighteenth century it was used more freely in reference to any stringed keyboard instrument.

chamber music　Music for a group of up to about ten players, with one person to a part.

characteristic music　Instrumental music based on a narrative or a poetic idea, sometimes explained in an accompanying text or program meant to be read by the listener before or during the performance.

chord　Combination of three or more pitches, heard simultaneously.

chromatic scale　Scale built of all twelve pitches in the octave.

chromaticism　The use of several notes of the chromatic scale in a composition or passage.

clavecin　French word that in the eighteenth century meant any stringed keyboard instrument, but today refers more specifically to the harpsichord.

clavichord　Keyboard instrument popular between the fifteenth and eighteenth centuries. The loudness, which depends on the force with which a brass blade strikes the strings, is under the direct control of the player.

Clavier (also spelled **Klavier**)　A German word used in the eighteenth century to refer to any stringed keyboard instrument.

coda　Final part of an instrumental movement, usually coming after the standard parts of the form are completed.

coloratura　Highly ornamented singing, with many notes sung to a single syllable of text.

commedia dell'arte　Italian improvised comedy, involving stock characters and plotlines.

concert aria　Aria for voice and orchestra written for performance as an independent composition.

Concert Spirituel　The most important and long-lasting concert series in eighteenth-century Paris, presenting concerts of vocal and instrumental music when the theaters were closed for religious holidays.

concerto　Instrumental work in several movements for solo instrument (or instrumental group) and orchestra.

conductor　Person who leads performances of musical ensembles. In the eighteenth century the conductor often presided at the keyboard, leading with a combination of gesture and sound.

consonance　Combination of pitches that provides a sense of stability in music.

counterpoint　The art of combining in a single texture two or more melodic lines.

courante　A dance in binary form and compound meter, one of the standard movements of dance suites of the seventeenth and early eighteenth centuries.

crook　An exchangeable segment of tubing in a brass instrument, used to change the length of fixed tube, altering the key in which it plays.

da capo aria An aria in the form **ABA**. Composers typically notated the first section only once; at the end of section **B**, they wrote "Da capo" (from the top). In requiring the musicians to perform section **A** second time, the composer gave the vocal soloist an opportunity to improvise embellishments of musical material now familiar to the players and the audience.

development In many sonata-form movements, the second section, in which the thematic material is fragmented and undergoes modulation through a range of keys.

diatonic Built from the seven pitches of a major or minor scale.

diminished seventh chord Chord built from a diminished triad and a diminished seventh, occurring naturally on the raised seventh step of a minor scale.

dissonance Combination of pitches that sounds unstable, in need of resolution.

Divine Office In the Roman Catholic liturgy, a series of prayer services that take place throughout the day. They include Vespers, Matins, and Lauds, all of which were the object of musical elaboration in the eighteenth century.

dominant In tonal music, the pitch a perfect fifth above the tonic, or the chord based on that note.

dominant seventh chord The chord form that occurs naturally on the dominant of a major key, consisting of a major triad and a minor seventh.

double stop The playing of two pitches simultaneously on a bowed string instrument.

drum bass Bass line, characteristic of galant music, with repeated eighth notes or quarter notes

dynamics Element of musical expression relating to the degree of loudness or softness, or volume, of a sound.

empfindsamer Stil The "sensitive style" cultivated by Carl Philipp Emanuel Bach in his keyboard music, involving frequent appoggiaturas, wide melodic leaps, and emphasis on the minor mode.

ensemble In opera, an extended number with multiple singers.

episode In a rondo, the episodes are the passages, usually in keys other than the tonic, heard between statements of the recurring rondo theme.

exposition Opening section of a sonata-form movement, in which the principal thematic material is set out. The first theme group is in the tonic key, and the second is generally in the dominant or the relative major.

falsetto Vocal technique whereby a man can sing above his normal range, producing a lighter sound.

fantasy, fantasia A musical work in an improvisatory style, often highly emotional and avoiding the standard forms.

fermata Symbol placed over a note, chord, or rest requiring it to be sustained longer than the indicated time value, at the performer's discretion.

finale 1) Last movement of an instrumental work. 2) An ensemble at the end of an act of an opera, depicting a series of events by means of several passages that differ in tempo, meter, key, and orchestration.

fonte A voice-leading schema, typical of galant music, involving a two-stage descending sequence, the first stage tonicizing a minor key, and the second stage tonicizing the major key one step lower, for example, a phrase in D minor followed by the same phrase in C major.

form Structure and design in music, based on repetition, contrast, and variation.

French overture A kind of overture popularized in the seventeenth century by the French composer Jean-Baptiste Lully, beginning with a slow section dominated by dotted rhythms and continuing with a fast section in which imitative textures predominate.

fugato A passage, within an otherwise homophonic movement, that uses the imitative techniques of the fugue.

fugue Polyphonic form in which one or more themes or "subjects" are treated in imitative counterpoint.

half step The distance between two adjacent keys on a piano; the smallest interval normally used in Western music.

harmonic progression Series of chords that are directed toward a harmonic goal, usually a stable, consonant sonority.

harmony Aspect of music that pertains to simultaneous combinations of notes, the intervals and chords that result, the succession of chords, and the underlying principles.

harpsichord Keyboard instrument, in use between the fifteenth and eighteenth centuries, in which the strings are plucked by quills instead of being struck with hammers like the piano.

impresario A person who manages a theater and oversees the production of operas.

intermezzo A comic opera, often for just two or three singers, intended for performance during the intermissions of a serious opera or a play.

interval Relationship or distance between two pitches.

Kapellmeister German term for the director of a musical organization and the conductor of an orchestra.

key In tonal music, the organization of pitches and chords around a central pitch, the tonic.

key signature Sharps or flats placed at the beginning of a piece to show the key or tonal center of a work.

learned style A term frequently used in the eighteenth century to refer to a style (associated particularly with composers born in the previous century) that valued counterpoint and fast harmonic rhythm.

Lent In Roman Catholicism, the penitential period of 40 days before Easter. Many of Europe's theaters were closed, leaving the field open for organizers of concerts. In Vienna and some other predominantly Catholic cities, Lent became the most important concert season of the year.

libretto (Italian, "little book") Text of an opera or oratorio.

lied (German, "song"; plural, *lieder*) Song with German words, often in strophic form. In Singspiel, lieder were accompanied by an orchestra; lieder written for performance outside the theater were

typically accompanied by a keyboard instrument.

liturgy The body of texts to be spoken or sung, and ritual actions to be performed, in a religious service.

Magnificat An important component of Vespers (part of the Divine Office), frequently set to orchestrally accompanied music during the eighteenth century.

major scale Scale consisting of seven different pitches in a specific pattern of whole and half steps. It differs from a minor scale primarily in that its third degree is raised half a step.

mass Musical setting of the texts from the most important service of the Catholic Church; usually in five movements, consisting of the Kyrie, Gloria, Credo, Sanctus, and Agnus Dei.

Matins One of the most important parts of the Divine Office, the first Office of the day, and the object of musical elaboration since the Middle Ages.

measure Recurring temporal unit that contains a fixed number of beats, indicated on the musical staff by barlines.

melody Succession of pitches, usually in several phrases that are perceived as a coherent, self-contained structure.

messa di voce The sustaining of a single pitch while gradually increasing and then decreasing the volume of sound.

meter Recurring patterns of strong and weak beats, dividing musical time into units of equal duration.

minor scale Scale consisting of seven different pitches in a specific pattern of whole and half steps. It differs from the major scale primarily in that its third degree is lowered.

minuet A dance in binary form and triple meter, usually presented with a second minuet in the form **ABA**. The second minuet (**B**) came to be called the "trio."

motive Short melodic or rhythmic idea; the smallest fragment of a theme that forms a recognizable unit.

movement Complete, self-contained segment of a larger musical work.

musico (Italian, "musician"; plural, *musici*) Male singer castrated before puberty to preserve his high vocal range and featured prominently in opera seria and Catholic church music.

nationalism Attitude or outlook that posits an identity for a group of people through characteristics such as common language, shared culture, historical tradition and institutions, and musical elements derived from folk or indigenous styles.

natural horn Ancestor of the modern French horn, characterized by lack of valves.

nocturne (French, "night piece") Type of character piece with slow tempo, flowing accompaniment, and broad lyrical melodies, associated especially with the solo piano music of John Field and Frédéric Chopin.

octave Interval between two pitches seven diatonic notes apart; the lower pitch vibrates half as fast as the upper.

opera Musical stage work that is generally sung throughout, combining the resources of vocal and instrumental music with poetry and drama, acting and pantomime, scenery and costumes.

Opéra Informal name for the Académie Royale de Musique; also the informal name of the theater in Paris where *tragédie lyrique* was performed.

opera buffa Italian comic opera, sung throughout, with recitatives, arias, and ensembles.

opéra-comique A French stage work, whether serious or humorous, with vocal and instrumental music and spoken dialogue.

opera seria Italian serious opera, on a serious subject but normally with a happy ending, and without comic characters and scenes.

opus number (abbrev. *op.*; plural, *opera* [*opp.*]) Number designating a work in chronological relationship to other works by the same composer; in the eighteenth century opus numbers were generally assigned only to published works.

oratorio Large-scale genre originating in the seventeenth century, with a libretto of religious or serious character; similar to opera but unstaged, performed by solo voices, chorus, and orchestra.

orchestra Performing group generally consisting of groups or "sections" of string instruments, with single, paired, or multiple woodwind, brass, and percussion instruments.

orchestration The study or practice of writing music for instruments, or adapting for orchestra music composed for another medium.

overture An orchestral piece introducing an opera or other long vocal work. See also *French overture, sinfonia.*

partimento A pedagogically conceived bass line above which a student of performance or composition improvised a melody; used by eighteenth-century teachers, especially in Naples, to familiarize their students with the wide array of voice-leading patterns used in the galant style.

pasticcio (Italian, "pie") Opera consisting of arias and ensembles by several composers

patronage Sponsorship of an artist or a musician.

perfect cadence Cadence that moves from a dominant to a tonic harmony, with chords in root position.

phrase Unit of a melody or of a succession of notes that has a distinct beginning and ending and is followed by a pause or other articulation.

piano quartet Chamber ensemble of piano, violin, viola, and cello, or a composition written for that ensemble.

piano trio Chamber ensemble of piano, violin, and cello, or a composition written for that ensemble.

pianoforte (Italian, "soft-loud"; also **fortepiano**) Early name for the piano, so called because of its ability to produce gradations of dynamics.

pizzicato Performance direction to pluck a string of a bowed instrument with the finger.

plainchant Monophonic, unmeasured vocal melody, part of the liturgy of the Roman Catholic Church.

polyphony Musical texture featuring two or more lines or voices.

prima donna (Italian, "first lady") Leading female singer in Italian opera.

Prinner Voice-leading schema common in eighteenth-century music in which a treble line descending from the sixth scale degree to the third is accompanied by a bass descending from the fourth scale degree to the first.

program music See *characteristic music.*

range Distance between the lowest and highest pitches of a melody, an instrument, or a voice.

realization Performing (or creating a performable edition of) music whose notation is incomplete, as in playing a basso continuo.

recapitulation In a sonata form, the third section, where material from the exposition is restated, now in the tonic key.

recitative Speech-like type of singing that follows the natural rhythms of the text; used in opera and oratorio. See also *accompanied recitative* and *simple recitative.*

relative major Scale or key whose initial note lies a minor third above the tonic of a minor scale, with which it shares all pitches.

relative minor Scale or key whose initial note lies a minor third below the tonic of a major scale, with which it shares all pitches.

responsory An item in the Catholic liturgy, associated most strongly with the Matins service. It consists of a respond followed by a verse. After the verse, the second half of the respond is repeated, resulting in the form **ABCB** (in which **C** is the verse). Composers who set responsories to music often preserved the **ABCB** structure.

retransition In sonata form, the passage at the end of the development that leads to and emphasizes the dominant in preparation for the return of the tonic at the recapitulation.

rhythm The particular pattern of short and long durations.

ritornello (Italian, "little return") A musical passage, first presented at the beginning of a movement, that recurs, in whole or in part, later in the movement. In eighteenth-century arias and concertos, ritornellos are typically played by the orchestra; the opening ritornello is also called the orchestral introduction.

romanesca In galant music, a voice-leading schema involving a descending bass line that typically traces the scale degress $\hat{1}-\hat{7}-\hat{6}-\hat{3}$.

rondo Musical form in which the first section recurs, usually in the tonic, between subsidiary sections.

sacred music Religious or spiritual music, for church or devotional use.

salon Gathering in a private home for a semipublic musical or literary event, attended by both aristocracy and the bourgeoisie.

sarabande Binary-form dance characterized by slow tempo, triple meter, and emphasis on the second beat of the measure.

scale Series of pitches arranged in ascending or descending order according to a specific pattern of intervals.

scherzo (Italian, "joke") Composition in ternary (**ABA**) form, usually in triple meter; usually a part of a multimovement chamber or orchestral work.

score The written form of a musical composition, containing musical notation as well as verbal and graphic indications for performance.

secondary dominant Dominant chord that resolves to or is directed toward a harmony that is not the tonic.

semitone See *half step.*

sequence Restatement of a musical idea or motive at a different pitch level.

simple recitative Recitative accompanied by basso continuo.

sinfonia (plural, *sinfonie*) Italian word for the early eighteenth-century opera overture, typically in three movements (fast-slow-fast)—the principal ancestor of the concert symphony.

Singspiel (German, "singing play") Genre of opera in Germany and Austria, featuring spoken dialogue interspersed with arias, ensembles, and choruses.

sonata (Italian, "played") Work for solo instrument or ensemble. Before 1750 the term was used mostly for multimovement works for chamber ensembles (see *trio sonata*); after 1750 it was applied increasingly to multimovement works for keyboard intruments alone or for keyboard instruments and other solo instruments.

sonata form The design of the opening movement of most multimovement instrumental works from the later eighteenth through the nineteenth centuries, consisting of themes that are stated in the first section (exposition), developed in the second section (development), and restated in the third section (recapitulation).

sonata-rondo A form that blends characteristics of sonata form and the rondo.

string quartet Chamber music ensemble consisting of two violins, viola, and cello, or a multimovement composition for this ensemble.

strophic Song or aria structure in which the same music is repeated for every stanza (strophe) of the poem.

subdominant In tonal music, the pitch a perfect fourth above the tonic, or the chord based on that pitch.

suite Work made up of a series of contrasting movements, usually dance-inspired and all in the same key.

suspension Embellishment created when a note is sustained while another voice moves to form a dissonance with it; the sustained voice descends a step to resolve the dissonance.

symphonie concertante A concerto, typical of the late eighteenth and early nineteenth centuries, for two or more solo instruments and orchestra.

symphony Large work for orchestra, usually in three or four movements.

syncopation Temporary shifting of the accent to a weak beat or a weak part of a beat.

tempo (Italian, "time" or "movement") Speed of a musical composition, or the designation of such in a musical score.

ternary form Musical form comprising three sections, with the outer sections being essentially the same, contrasting with a middle section: **ABA**.

texture The interweaving of melodic and harmonic elements in a musical work.

theme Melody or other well-defined musical element used as basis for a composition or movement; in a fugue, the theme is often called a subject.

theme and variations See *variation form*.

through-composed Descriptive term for songs that are composed from beginning to end, without repetitions of large sections.

timbre The sound quality or character that distinguishes one voice or instrument from another.

tonality The system by which a piece of music is organized around a central note, chord, and key (the tonic), to which all the other notes and keys in the piece are subordinate.

tonic (1) The first and central pitch of a scale. (2) The main key area in which a piece or movement begins and ends and to which all other keys are subordinate.

topics Term for the different and contrasting styles in music that serve as subjects for musical discourse.

tragédie lyrique (also known as **tragédie en musique**) French seventeenth- and eighteenth-century form of opera, pioneered by Jean-Baptiste Lully, that combined the French classic drama and ballet traditions with music, dance, and spectacle.

transvestism A practice common in eighteenth-century opera involving a female singer portraying a male character or a male singer (typically a musico) portraying a female character. Within the plots of operas we find another kind of transvestism, with male characters pretending to be women and female characters pretending to be men.

tremolo (Italian, "trembling") Very rapid repetition of a tone or alternation between two pitches.

triad Common chord type, consisting of three pitches, normally a third and a fifth apart. The common forms are major, minor, diminished, and augmented.

trio (1) Piece for three players or singers. (2) The second of two alternating sections in a minuet or scherzo movement.

trio sonata A genre favored by composers in the learned style, for two treble instruments and basso continuo. A performance may involve more than three players if, as is commonly the case, the bass part is played by two or more musicians.

triplet Group of three equal-valued notes played in the time of two.

tritone Interval spanning three whole steps or six half steps, such as F to B; a component of the diminished seventh chord.

variation form, variations Musical form that presents a series of transformations of a theme, usually preserving the theme's length and phrasing, but altering its melody or harmony. Also referred to as *theme and variations*.

vaudeville A popular tune to which a new text was fitted, an essential part of early *opéra-comique*.

virtuoso Performer of extraordinary technical ability.

walking bass A bass line, characteristic of the learned style, that moves steadily and continuously with notes of one duration.

whole step Musical interval equal to two half steps.

woodwind Musical instrument that produces sound when the player blows air through a mouthpiece that has a sharp edge or a reed, causing the air to vibrate in a resonating column.

ENDNOTES

CHAPTER 1

1. "the fine arts": *The Letters of Mozart and His Family*, 3rd ed., trans. Emily Anderson (New York: Norton, 1985), 266.

1. "managed by—*philosophes*": Jacques Barzun, *From Dawn to Decadence, 1500 to the Present: 500 Years of Western Cultural Life* (New York: HarperCollins, 2000), 359–92.

2. "without knowing why": *The Letters of Mozart and His Family*, 833.

2. "sophistication, and clemency": Antonio Planelli, *Dell'opera in musica* (Naples: Donato Campo, 1772), 72.

4. "musical encyclopedia": Friedrich Wilhelm Marpurg, *Historisch-Kritische Beyträge zur Aufnahme der Musik* (Berlin: Schützen, 1754), I:v.

5. "visit foreign lands": William S. Newman, "Emanuel Bach's Autobiography," *Musical Quarterly* 51 (1965): 367–68.

5. "loathsome fish-tail": Voltaire, *Oeuvres completes* (Paris: Garnier Frères, 1880), 39:454.

14. "induced by performance": Dennis Libby, "Italy: Two Opera Centres," in *The Classical Era: From the 1740s to the End of the Eighteenth Century*, ed. Neal Zaslaw (Englewood Cliffs, NJ: Prentice Hall, 1989), 15–16.

CHAPTER 2

20. "truth in music": David Yearsley, *Bach and the Meanings of Counterpoint* (Cambridge: Cambridge University Press, 2002), 228.

23. "small figures and quick notes": Daniel Heartz, *Music in European Capitals: The Galant Style, 1720–1780* (New York: Norton, 2003), 47.

24. "unquestionably receive preference": Heartz, *Music in European Capitals*, 47.

24. "the manner of the time": Ibid., 48.

25. "the same note": Johann Joachim Quantz, *On Playing the Flute*, trans. Edward R. Reilly (New York: Schirmer, 1966), 326.

26. "meant to say": Johann David Heinichen, *Thorough-Bass Accompaniment*, ed. George J. Buelow (Lincoln: University of Nebraska Press, 1992), 316.

26. "art [that is, artifice]": *The New Bach Reader: A Life of Johann Sebastian Bach in Letters and Documents*, ed. Hans K. David, Arthur Mendel, and Christoph Wolff (New York: Norton, 1998), No. 343.

27–28. "essential thing in music": Paul Nettl, *Forgotten Musicians* (New York: Philosophical Library, 1951), 301.

28. "the comic ones": Nettl, *Forgotten Musicians*, 267–68.

CHAPTER 3

30. "powers of description": Michael Kelly, *Reminiscences*, 2nd ed., 2 vols. (London: Henry Colburn, 1826; repr., New York: Da Capo, 1968), I:23–24.

31. "what makes genius": Jean-Jacques Rousseau, *Dictionnaire de musique* (Paris: Veuve Duchesne, 1768), 227.

36. music of the other world: John A. Rice, "Sense, Sensibility, and Opera Seria: An Epistolary Debate," *Studi musicali* 15 (1986): 120.

36–37. "not the master's [composer's]": Frederick C. Petty, *Italian Opera in London, 1760–1800* (Ann Arbor: UMI, 1980), 258.

37. "in a quiet room": Burney, *France and Italy*, 355–56.

38. "strings and organ": Thomas Griffin, *Musical References in the Gazzetta di Napoli, 1681–1725* (Berkeley, CA: Fallen Leaf Press, 1993), 69.

40. "laboured contrivance": Charles Burney, *A General History of Music*, 4 vols. (London: by author, 1776–89), IV:547.

42. "ease, grace, and taste": Charles de Brosses, *Lettres d'Italie*, ed. Frédéric d'Agay, 2 vols. (Paris: Mercure de France, 1986), II:315.

42. "truth was revealed": André Grétry, *Mémoires, ou Essai sur la musique* (Paris: by author, 1789), 507.

CHAPTER 4

51. "more than a month": Charles de Montesquieu, *Voyages*, 2 vols. (Bordeaux: Gounouilhou, 1894), I:220.

54. "man's heart is proof": Jean-Jacques Rousseau, *The Confessions*, trans. J. M. Cohen (London: Penguin, 1953), 295–96.

55. "in Great Britain": Charles Burney, *Memoirs of the Life and Writings of the Abate Metastasio*, 3 vols. (London: Robinson, 1796), I:101.

55–56. "the minister's harem": Bruce Alan Brown, *Gluck and the French Theatre in Vienna* (Oxford: Clarendon, 1991), 47, 117.

56. "a worthy partner to her": Daniel Heartz, *From Garrick to Gluck: Essays on Opera in the Age of Enlightenment*, ed. John A. Rice (Hillsdale, NY: Pendragon, 2004), 292.

57. "old woman": John A. Rice, "Sense, Sensibility, and Opera Seria: An Epistolary Debate," *Studi musicali* 15 (1986): 109.

CHAPTER 5

63. "by the hammer": Percy A. Scholes, *The Oxford Companion to Music*, 10th ed. (London: Oxford University Press, 1970), 459.

63. "full five minutes": Charles Burney, *France and Italy*, 216.

64. "judgment and delicacy": Burney, *France and Italy*, 213.

68. "manner of the time": Daniel Heartz, *Music in European Capitals: The Galant Style, 1720–1780* (New York: Norton, 2003), 48.

68–69. "rules of composition": Charles Burney, *A General History of Music*, 4 vols. (London: by author, 1776–89), IV:664; Frances Burney, *Memoirs of Doctor Burney* (Philadelphia: Key & Biddle, 1833), 15.

69. "wild but masterly composer": Charles Burney, *A General History of Music*, IV:664; Frances Burney, *Memoirs of Doctor Burney*, 15.

71. "harmonious poetic song": Saverio Mattei, *Memorie per servire alla vita del Metastasio* (Colle: Martini, 1785), 59, quoted in translation (slightly altered here) in Heartz, *Music in European Capitals*, 992–93.

CHAPTER 6

75. "un plaisir unique": Voltaire, *Le Mondain* (1736), quoted in Daniel Heartz, *From Garrick to Gluck: Essays on Opera in the Age of Enlightenment*, ed. John A. Rice (Hillsdale, NY: Pendragon, 2004), 272.

77. "name of Opéra-Comique": *History of Opera*, ed. Stanley Sadie (New York: Norton, 1989), 116.

77. "all decent folk": *The Age of Enlightenment, 1745–1790*, ed. Egon Wellesz and Frederick Sternfeld (New Oxford History of Music, vol. 7; London: Oxford University Press, 1973), 207.

83. "excel in his concerts": Jean-François Marmontel, *Oeuvres postumes: Mémoires*, 4 vols. (London: Peltier, 1805), I:313.

CHAPTER 7

88. "pay well for it": Johann Mattheson, *Das neu-eröffnete Orchestre* (Hamburg: by author, 1713), 211, 219.

93–94. "end of the opera": Frederick C. Petty, *Italian Opera in London, 1760–1800* (Ann Arbor: UMI, 1980), 142.

99. "in Soho-square": Daniel Heartz, *Music in European Capitals: The Galant Style, 1720–1780* (New York: Norton, 2003), 910.

100. "I ever gave": John A. Rice, "The Blind Dülon and His Magic Flute," *Music & Letters* 71 (1990): 30–31.

101. "both Their Majesties": Rice, "The Blind Dülon," 30.

102. "travels through Italy": *Twelve sonatas for two violins and a bass or an orchestra composed by Gio. Batta. Pergolese, the author of the Stabat Mater* (London: Bremner, [1780]).

CHAPTER 8

108. opposite sides of the learned/galant divide: Robert Freeman, *Opera without Drama: Currents of Change in Italian Opera, 1675–1725* (Ann Arbor: UMI Research Press, 1981), 208.

110. "singing or acting": Daniel Heartz, *Haydn, Mozart, and the Viennese School, 1740–1780* (New York: Norton, 1995), 136.

111. "delightful and less heavy": Heartz, *Haydn, Mozart, and the Viennese School*, 135–36.

113. "turn the pages for me": *The Letters of Mozart and His Family*, 3rd ed., trans. Emily Anderson (New York: Norton, 1985), 6; Heartz, *Haydn, Mozart, and the Viennese School*, 113.

114. "mein cook, Waltz": Charles Burney, *An Account of the Musical Performances in Westerminster-Abbey* (London: Printed for the Benefit of the Musical Fund, 1785), 33.

116. "besides the organ": Charles Burney, *The Present State of Music in Germany, the Netherlands, and United Provinces*, 2nd ed., 2 vols. (London: Becket, 1775), I:226–27.

116. "edified, convinced, and wiser": Bruce Alan Brown, "Maria Theresa's Vienna," in *The Classical Era: From the 1740s to the End of the Eighteenth Century*, ed. Neal Zaslaw

(Englewood Cliffs, NJ: Prentice Hall, 1989), 108–9.

116. "the best models": Quoted in Paul Bryan, *Johann Wanhal, Viennese Symphonists: His Life and His Musical Environment* (Hillsdale, NY: Pendragon, 1997), 5.

117. "constantly preserved": Charles Burney, *A General History of Music*, 4 vols. (London: by author, 1776–89), IV:599.

117. "*Shoo fly, don't bother me*": Bruce C. MacIntyre, "Johann Baptist Vanhal and the Pastoral Mass Tradition," in *Music in Eighteenth-Century Austria*, ed. David Wyn Jones (Cambridge: Cambridge University Press, 1996), 130.

118. "vividness of her playing": *Journal de Paris*, 24 April 1784.

118. "thoroughly musical": *The Letters of Mozart and His Family*, 236.

118. "And there she is right": *The Letters of Mozart and His Family*, 748.

119. "artistry and facility": Michael Lorenz, "The Jenamy Concerto," *Newsletter of the Mozart Society of America* 9, no. 1 (2005): 1–3.

CHAPTER 9

124. "not suited to comedy": Johann Friedrich Reichardt, *Über die deutsche comische Oper* (Hamburg: Bohn, 1774), 7.

126. "all over Germany": Reichardt, *Über die deutsche comische Oper*, 61.

127. hoped that a stint in the army would cure him: Gerhard Ritter, *Frederick the Great: A Historical Profile* (Berkeley: University of California Press, 1968), 26.

128. "anyone but the king": Daniel Heartz, *Music in European Capitals: The Galant Style, 1720–1780* (New York: Norton, 2003), 374.

128. "for the accompaniment": Kurd von Schlözer, *General Graf Chasot: Zur Geschichte Friedrichs des Großen und seiner Zeit*, 2nd ed. (Berlin: Hertz, 1878), 227.

129. "ever before existed": Ernest Eugene Helm, *Music at the Court of Frederick the Great* (Norman: University of Oklahoma Press, 1960), 110.

130. "an equal partner": Mary Oleskiewicz, "The Trio in Bach's Musical Offering: A Salute to Frederick's Tastes and Quantz's

Flutes?" in *The Music of J. S. Bach: Analysis and Interpretation*, ed. David Schulenberg (Lincoln: University of Nebraska Press, 1999), 80.

130. "old Bach has come": Christoph Wolff, *Johann Sebastian Bach: The Learned Musician* (New York: Norton, 2000), 427.

130. "with equal perfection": Burney, *Germany*, II:152–53.

131–32. "Ch[ristian] r[eligion]": Pierpaolo Polzonetti, *Italian Opera in the Age of the American Revolution* (Cambridge: Cambridge University Press, 2011), 112.

134. "created a masterpiece": Heartz, *Music in European Capitals*, 368.

134. "king of Prussia": William S. Newman, "Emanuel Bach's Autobiography," *Musical Quarterly* 51 (1965): 366.

136. "in my opinion": Newman, "Emanuel Bach's Autobiography," 372.

137. "from his countenance": Burney, *Germany*, II:269–70.

CHAPTER 10

140. cello, and double bass: Eugene K. Wolf, *The Symphonies of Johann Stamitz: A Study in the Formation of the Classical Style* (Utrecht: Bohn, 1981), 19.

140. "not repressed by cultivation": Burney, *The Present State of Music in Germany, the Netherlands, and United Provinces*, 2nd ed., 2 vols. (London: Becket, 1775), II:12–13.

140. "fire and genius": Burney, *Germany*, I:93.

141. two clarinetists available as well: Spitzer and Zaslaw, *The Birth of the Orchestra*, 260–61.

141. "storm of the strings": Eugene K. Wolf, "The Mannheim Court," in *The Classical Era*, 228.

141. "as to fight it": Burney, *Germany*, I:94–95.

146. "the Italian language": *Haydn: Two Contemporary Portraits*, ed. Vernon Gotwals (Madison: University of Wisconsin Press, 1968), 12.

146. "exactly right": *Haydn: Two Contemporary Portraits*, 10.

146. "every amateur": Ernst Ludwig Gerber, *Historisch-Biographisches Lexicon der Tonkünstler*, 2 vols. (Leipzig: Breitkopf, 1790–92), I, column 910.

147. provisions of Haydn's contract with Paul Esterházy: Karl Geiringer, *Haydn: A Creative Life in Music*, 3rd ed. (Berkeley: University of California Press, 1982), 43–45.

148. "in public concerts": Johann Joachim Quantz, *On Playing the Flute*, trans. Edward R. Reilly (New York: Schirmer, 1966), 211.

150. "depart from Eszterháza": *Haydn: Two Contemporary Portraits*, 19.

151. "had to be original": Ibid., 17.

CHAPTER 11

153. "the dance of victory": Howard Brofsky, "Rameau and the Indians: The Popularity of Les Sauvages," in *Music in the Classic Period: Essays in Honor of Barry S. Brook*, ed. Allan W. Atlas (New York: Pendragon, 1985), 43–60.

154. "a frightful noise": *Mémoires de Frédérique Sophie Wilhelmine, Margrave de Bareith*, 2 vols. (Brunswick: Vieweg, 1810), II:113.

154. "the greatest justness": Colin Dyer, *The French Explorers and the Aboriginal Australians, 1772–1839* (St. Lucia: University of Queensland Press, 2005), 90–91.

155. "the confusion of hell": Rogério Budasz, "Black Guitar-Players and Early African-Iberian Music in Portugal and Brazil," *Early Music* 35 (2007): 3–21.

155. "all night along": Douglas Hall, *In Miserable Slavery: Thomas Thistlewood in Jamaica, 1750–86* (Kingston: University of the West Indies Press, 1999), 37.

156. "precious pearl of Brazil": Simam Ferreira Machado, *Triunfo Eucharistico* (Lisbon: Officina da Musica, 1734), 24–25; facsimile edition in Affonso Ávila, *Resíduos seiscentistas em Minas*, 2 vols. (Belo Horizonte: Centro de Estudos Mineiros, 1967), I. This translation from C. R. Boxer, *The Golden Age of Brazil, 1695–1750: Growing Pains of a Colonial Society* (Berkeley: University of California Press, 1962), 162–63.

156–57. "small numbered parcels": Josinéia Godinho, "The Mariana Organ," www.orgaodase.com.br.

159. military drum, fife, and trumpet: Ferreira Machado, *Triunfo Eucharistico*, 47–48, 57–59, 68.

164. "drumming last night": Hall, *In Miserable Slavery*, 12, 18, 131, 182, 293.

164. "buried in this parish": *The History of Jamaica, or, General Survey of the Antient and Modern State of that Island*, 3 vols. (London: T. Lowndes, 1774), II:5, 7, 117.

164. "Poetry, Painting, and Music": Howard E. Smither, *A History of the Oratorio*, vol. 3, *The Oratorio in the Classical Era* (Chapel Hill: University of North Carolina Press, 1987), 315.

166. "in their company": Sarah Eyerly, "Singing from the Heart: The Musical Utopias of the Moravian Church," *Society for Eighteenth Century Music Newsletter* 6 (April 2005): 1.

CHAPTER 12

174. "such a magnificent choir in Italy": Marina Ritzarev, *Eighteenth-Century Russian Music* (Aldershot: Ashgate, 2006), 82.

176. "so complete": Daniel Heartz, *Music in European Capitals: The Galant Style, 1720–1780* (New York: Norton, 2003), 940.

176. "It passes understanding": Heartz, *Music in European Capitals*, 943–44.

177. "as short as possible": Giovanni Paisiello, *Il barbiere di Siviglia*, 2 vols., ed. Francesco Paolo Russo (Laaber: Laaber-Verlag, 2001), I:5.

179. "Count Sheremetev's serfs": R. Aloys Mooser, *Annales de la musique et des musiciens en Russie au XVIIIe siècle*, 3 vols. (Geneva: Mont-Blanc, 1948–51), 843.

183. "or a slave": C. F. P. Masson, *Mémoires secrets sur la Russie*, 2 vols. (Paris: Pougens, 180), II:60–62.

183. "a mechanical performance": Elisabeth Vigée Lebrun, *Memoirs*, trans. Lionel Strachey (New York: Braziller, 1989), 89.

CHAPTER 13

192. "and went home": *The Letters of Mozart and His Family*, 3rd ed., trans. Emily Anderson (New York: Norton, 1985), 557–58.

193. "simply unbearable": *The Letters of Mozart and His Family*, 522.

194. "burned to the ground": Jeremy Black, *The British Abroad: The Grand Tour in the Eighteenth Century* (New York: St. Martin's Press, 1992), 327.

CHAPTER 14

200. "best place in the world": *The Letters of Mozart and His Family*, 3rd ed., trans. Emily Anderson (New York: Norton, 1985), 271.

202. "important feastdays": Carl Maria Brand, *Die Messen von Joseph Haydn*, 2 vols. (Würzburg: Triltsch, 1941), II:193.

204. "get to know me": *The Letters of Mozart and His Family*, 718.

204. "Just as many, Your Majesty, as are needed": Franz Xaver Niemetschek, *Lebensbeschreibung des K. K. Kapellmeisters Wolfgang Amadeus Mozart* (Prague: in der Herrlischen Buchhandlung, 1808; facsimile reprint, Laaber: Laaber Verlag, 2005), 34.

205. published in 1784: Quoted in translation in H. C. Robbins Landon, *Haydn: Chronicle and Works*, 5 vols. (Bloomington: Indiana University Press, 1976–80), II:214.

206. "some other house": *The Letters of Mozart and His Family*, 888–89.

207. "supervise the copying": Ibid., 885–86.

210. "understood the science": Michael Kelly, *Reminiscences*, 2nd ed., 2 vols. (London: Henry Colburn, 1826; repr., New York: Da Capo, 1968), I:197.

212. "three attentive people": Quoted in translation from the *Journal des Luxus und der Moden* (Weimar, 1788) in Mary Sue Morrow, *Concert Life in Haydn's Vienna: Aspects of a Developing Musical and Social Institution* (Stuyvesant, NY: Pendragon, 1989), 19.

212. "lively in the extreme": Kelly, *Reminiscences*, I:240–41.

214. "knowledge of composition": *The Letters of Mozart and His Family*, 886.

216. "accurate judge of it": Kelly, *Reminiscences*, I:207.

216. "whenever they appear": John A. Rice, *Antonio Salieri and Viennese Opera* (Chicago: University of Chicago Press, 1998), 344.

217. "source of innate genius": *Mozart: A Documentary Biography*, ed. Otto Erich Deutsch (Palo Alto: Stanford University Press, 1965), 278.

CHAPTER 15

224. "a very good performer": Burney, *Germany*, II:3–5.

225. "settings are excellent": Thomas Forrest Kelly, *First Nights at the Opera* (New Haven, CT: Yale University Press, 2004), 118.

225–26. "as from a single soul": Kelly, *First Nights at the Opera*, 90.

227. "the best concerts": Franz Xaver Niemetschek, *Lebensbeschreibung des K. K. Kapellmeisters Wolfgang Amadeus Mozart* (Prague: in der Herrlischen Buchhandlung, 1808; facsimile reprint, Laaber: Laaber Verlag, 2005), 34–35.

227. "a great honor for me": *The Letters of Mozart and His Family*, 3rd ed., trans. Emily Anderson (New York: Norton, 1985), 903.

227. "one of the finest in his life": Niemetschek, *Lebensbeschreibung*, 40.

229. "that is, yesterday": *The Letters of Mozart and His Family*, 911.

230. "how Mozart wanted it": Kelly, *First Nights at the Opera*, 108.

230. "that's how to scream": John A. Rice, *Mozart on the Stage* (Cambridge: Cambridge University Press, 2009), 156.

241–42. "to be played on the different evenings": Quoted from the journal of Charlotte Papendieck, the wife of a flutist, in Landon, *Haydn: Chronicle and Works*, III:52.

242. "his residence in England": Landon, *Haydn: Chronicle and Works*, III:49–50.

244. "that Haydn heard under its creator's direction": Daniel Heartz, *Mozart, Haydn, and Early Beethoven, 1781–1802* (New York: Norton, 2009), 471.

247. what has been called the "London Pianoforte School": Alexander Ringer, "Beethoven and the London Pianoforte School," *Musical Quarterly* 56 (1970), 742–58.

249. "whatever their director could require": Harold C. Schonberg, *The Great Pianists* (New York: Simon & Schuster, 2006), 64.

249. *The Sufferings of the Queen of France*: London: Corri, Dussek & Co., 1793; facsimile edition in *The London Pianoforte School 1766–1860*, ed. Nicholas Temperley (New York: Garland, 1985), VI.

CHAPTER 16

237. "shelter to England": H. C. Robbins Landon, *Haydn: Chronicle and Works*, 5 vols. (Bloomington: Indiana University Press, 1976–80), III:214.

238. Professional Concert program of February 15, 1790: From a facsimile of the advertisement in Meredith MacFarlane and Simon McVeigh, "The String Quartet in London Concert Life, 1769–1799," *Concert Life in Eighteenth-Century Britain*, ed. Susan Wollenberg and Simon McVeigh (Aldershot: Ashgate, 2004), 163.

239. "conclude an agreement": *Haydn: Two Contemporary Portraits*, ed. Vernon Gotwals (Madison: University of Wisconsin Press, 1968), 119.

239. "all over the world": *Haydn: Two Contemporary Portraits*, 119–20.

240. "astonished me": *The Collected Correspondence and London Notebooks of Joseph Haydn*, ed. H. C. Robbins Landon (London: Barrie and Rockliff, 1959), 112.

240. London events announced in the *Public Advertiser*: Landon, *Haydn: Chronicle and Works*, III:41.

CHAPTER 17

256. "*Mozart's spirit from Haydn's hands*": *Thayer's Life of Beethoven*, ed. Elliot Forbes (Princeton, NJ: Princeton University Press, 1967), 115.

256. "Haydn's humorous caprice": John A. Rice, *Empress Marie Therese and Music at the Viennese Court, 1792–1807* (Cambridge: Cambridge University Press, 2003), 243.

257. "English grand pianoforte": Mary Sue Morrow, *Concert Life in Haydn's Vienna: Aspects of a Developing Musical and Social Institution* (Stuyvesant, NY: Pendragon, 1989), 284.

259 "mostly gives choral works by him": H. C. Robbins Landon, *Haydn: Chronicle and Works*, 5 vols. (Bloomington: Indiana University Press, 1976–80), 28.

259–60. "richness of orchestration": John A. Rice, "Did Haydn Attend the Handel Commemoration in Westminster Abbey?" *Early Music* 40 (2012): 73–80.

262. "The whole thing should have two fugues": John A. Rice, *Empress Marie Therese and Music at the Viennese Court, 1792–1807* (Cambridge: Cambridge University Press, 2003), 198.

265. "tore it in two and threw it on the floor": *Thayer's Life of Beethoven*, 348–49.

266. "heroes of different types and different situations": Lewis Lockwood, *Beethoven: The Music and the Life* (New York: Norton, 2005), 213.

267–68. "free to do as he wishes with the piece": *Letters to Beethoven and Other Correspondence*, 3 vols., ed. Theodore Albrecht (Lincoln: University of Nebraska Press, 1996), I:86.

271. Beethoven concert announced in *Wiener Zeitung*: *Thayer's Life of Beethoven*, 446.

273. "the sky begins to clear": John A. Rice, "New Light on Dittersdorf's Ovid Symphonies," *Studi musicali* 29 (2000): 486.

PHOTOGRAPHS

11 *The Enraged Musician*, 1741, commons.wiki-media.org 17 bpk, Berlin/Art Resource, NY 18 Universal History Archive/Getty Images 19 Bildarchiv Monheim GmbH/Alamy 25 © Victoria and Albert Museum, London/Harry R. Beard Collection 31 Photodisc/Getty Images RF 47 Pietro Domenico Oliviero. The Royal Theater, Turin, commons.wikimedia.org 50 Courtesy of author 51 The Pierpont Morgan Library/Art Resource, NY 52 Alfredo Giovine, "Musicisti e Cantanti Baresi", Bari, Archivio delle tradizioni popolari baresi, 1968. Archivio fotografico Centro Studi Baresi di Felice Giovine 62 © The British Library Board, R.M.20 fl 66 National Music Museum, South Dakota 70 Sibley Music Library, Eastman School of Music, University of Rochester 74 Réunion des Musées Nation-aux/Art Resource, NY 76 Wikipedia, Gift of Elizabeth Paine Card, in memory of her father, Robert Treat Paine 2nd Museum of Fine Arts, Boston 80 Virginia Historical Society 83 © The Metropolitan Museum of Art/Art Resource, NY 85 Wikipedia, Bibliothèque Nationale de France 92 Lebrecht Music & Arts 95 © Victoria and Albert Museum, London/Harry R. Beard Collection, given by Isobel Beard 100 © The Trustees of the British Museum 101 HIP/Art Resource, NY 110 Imagno/Getty Images 112 Kunsthistorisches Museum, Vienna 113 Granger Collection 123 Foto Marburg/Art Resource, NY 128 Bildarchiv Preussischer Kulturbesitz/BPK, Berlin/Art Resource, NY 131 Wikipedia. Deutsche Staatsbibliothek, Berlin, http://commons.wikimedia.org/132 © Lebrecht Music & Arts 132 © Lebrecht Music & Arts 136 © The Metropolitan Museum of Art/Art Resource, NY 142 Photo by John Rice 144 Erich Lessing/Art Resource, NY 150 Imagno/Getty Images 155 Abby Aldrich Rockefeller Folk Art Museum, Williamsburg, Virginia 157 Photograph by Louise Rice (reproduced with permission) 158 Photo by Eduardo Trópia 162 Madero Street, Mexico, December 2006. Photo by Juan Fernando Ibarra. commons.wikimedia.org 165 © The Trustees of the British Museum 172 Map of St. Petersburg by Johann Baptist Homann, ca. 1720. University of Wisconsin-Milwaukee, commons.wikimedia.org 173 Photo by Mariza de Andrade 179 © culture-

MUSICAL EXAMPLES

INDEX

Note: Page numbers in *italics* indicate illustrations or musical examples. Page numbers followed by an *italic t* indicate tables.

A19